Nuclear Export Controls in Europe

Collection "La Cité Européenne"

n°6

Harald Müller
(ed.)

Nuclear Export Controls in Europe

EUROPEAN INTERUNIVERSITY PRESS

Brussels

ISBN 90 - 5201 - 413 - 2
D/1995/5678/09

Table of Contents

PREFACE

Since PRIF started its programme on a European Non-Proliferation Policy in 1986, it has published five books, including the present one. The four predecessors were : *"A Survey of European Nuclear Policy, 1985-87"*, London (The Macmillan Press) 1989, *"Western Europe and the Future of the Nuclear Non-Proliferation Treaty"*, Brussels (coedited by Peter Lomas and produced in collaboration with the Centre for European Policy Studies), *"How Western European Nuclear Policy Is Made. Deciding on the Atom"*, London (Macmillan) 1991, *"European Non-Proliferation Policy, 1988-1992"*, Brussels (European Interuniversity Press) 1993, all edited by the present editor. As the book titles suggest, the programme aims at watching, and assisting in, the emergence of a common European policy in a field that affects the security of Europe immediately and decisively.

"Europe", as we see it, consists of the members of the Union and those with a perspective to accede. This is why this volume contains chapters on three non-members, Hungary, Poland, and Estonia. That some member states are not included is by no means in disregard to their significance, or their commitment to non-proliferation. Rather, the incident of finding or not finding collaborators in these countries has, in some cases, prevented an otherwise needed inclusion of these countries.

Since its beginning the programme has enjoyed the support of various institutions. For the present volume, we are grateful for such support from the Rockefeller Brothers Fund, The John Merck Fund, the W. Alton Jones Foundation, and the Rockefeller Foundation. I wish to express my deepest gratitude to Hilary Palmer, the former program officer at the Rockefeller Brothers Fund. It was her personal commitment and hard effort that has created an international non-governmental non-proliferation community that makes now an essential contribution to the global non-proliferation regime. In two decades of work, I have not seen a single case where a foundation person has had such a unique impact on an issue area. Hilary's work must duly serve as a model how foundations can and should operate. My colleagues and I remain deeply indebted to her for her great and effective support, and for the smooth and friendly way in which she helped us.

Many people who do not show up in the list of contents have contributed to the success of this study. Long-time programme collaborators David Fischer, William Walker, Alain Michel, Michel Amory and Julien Goens have helped with lucid comments, as have Paul Eavis and Marc Schmitz. Matthias Dürr and Peter Lennon of the European Commission have explained the intricacies of the Union regulation on dual-use goods to the editor. Gerard Holden has polished the styles and eliminated the idiosyncratic mistakes of so many non-native speakers competently, smoothly, and without complaints about the bloody wounds we have afflicted to his mother tongue. Katja Frank, Sylvia Meier and Simone Wisotzki assisted in the preparatory work. Gudrun Weidner, in her usual ingenious mode, has managed the production process and prepared the study for publication. I thank them all.

As before, working with this team of true Europeans gives enormous satisfaction, and I look forward to continuing our common work.

Harald MÜLLER

NUCLEAR EXPORT CONTROLS IN EUROPE : AN INTRODUCTION

Harald Müller

1. Introduction : Why Export Controls ?

Export controls have been criticised from two directions. First, developing countries have suspected that these controls are aimed at preserving a technological oligopoly on the part of the industrialized world and impeding Third World development. These countries have consistently asked for them to be removed, even though in the context of NPT Review Conferences a huge number of Third World countries have endorsed existing export control practices, for example the work of the Zangger Committee, and even calls for strengthening the supervision of international nuclear transfers. It is no surprise that such criticism has drawn applause from countries that - in contrast to the vast majority of the nonaligned - have really suffered from export restrictions and denials, such as India. Second, supporters of non-proliferation have argued that export controls are an insufficient instrument since they can be circumvented, since second-tier suppliers do not participate, since proliferators can produce important items by themselves, and so on.[1]

---

[1] BAILEY K., **Strengthening Nuclear Non-Proliferation**, Westview, Boulder, 1993, Chapter 3.

However, this criticism would only be valid if export control were seen as the central instrument of the non-proliferation regime. This, of course, is not the case. Export controls for nuclear and nuclear-capable dual-use material, equipment, and technology contribute, together with other instruments such as safeguards, regional diplomacy, disarmament, security assurances etc. to the strength of the regime, but they are by no means its only or even its main pillar. The contributions they make to the regime are the following :

- Export controls can delay the process of proliferation and thus create a "breathing space" during which diplomatic efforts can be made to diffuse the motivations for proliferation, or during which the government interested in nuclear weapons may disappear.

- Export controls, by forcing the proliferator to set up extensive procurement networks or to invest heavily in a domestic infrastructure, drive the costs of a nuclear weapons programme beyond what would have been necessary if all the required goods had been available on the market.

- Deterrence : the threat to punish violations of foreign trade restrictions creates a strong deterrent effect. This effect can work against both the exporting individual or company and the importing individual, company or country, if two conditions are met. There must be some probability of detection, and the severity of the punishment must outweigh the potential benefit multiplied by the probability of detection.

- Export controls serve to deter companies and businessmen as well as, to a degree, proliferators. This means, of course, that violations of export control rules must be threatened by serious punishment.

- Export controls serve as a means of enhancing intelligence about ongoing procurement activities ; without export controls, the IAEA system of universal reporting on nuclear transfers could not function.[2]

- A reasonably effective export control system, together with IAEA safeguards and national intelligence, can enhance confidence about the nuclear capabilities of other countries, and reassure the world that these capabilities remain within the permitted boundaries for non-nuclear weapon states, if no violations of export controls have been reported.

- By controlling the foreign trade activities of their subjects, states fulfil their obligation under Art.II.3 NPT, as interpreted by various Review Conferences. Main Committee III of the 1990 Review Conference, for example, reached the following consensus :

«The Conference notes that a number of States Parties engaged in the supply of nuclear material and equipment have met regularly as an informal group which has become known as the Zangger Committee in order to coordinate their implementation of Art.III.2. To this end, these States have adopted certain requirements, including a list of items triggering IAEA safeguards for their export to non-nuclear weapon States not party to the Treaty... The Conference urges all States to adopt these requirements in connection with any nuclear cooperation with non-nuclear weapon States not Party to the Treaty. The Conference recommends that the list of items triggering IAEA safeguards and the procedures for implementation be reviewed from time to time to take into account advances in technology and changes in procurement practice. The Conference recommends the States Parties to consider further ways to improve the measures to prevent diversion of nuclear technology for nuclear weapons, other nuclear explosive purposes or nuclear weapon capabilities.»[3] «The Conference recognizes that there

---

[2] For a discussion of reporting requirements concerning the export and import of sensitive equipment, see : SCHEINMAN L., *"Assuring the Nuclear Non-Proliferation Safeguards System"*, Occasional Paper Series, The Atlantic Council, Washington, October 1992, p.17.

[3] Reprinted in HOWLETT D. & SIMPSON J. (eds), **Nuclear Non-Proliferation. A Reference Handbook**, Longman, Harlow, 1992, p.354.

are items of equipment and materials, including tritium, not identified in NPT Article III.2 which are relevant to the proliferation of nuclear weapons and therefore to the NPT as a whole. Without prejudice to the existing principles guiding international cooperation in the peaceful uses of nuclear energy, especially Article IV of the NPT, the Conference in this regard calls for early consultations among States to ensure that their supply and export controls are appropriately coordinated.»[4]

- Export controls help suppliers to trigger the call for safeguards in the recipient country.[5] The 1975 Review Conference observed in its final document :

«The Conference urges that [...] in all achievable ways, common export requirements relating to safeguards be strengthened, in particular by extending the application of safeguards to all peaceful nuclear activities in important States not Party to the Treaty.»[6]

For all these reasons, export controls are indispensable to any non-proliferation regime ; without them, the regime would suffer an information and confidence gap that could not be bridged in any other way. While such controls, particularly if imposed unilaterally by a state or a group of states, are bound to create distrust among the other parties, this is an objection to a certain political style, not to such controls *per se*.

2. Export Controls : The European Record

In the past, European suppliers have frequently been a source of concern for the non-proliferation regime. The most striking case was French assistance to the Israeli nuclear weapons programme. France

---

[4] *Ibid.*, p.353.

[5] For the connection between Art.III.2 NPT requirements and export controls, see : FISCHER D. & SZASZ P., **Safeguarding the Atom : A Critical Appraisal**, Taylor & Francis for SIPRI, London, 1985, p.101ff.

[6] HOWLETT & SIMPSON, *Op.cit.*, 1992, p.354.

served also as a supplier to Iraq - the research reactor in question was finally bombed by the Israeli air force in 1981. German cooperation contributed to nuclear weapon programmes in South Africa, Pakistan, Brazil and Iraq and helped the nuclear sectors in India, Argentina, and Iran. Belgium was involved in Pakistan and was tempted to assist Libya with sensitive nuclear technologies. Italy supplied technology to Iraq, Argentina and Pakistan. Pakistan's most prominent bomb maker learned centrifuge technology in the Netherlands, and Dutch experts apparently worked at least temporarily in the Brazilian centrifuge programme. British firms were also implicated in Iraq's nuclear weapon programmes. Spanish companies had some dealings in Pakistan and in Iraq. As an industrial powerhouse, Europe is capable of supplying the full range of nuclear fuel cycle and dual-use facilities, equipment, material and technology and also help in critical weapons technology. A European policy of export controls is thus a *sine qua non* of the maintenance of a credible nuclear non-proliferation regime.[7]

Europe's non-nuclear weapon states were more or less restive participants in the negotiations leading up to the NPT, and were particularly concerned to keep restraints on their nuclear industries to a minimum. Germany and Belgium were among the protagonists of an interpretation of Article III.2 of the NPT that refused to understand its language as requiring full-scope safeguards as a condition of all nuclear supply ; rather, in their view, this article required safeguards on exported items only, other - unsafeguarded - nuclear activities in the recipient countries notwithstanding. It was on this basis that the huge deal between Germany and Brazil in 1975 was conceived. Non-NPT France followed the same line, as shown by its exports to Pakistan and India.[8] It was only in 1990-1992 that these European suppliers finally convinced themselves that only a full-scope safeguards export policy was compatible with the letter and spirit of their non-proliferation commitments (and interests).

---

[7] E.g. ALBRIGHT D. & HIBBS M., *"Iraq's shop-till-you-drop nuclear program"*, in : **Bulletin of the Atomic Scientists**, Vol.48, No.3, April 1992, pp.26-37.

[8] GOLDSCHMIDT B., **The Nuclear Complex. A Worldwide History of Nuclear Energy**, American Nuclear Society, LaGrange Park, 1981, pp.181-212.

Another sensitive point in the history of European supply policy was the avowed readiness to export sensitive equipment and technology to non-NPT parties. Germany did this vis-a-vis Brazil and - until about 1974 - tolerated enrichment cooperation with South Africa. France was ready to supply reprocessing technology to Pakistan and South Korea, before it changed its policy in 1976 (Germany followed suit one year later).[9]

We can also discern a pattern of supply policy which would stop exports not on their merits (or dangers), but only after the items in question were duly written into international lists. This is why German heavy water technology found its way into India, and why Italian hot cells could be supplied to Iraq, both without safeguards, because at the time of the transfer these items were not on the Zangger list.[10]

It was also European - mainly French and German - concerns that prevented the London Suppliers Group from reconvening between 1977 and 1991. European suppliers worried that developing countries, already greatly upset both by the multilateral "changing of the rules" through the London Group and by the unilateral "changing of the rules" through the US Nuclear Non-Proliferation Act of 1978, would be antagonized even more if the London Group were in any way institutionalized.[11] The strong controversies on nuclear cooperation during the International Fuel Cycle Evaluation (INFCE), between 1977 and 1981, the 1980 NPT Review Conference, the IAEA Committee on the Assurances of Supply in the first half of the eighties, and the United Nations Conference on International Cooperation in the Peaceful Uses of Nuclear Energy of 1987 seemed to substantiate this fear.[12] Thus, while proliferators were anxiously developing and refining their circumvention strategies for procure-

---

[9] *Ibid.*, pp.399-411.

[10] MÜLLER H., *"After the Scandals : West German Nonproliferation Policy"*, **PRIF Reports** No.9, PRIF, Frankfurt, February 1990.

[11] BERKHOUT F., *"The NPT and Nuclear Export Controls"*, in : HOWLETT & SIMPSON, 1992, pp.45-50.

[12] On CAS and PUNE, see : MÜLLER H., FISCHER D. & KÖTTER W., **Nuclear Non-Proliferation and Global Order**, Oxford University Press, Oxford, 1994, pp.33-34.

ment, the suppliers, including the Europeans, evolved their control systems in a far less dynamic way, if at all.

On the plus side, all European member states (with the exception of Ireland) had some form of export controls, mainly closely conforming to COCOM, with minor adjustments for the specific requirements of Art.III.2 of the NPT. When, in the eighties, all EC members joined the Nuclear Suppliers Group, their export principles and lists began to resemble each other more closely, though they did not become completely identical. In addition, most EC countries participated in the Zangger group. Yet despite all these activities, it became clear at the beginning of the nineties, that a major overhaul was required. This applied above all to the problem of dual-use nuclear capable equipment and technology, since this had proved to be the preferred circumvention route for would-be nuclear weapon states.

3. The Legal Foundations of Common Export Control Policy in the EU

Within the European Union, the area of export control is characteristically a battlefield between the Commission and member states - notably France and Britain, where Commission authority competes with national sovereignty. The Treaty of Rome, in its Article 223, exempts strategic goods from Community law. Weapons and munitions are thus regulated exclusively by the states, guided, at best, by guidelines agreed in intergovernmental consultations. Goods that have civilian and military applications - dual-use goods - can be argued to have strategic value and thus be exempt under Art.223, while on the other hand they are widely used in civilian industry and thus fall under Community law. Goods specially designed for use in the civilian nuclear industry are subject to the specific rules of the EURATOM Treaty.[13]

---

[13] MÜLLER H., *"The Export Controls Debate In the "New" European Community"*, in : **Arms Control Today**, Vol.23, No.2, March 1993, pp.10-14.

Since 1984, a special regime has applied to so-called sensitive items, namely plutonium, highly enriched uranium, and reprocessing, enrichment, and heavy water production plants and technology. In the light of political obligations undertaken at that time by some, but not all, members of the Community under the London Suppliers Guidelines, it was resolved by the Council that such items, if transferred between member states of the European Community, would be subject to national controls.[14]

The Single European Act and to an even greater extent the Maastricht Treaty served to underline how questionable the distinction between the economic and political aspects of security is. In calling for a Common Foreign and Security Policy (CFSP), these legal documents profoundly challenge the persistence of national decision-making over conventional arms transfers. For how can a Union CFSP be developed, both regionally and in particular for the non-proliferation of weapons of mass destruction, if an essential instrument (or, conversely, disturbance) of foreign and security policy such as arms transfers cannot be touched upon ?

In other words, the failure to draw up a common policy on arms exports remains a bleeding wound in the brittle corpus of CFSP. This is all the more true as the member states supply almost a third of the arms sold to the Third World and thus have a considerable impact on regional arms races and wars. When considered in the light of this grave responsibility, the policy instruments developed so far are simply not adequate.

Common guidelines for the licensing of conventional arms exports were agreed at the Luxembourg summit in 1991 and amended in 1992. They contain eight criteria that member states are supposed to apply in national licensing decisions : 1. International commitments of member states, notably UN sanctions. 2. The human rights situation in the recipient state. 3. The internal stability of the recipient. 4. Regional security and stability in the recipient's region. 5. The national security interests of EU member states. 6. The re-

---

[14] Reprinted in HOLST J.J. *et al.*, **Blocking the Spread of Nuclear Weapons. American and European Perspectives**, Council on Foreign Relations, Washington, D.C., 1986, pp.127-129.

cipient's attitude towards terrorism and international law. 7. The risk of diversion and undesirable re-exports. 8. The appropriateness of the transfer in the light of the recipient's security situation.[15]

Notwithstanding these criteria, arms export policy within the EU remains painfully disparate, as the following differences in national behaviour in the last two years reveal. Germany refused to transfer weapons to Taiwan, while France was pleased to deliver Mirage fighters and frigates. Germany and Britain have sold warships and aircraft, respectively, to Indonesia, a country embargoed by both Portugal and Italy. Export policy for the Middle East is in complete disarray. French soldiers may confront French weapons in Ruanda, while the Belgians stopped propping up Ruanda's governmental forces in 1990. And France, Belgium and Germany have self-imposed moratoria for antipersonnel mines, while Italy is one of the world's top suppliers of this deadly ordnance.

In the negotiations leading to the Maastricht Treaty, some countries (Belgium and Germany among them) proposed the elimination of Art.223. France and the United Kingdom would not agree. As long as this illogical exemption stands, the temptation to misuse arms exports for commercial gain or for purely national - as opposed to Union - foreign and security policy ends will remain irresistible. And all attempts to develop a CFSP, of which non-proliferation policy will be a vital component, will be incomplete if the handling of conventional arms transfers is not integrated.

4. The Development of a Common Export Control System for Dual-use Goods in the EU

Controlling arms exports is one thing. It may be politically difficult, but it is technically and legally straightforward : a weapon is a weapon is a weapon, it is made to kill, and restraining its transfer is contingent more on political will and interest than on complex, difficult and balanced technical and legal judgements. Not so for the most intricate object of export controls, dual-use equipment. Such

---

[15] MÜLLER H., *Op.cit.*, March 1993, pp.10-14.

items can be employed for completely innocent, civilian and peaceful purposes. Or they can be integrated into military programmes and can play, as the Iraqi case convincingly demonstrated, the crucial role in a state's attempt to acquire weapons of mass destruction. Distinguishing between the purposes of civilian and military users is a difficult task. It is even compounded in the nuclear field, where dual-use acquires a double meaning : an item may have nuclear and non-nuclear applications, independent of their civilian or military character, and it may be usable in military or civilian nuclear projects. It is no surprise that export controllers find it difficult to resolve this problem on a case-by-case basis.

As the project of a single market approached realisation, it became obvious that the regulation of dual-use transfers was becoming a major political issue. On the one hand, the single market required the unimpeded movement of goods for the civilian industries of member states, if it was to be truly "single". On the other hand, the removal of export controls on such goods where they cross national borders may open a Pandora's Box of uneven control standards, creating welcome routes for proliferators to procure goods via a series of European transit stations, illegally or even legally. It goes without saying that this dilemma became ever more apparent as the lessons of the Iraqi case became clearer.

Since 1991, the European Commission and the member states have struggled to draw up a regulation concerning dual-use goods. Debates on the first Commission draft from August 1992 revealed major differences among the member states on key issues of the regulation. These issues were[16] :

- The degree of centralization or "unionization" of the issue (role of the Commission) ; some member states started from the assumption that dual-use goods, having strategic importance, would fall entirely under Art.223 of the Rome Treaty and thus must be exempted from all Commission authority.

---

[16] *Ibid.*

- The handling of non-listed dual-use items. Some countries insisted on a catch-all clause subjecting non-listed items that were destined for military end-use to licensing, while others believed that such items should not be controlled at all.

- The definition of technology, notably the inclusion of intangible technology transfer such as engineering services on-site, modem-transferred information, the training of operators in the country of origin and the like.

- The treatment of transit (whereby the item passes through Union territory, but has neither its point of origin nor its destination there and transit trade transactions (where Union companies or individuals act as intermediaries, but the item never passes through Union territory).

- The risk of "licence-shopping", whereby an exporter would apply in the country with the lowest export control standards for licences covering goods produced in a country with higher standards. Since licences were to be valid for the whole Union territory, the countries where the goods originated would have no way of stopping such exports.

- The exclusion of certain goods from the regulation, i.e. their continued submission to national rather than Union control procedures.

- The length of the transition period, i.e. the time when some intra-Union controls (though no border controls) would still be permitted. Some countries would have preferred an open-ended transition period, others, plus the Commission, pleaded for a very short, limited time-frame.

The debate on these issues revealed deep differences between the member states, touching in some cases upon constitutional principles (such as the question of whether the extraterritorial application of criminal law, as in the case of on-site services, was admissible at all) or legal philosophy (such as the issue of whether licence requirements for non-listed items in case of their military end-use created too indeterminate an action to subject violations to a criminal penalty). It is thus no surprise that it took a long time to reach an agreement, and that the agreement that was finally drawn up at the Corfu summit in June 1994 fell somewhat short of initial expectations. Nevertheless, there is now a starting point for a Union export control system, and the system contains enough instruments for review and further development to make improvements appear possible.

The above controversies were resolved as follows :

- "Unionization" : the system was set up in two parts, a regulation of Community law, concerning the trade issue, and an intergovernmental "Joint Action" according to Part J of the Maastricht Treaty, containing the lists of goods and destinations and the criteria for licensing, i.e. those aspects that, according to the majority view, fell into the competence of the member states as "strategic".

- Catch-all clause : exporters need a licence for non-listed goods destined for use in the production, maintenance etc. of weapons of mass destruction and missiles if they have been informed by their governments of this end-use. If they themselves have knowledge of such an end-use, they must tell the government. Member states may set rules on a national basis for cases where exporters have reason to assume such an end-use, but no definite knowledge. Whether violations will be punished, and how, is to be decided by the member states.

- Technology : only blueprints and software were included and treated like goods. The question of intangible technology was left to member states, with a declaration of intent to reconsider its possible inclusion in the near future.

- Neither transit nor transit trade transactions were regulated ; thus it falls to member states to deal with these issues.

22

- Licence shopping : licences for exports to extra-Union destinations are principally valid for Union territory as a whole. They will be issued by the country of residence of the exporter. If the goods in question are located in another member state, or are to be shipped through another member state, that state can reject the licensing by the state of residence, and such a rejection is binding. Moreover, if the export violates the essential interests of any other member state, that state can request the licensing member state not to issue, or to revoke, the licence. If a member state is asked by the exporter to execute the licence approved in another member state, and has reason to believe that the granting of this licence was based on insufficient information, or that the situation has changed since the licence was granted, it can delay customs action for ten days and ask the state which approved the licence to revoke it. If the state of origin refuses, the requesting state must process the exported item, unless it believes that its supreme foreign policy or security interests, or its international obligations would be hurt by the export. In this case, it has the right to stop it. The item in question must be returned to the exporter.

- Intra-Union licensing : the Joint Action annex distinguishes between two types of goods for which national controls can be maintained during the transition period. "Normal" dual-use goods require, for intra-Union transfers, a written certification that the export of such goods to extra-Union destinations will require a licence. Member states are also entitled to ask for a licence if they know that the final destination of an item transferred within the Union is a non-Union recipient, and if the transferred item is subject to licence if exported from the Union (this is another obstacle to licence-shopping). For a small list of particularly sensitive dual-use goods, Union members can decide to require licences even for intra-Union transfers for a transition period, after which this rule will be reconsidered. Intra-Union movements of Plutonium, weapons-grade Uranium and sensitive nuclear technology (reprocessing, enrichment, and heavy-water production) remain under licence according to the 1984 Council regulation. These exemptions from the "single market" rule must not amount to border controls at intra-Union borders, but must be part of a surveillance system that applies to member states' entire territories and does not discriminate between trade within the member state and trade between member states.

The length of the transition period is fixed at three years. At the end of this period, a consideration of whether the measures in the preceding paragraph shall apply further is required. The Commission retains the right to ask for a revision sooner if there is agreement between the member states. The basis for a revision will be a Commission report on the harmonization of the export control policies of member states, on the understanding that only a high uniform standard will justify the complete elimination of intra-Union controls. For sensitive nuclear and other highly sensitive dual-use goods, a special system of supervision is envisaged ; on request, individual member states may continue to ask for single licences.

The member states and the Commission must provide for adequate cooperation between their licensing and customs authorities, in order to achieve the most uniform practices in the application of the regulation and the joint action. Each member state informs the Commission on its internal ordnances for the implementation of the regulation. The Commission distributes this information to all member states and provides a report on implementation to the Council and the European Parliament every two years. A coordination group, chaired by the Commission, reviews all issues concerning implementation that are submitted either by the chair (i.e. the Commission) or a member state. This includes, in particular, measures to inform exporters about the obligations derived from this regulation.[17]

The regulation is a reasonable start, provided the revision mechanism is used. The greatest danger, the risk of licence-shop-

---

[17] For a concise description of the new regulation, see : KRENZLER H.G., *"Die Handelspolitik der Europäischen Gemeinschaft als Instrument der Friedenssicherung"*, in : EITEL T. *et al.*, **Rechtliche Aspekte internationaler Friedenssicherung, Sitzungsbericht Q zum 60**. Deutschen Juristentag, München (Beck), 1994, pp.37-52, partic. pp.43-46.

ping, appears to have been effectively foreclosed. Since national regulations are permitted for transit and transit trade as well as for intangible technology, and because controls, though no customs action, remain legal for the transition period, the danger that lowest common denominator solutions could eliminate high standards in some Union countries without a commensurate gain in the others now appear all but excluded. Moreover, this overall positive assessment should not blind us to the weaknesses of the system. It remains incomprehensible why, despite the strong and obvious lessons from the Iraqi case (and other incidents as well), no agreement was possible on transit trade, intangible technology, and a catch-all clause for all military projects (remember the Iraqi "super-gun"). That penalties are completely left to the member states, with the very vague injunction that sanctions must be "effective, appropriate, and deterring" need not, but could, create a major loophole. The division of the system into a regulation and a joint action points again to the parochialism of certain European countries, who follow a 19-century understanding of "national sovereignty" to the detriment of the Union as a whole and, consequently and ultimately, of the interests of their own nations.

5. National Export Policies of European Countries : The Situation at End-1994[18]

5.1. Common Features

In comparing the status of national export policies in selected European countries as the new EU regulation and joint actions are introduced, some general observations are in order. The general framework of rules is already not only similar, but identical : the Zangger list, London list and Suppliers Group dual-use list are uniformly applied. That this is true even for a non-member of these groups, the young Estonian democracy, is a proof of the strong "pull" effect of existing international regimes on new states looking for acceptance as normal and equal members of the international community. As the leading members of this community all adhere to

---

[18] In this section I rely on the country studies in this book.

the rules quoted, it was seen as desirable that Estonia should quickly and demonstrably follow the same rules - even if the country's internal capability to implement them was and still is not sufficiently developed.

The attraction of the European Union and the need to gain full access to Western markets and technology was a driving force behind the adoption of strong export control policies in Hungary and also Poland. That Hungary introduced the stratified European "Joint Action" list even before the Union had finally resolved to adopt it is a convincing indication of this attraction. It can be expected that the whole of the EU regulation will be integrated into the current Polish and Hungarian nuclear export systems.

A second striking finding is that some strengthening of export control legislation, regulation and administration is reported from all countries under review. Indeed, one country, Germany, which had been involved in many undesirable transfers before 1990, has gone so far that voices warning against undue competitive disadvantages have grown louder, and signs of a certain retreat from the very advanced steps that had been taken are noted.

The Gulf War and the end of the East-West conflict had a decisive impact on convincing governments and publics that improvements were needed. The Gulf War exposed the risks of insufficient precautions against the ever more sophisticated procurement strategies of proliferators, and the blatant insufficiency of policies that would attempt to follow the letter of the rules rather than to realize their objectives and meaning. The fading-away of the Cold War aroused in many observers the fear that export controls might be generally weakened because of the profound obsolescence of COCOM, on which the major part of export control systems hinged. In fact, opposite seems to have happened : the end of this contest has focused attention far more on the dangers of proliferation, and has freed countries from the perceived need to compromise on export controls in order to gain or maintain allies around the world. In addition, far closer coordination of policies among former enemies has become not only possible, but indeed the cherished practice of

Eastern countries, as the examples of Poland, Hungary and also Estonia prove.

If anything, this comparison confirms the value of the EU regulation/joint action, not least where regarding one of the most touchy issues, the catch-all clause is concerned. The necessity of this device, though hotly contested, is beyond doubt in the light of experiences in Iraq and Pakistan. For recipient countries with a modestly developed industrial infrastructure and a government strongly dedicated to developing weapons of mass destruction, dual-use rather than military-use equipment is the key to success. A catch-all clause secures the "lower end" of the technology spectrum against this circumvention strategy, and protects export control systems against the persistent risk that in drawing up lists something significant might be overlooked. Prior to the Union regulation, catch-all clauses were absent in France, Belgium, Poland, Greece, Denmark, Sweden and Italy. Only the UK, Germany, and Spain (here it depended on prior information provided by the government) had one. As a consequence of the regulation, such clauses have now been introduced into Belgium and Italy, and the other countries of the Union, and most likely their neighbours, too, will follow.

Some countries had - and have - another instrument to substitute for, or to complement, a catch-all clause : a single-case intervention authority for the government. This instrument does not threaten an exporter preparing an export in full awareness of the intended utilization of the transfer in the recipient country ; neither does it oblige this exporter to inform the government and thus to enhance governmental knowledge about ongoing procurement activities, a strong advantage of the catch-all clause as written in the EU regulation. But with a single-case intervention authority, a government that knows about the intended use of the item in a nuclear weapons programme is at least not helpless against the undesired transfer of non-listed items. Such single case intervention authority is available in France, the UK, Belgium, and Germany.

Even with the catch-all clause concerning projects for weapons of mass destruction being introduced in all European countries, its effectiveness remains to be seen. As the regulation leaves it to governments to punish any failure of companies to fulfil their reporting obligations, the application of the clause may vary widely in practice.

5.2. Major Differences

Several issues that had been heavily contested and will continue to be discussed in the coming years have been left open by the regulation. The first is the issue of the extraterritorial reach of national criminal law, an issue that affects both transit trade transactions (extraterritorial brokerage) and intangible technology transfer, notably rendered services on-site in the proliferating country. The former is a valuable tool for the procurement agencies of proliferating countries, while the latter becomes all the more indispensable the more the recipients rely on buying parts rather than complete items that are on the control lists, dual-use technology and their own production capacities to produce the goods needed for nuclear weapon programmes. On both issues, the differences between the European countries are vast.

Transit trade transactions appear to be subject to governmental control in France and Germany only. On intangible technology transfer, the only country except Germany that appears to apply controls is Belgium, and curiously, this applies to dual-use but apparently not to specifically nuclear technology. It remains to be seen whether, on both accounts, the minority will be able to convince the majority of the need to enhance their own systems, and if they can resist the temptation to abandon their own present regulations if they cannot be generalized across the Union (the pressure in Germany is high indeed when intangible technology is concerned).

A second area left unregulated by the regulation is the legal consequences of breaches of it. The first aspect here relates to the scope of action that is covered by the law. While all countries threaten to punish the main act of intentional breach of law, the situation is more ambiguous concerning unintentional breaches, or secondary acts such as instigation, support and assistance. The results of our studies are somewhat unclear, as, depending on the legal system of the state, this question needs either to be clarified in the special law on export controls or, alternatively, to be automatically covered by stipulations in the general criminal code. Clear provision for the punishment of secondary acts is made in France, Denmark, Germany, and Italy, but not in the other countries.

Vast differences remain in the severity of punishment. Maximum prison terms range from 2 years in Greece and Denmark through 3 years in France, 5 years in Belgium and Poland, 6 years in Italy and Spain, 7 years in the UK to the maximum of 10 years in Germany, where in exceptional cases the delivery of special parts of nuclear weapons may be punished by up to 15 years in prison.

Fines vary as well, but generally it can be said that these will be lower than the likely profits from major transfers to countries eager to develop their nuclear weapon programmes. Consequently, some, but not all, countries have the possibility of seizing the profits, or the sale value, of the goods involved : Italy, Germany, Greece and Poland can do this. In Spain, twice the value of a sale can be seized, and the French authorities can go so far as to request three times the value of an illegally exported item.

5.3. Organizational Aspects of Export Controls

A lot of commonality can be observed in the licensing process. Usually, the executive agency is a special regulatory body or an office attached to, or under the authority of, the economics, industry or foreign trade ministry ; the country with the youngest export control effort, Estonia, where it is attached to the Foreign Ministry, is a remarkable exception. Decision-making on export licensing is subject to an interagency process, usually operating through a multi-agency committee. Remarkably, the role of foreign offices has become very strong in this process of interagency organization, and in most cases the foreign ministry holds either the chair or a veto power over decisions. This bodes well for a more effective, security-oriented export control policy : an earlier comparative study showed that where foreign offices have dominated non-proliferation policy in the past, that policy was stronger than in those countries where foreign ministry involvement was rather weak.[19]

Another important organizational aspect is government-industry relations. Four models appear to exist : there is a directional model, whereby the government either owns industry or is capable of giving clear guidance from above and can expect obedience from below. This is apparently the case in centralist France. A second model is the close corporatist one, where government and industry cooperate closely and industrial organizations are immediately involved in decision-making, rule-drafting and implementation. This is the Danish model, and up to a certain point the Swedish too.

The third model is a hybrid, mixing elements from the first two. The UK and Germany (formerly rather corporatist in this respect) fit it. They are directional in so far as they have established procedures - notably the role of the "export responsible" in companies, a manager who would bear the blame personally if a breach of the rules were to be discovered - that help the government to make its wishes known on export matters. Industrial organizations are used as transmission mechanisms for "early warning" on procurement activities. On the other hand, industrial associations and major companies are involved in government/industry review panels for export control practices and provide a significant input in the evolution of legislation. Spain may also come close to this model, with the weight more on the "directional" side.

A weak educational relation characterizes the fourth model : here, government restrains itself largely to training or to the provision of information to industry. This appears to be the case in both Poland and Hungary.

Finally, there is little or no organized relationship reported from Belgium, Greece and Italy.

---

[19] Cf. MÜLLER H., *"How Western European Nuclear Policy Is Made : A Comparison"*, in : *idem* (ed.), **How Western European Nuclear Policy Is Made. Deciding on the Atom**, Macmillan, London, 1991.

5.4. Special Features in Individual Countries

There are some particular features that are specific to one or a few countries. The lack of publicity and parliamentary control prevailing in this area in France is remarkable, particularly in the light of France's relatively successful export control policy. A strange loophole is reported from Belgium, where the requirement for Authorization and Licence is not the same for all goods, and consequently unlicensed goods that carry an authorization could leave the country ; it is unclear whether this loophole can be upheld in the light of the requirements of the EU regulation, and it would be recommendable to close it. The same applies to the curious "privilege" afforded by German law to lawbreakers in the nuclear sector as compared to their peers smuggling items for biological or chemical weapons.

The understaffing of the relevant agencies in Spain and Greece, exacerbated in the latter case by insufficient training of the inspectors, remains a reason for concern. On the other hand, the Spanish practice - echoed in France - of requiring prior authorization before companies enter into negotiations on long-term contracts is a useful feature ; other countries, e.g. Germany, handle this in a more informal way. Similarly, the Spanish and German practice of preparing and updating registers of exporters is useful in order to keep the authorities informed about the capabilities of companies ; in Spain, registration is even required before any licence can be obtained.

5.5. A Speculative Assessment of System Efficiency

It is hard, of course, to judge or predict the efficiency of recently revamped control systems. If we consider their preventive capabilities, we can assume that these are determined by a combination of the severity of possible punishment, the probability of detection (i.e. the quality of the controlling agencies), and the government-business relationship. This relationship may enhance detection capability through collaboration and enhance deterrence by introducing the risk that a perpetrator may be cut off from fruitful relations with the rest of the business community. Where all three or at least two of these aspects are strong, a system can be expected to be reasonably effective ; for example, prison terms in France are relatively short, but the directional control over industry and the competence of staff - usually considered to be high - may compensate for this weakness. Where all three or two aspects are weak, we must have some concerns.

In Belgium, for example, a breach of the requirement to obtain an authorization will earn the perpetrator a maximum of 5 years, and failure to obtain a licence only a very brief 1 year in prison ; but it is theoretically quite possible to transfer goods with an authorization, but without a licence. Under these circumstances, the reported lack of strong formal government-industry relations may prove fatal even if the staff responsible is of high quality.

For Spain, the level of punishment is satisfactory, but understaffing give grounds for concern. The question here is whether the directional mode of industry-government relations, in particular the registration tool, gives the authorities an adequate compensatory instrument.

Denmark's export controls have so far worked well despite a very low level of punishment ; the main reason for this has obviously been the organic corporatist system of export controls. The size and quality of staff has not been a serious issue here. However, under single market conditions, the Danish authorities may be either forced to provide for longer prison sentences or to review seriously their administrative and investigative capabilities, in order to protect themselves against unpleasant surprises. In Poland, the technical capabilities of control agencies and relatively weak government-industry relations justify improvements in the light of reasonable, though not extraordinarily heavy, punishments. The same applies to Italy.

According to our comparison the Greek system looks weak, even though we have to appreciate that Greece has not had a major problem with illegal exports in the past, in contrast to some of the countries that look stronger after recent reforms, such as Germany or the UK. But analysis of the Greek export control system reveals low punishment levels, weak government-business relations on export controls, and significant staff weaknesses. External assistance to help with the last problem would be highly commendable.

6. Conclusion : A Look Into the Future

The success of the member states and the European Commission in creating a joint approach to nuclear and dual-use export controls is a major achievement, all the more so as it was achieved in the face of national idiosyncrasies, sovereignty prerogatives, vastly differing philosophies of law, and commercial interests. However, essential questions remain, as the foregoing section on major differences and the overall assessment have clearly demonstrated. The question of intangible technology looms largest, in the light of its increasing significance for proliferators' programmes. In addition, it remains to be seen how the regulation will be translated into national law, regulation, and organization, and how it will be implemented in the practice of administrations and, eventually, of the courts.

It is for this reason that the review process is of the utmost importance. This process cannot be confined to the scrutiny of reports on implementing legislation. It must be possible to discuss administrative and court practice as well and to demand changes where they are necessary. If practice is not harmonized and weaknesses in certain countries are not eliminated, the spectre of "licence-shopping" will arise anew, despite the prudent precautions taken in the regulation. Improved harmonization of criminal law, that is, to say of prison sentences, though without precedence in the history of the Community/Union, might be inevitable in the end.

Beyond the nuclear sector proper, two issues are looming on the horizon. One is raised in Alessandro Politi's paper : the involvement of financial institutions. Without their involvement, a good number of illegal transfers would not be possible. Without their input, the information available to governmental agencies (and, incidentally, to the courts) will remain incomplete. Yet banks enjoy an extra-ordinary liberty to keep secrets, even where this affects national interests. Most likely, stronger regulation will be needed in this sector sooner or later.

Secondly, a common policy on arms transfers is the necessary and logical complement to proliferation control. It is complementary since countries that pursue the acquisition of weapons of mass destruction are usually also among those that overarm conventionally. Moreover, a strong conventional threat that creates regional imbalances is frequently a great incentive to try to compensate with nonconventional weapons. While weapons of mass destruction are the weapons that threaten most damage, conventional arms are those that kill in practice. A Common Foreign and Security Policy is an absurdity without a common arms transfer policy ; arms transfers affect both foreign policy objectives and the security of the Union, and they will become an even greater factor whenever the Union makes good on its promise to offer military assets to the United Nations. The political guidelines for arms transfers adopted in Luxembourg and Lisbon in 1991 and 1992 respectively are non-binding, vague, and subject to vastly different interpretations. They provide a broad framework, but do not help much unless they are considerably fleshed out. The elimination of Art.223 of the Rome Treaty has often been proposed and equally often rejected by individual governments.[20] Maybe the model of the dual-use system, a combination of Community and intergovernmental elements, could serve as an example to deal with this sensitive area.

---

[20] BAUER H. *et al.*, **Arms and Dual-Use Exports From the E.C. : A Common Policy for Regulation and Control**, Saferworld Foundation, London, 1992.

FRANCE

Philippe Richard

1. Introduction

When we consider the nuclear export control procedure in a given country it is necessary to distinguish between :

a) the international level of control (the country's international commitments), and
b) the national level (internal regulations and legislation).

Obviously, those two levels are strictly interdependent. The international level provides diplomatic justification for state intervention in free trade, ensures cohesion of actors and coordinates common decisions, whether they are a matter of support or of sanction. The national level provides technical realization and effective control. This paper investigates the interaction between these two levels in France. Such an interaction does not stand to reason. In some cases, shared international interests may contradict particular national interests.

2. International Regimes

Nuclear non-proliferation is by nature an international question. Its implementation depends on the political will expressed by the international community, which affirms itself in the framework of narrow cooperation. The principle of such cooperation is dependent on a number of international legal instruments that France has joined over the years.

Non-proliferation concerns three sorts of sensitive transfers, each governed by a specific regime and negotiated in a different forum :

- nuclear transfers (NPT, NSG) ;
- chemical and bacteriological transfers (Australia Group) ;
- missile technology transfers (MTCR).

To these three kinds of transfers dual-use technology, governed by COCOM, and conventional war materials and equipment, subject to no particular international regime, with the exception of transparency measures embedded in the UN conventional arms register, have to be added.

Our research is focused on nuclear technology. We will deal with those international regimes relating to nuclear non-proliferation of which France is a member : NPT, MTCR and COCOM (dual-use).

The NPT is the international treaty of reference in the matter. France signed this treaty in 1991, and it was ratified by Parliament in 1992. This adhesion did not appear to change anything in the practice of French policy, since France, a founding member of the Suppliers Group in 1977, already followed NSG recommendations consistently. Rather, signing the treaty reinforced the image that France seeks to promote abroad, that of a country which wants to participate efficaciously in the struggle against nuclear proliferation. This was also the reason why France adopted the rule of full-scope safeguards as a condition for authorizing new civilian nuclear contracts (as applied to Pakistan)[1] and ratified Protocol No.1 of the Tlatelolco Treaty, which prohibits nuclear weapons in Latin America. The principle of full-scope safeguards confirmed a policy that France had been following for some years, i.e. not to export to

---

[1] «Le Président pakistanais plaide son dossier nucléaire auprès de François Mitterrand», in : Le Monde, 03.06.1994.

India, Pakistan or Israel. But it eliminated all uncertainty about a possible change in this policy. And it deprived India of its supplier of fuel for the Tarapur light water reactor power station.

Concerning the Missile Technology Control Regime (MTCR), an informal agreement exists to which France adheres. But this regime remains rather fragile.

France also follows COCOM guidelines with regard to dual-use technology transfers. Three lists have been drawn up by COCOM : the war materials list, the Atomic Energy list which covers fissile material for civilian as well as military use, and the Industrial list, which is the most important and which covers civilian and military dual-use goods.

Even after COCOM disappears, the Industrial list will remain. France uses these three lists in the framework of its own legislation (*"Avis aux exportateurs"*, Notice to exporters), which is in the process of being revised.

3. National Regimes

This second part is the most specific aspect of our research. Before providing details it seems useful to present briefly the structure of definition of French external nuclear policy.

3.1. The Definition of French External Nuclear Policy

At the highest level French nuclear policy is defined by the Council for Foreign Nuclear Policy (*Conseil de politique nucléaire extérieure*, CPNE). «The need to ensure that such exports do not result in the proliferation of nuclear weapons led the Head of State to set up, in 1976, under his chairmanship this specialized Committee. The task of this council is to define the major principles of French foreign nuclear policy, especially with regard to the export of sensitive nuclear technology, equipments and products».[2] It is composed of the President of the Republic (chairman), the Prime Minister, the ministers of External Affairs, Economy, Defence, Industry, External Trade and the Administrator of the CEA (*Commissariat à l'Energie Atomique*). This organogram is very interesting. It shows that all aspects of nuclear policy in France are under the direct control of the Head of State. However, this council only expresses its opinion on the main lines of this policy, which is implemented at a lower level. In 1982 CPNE adopted a *"Document de Référence"* (unpublished) on French external nuclear policy. This Document constitutes French doctrine in matters of external nuclear policy. The French authorities always refer to this Document for elaboration of governmental agreements. For example, this Document states that, in agreeing to the London Guidelines, France at the same time refused to accept IAEA rules for control of all nuclear plants (full-scope safeguards). It also recommended the export of the French enrichment technique by chemical processing that is thought to be more proliferation-resistant than other enrichment technologies, but has neither been used on a commercial scale nor ever been exported.[3] France also evokes some unspecific restrictions concerning research reactors. Relating to the end of the fuel cycle (for plants or fuel sold by France) this Document does not state any clear policy. Lastly, this Document makes no reference to foreign persons under instruction in France. This problem is crucial. When we think about non-proliferation we always speak in terms of physical transfers (material, equipment, technology). We rarely take into consideration immaterial and invisible transfers such as intellectual instruction or know-how. It is possible to invite engineers or physicists to French research laboratories in total discretion and to give them an excellent training in the nuclear field. In the past France has collaborated with countries such as Iraq, and has participated in the scientific training of experts from those countries in France. The same applies to military personnel handling nuclear weapons, e.g. air force pilots. According to the 1992 Annual Report of the CEA,

---

[2] See "The regulation of nuclear trade", non-proliferation supply safety, Nuclear Energy Agency, OCDE/OECD, vol.II national regulations, France, p.84, Paris, OECD, 1988.

[3] It is remarkable that Iraq tested this technique in its nuclear weapon program, but abandoned it in favour of centrifuge and electromagnetic enrichment.

there were 970 "young scientists" preparing theses in its laboratories at the end of 1992. Among them were 145 foreigners, of whom 50 were from European Union countries. Topics of research covered all activities of CEA, such as advanced technologies, nuclear reactors, the fuel cycle, military applications and nuclear safety.[4] It is important to add that, for the CEA, there is no frontier between civilian and military research.[5]

We can state that the Document of Reference is very ambiguous on this point. There is a real risk of intellectual nuclear proliferation from France. The Document now seems outdated. It no longer corresponds to the practice and commitments of France in the field of non-proliferation. France has now signed the NPT, accepted full-scope safeguards, broken off exports of chemical enrichment facilities (because this involved serious proliferation risks) and has passed a new law on reprocessing of irradiated fuel which establishes the principle of the return of waste. The difference between the Document and France's current level of engagement creates uncertainties in the decision-making process. Decisions relating to nuclear exports may lack coherence.

It is also necessary to make clear that CNPE is not actually a living structure. After 18 meetings held between 1978 and 1983 (two or three meetings each year), this body ceased to meet. In 1984, 1985 and 1986 its Secretariat published some documents concerning different subjects : nuclear cooperation with India, plutonium management, cooperation with Canada in the matter of naval propulsion. It would be a good idea to revitalize CPNE. Its first priority would be to produce a new *"Document de Référence"*, and it would be recommendable to make this document public. Confidentiality is always a source of doubt and ambiguity. The efficacity of a nuclear non-proliferation policy depends on transparency and the possibility of democratic control.

---

[4] Rapport Annuel de CEA 1992, pp.58-59.

[5] See : DAVIS M., **Guide de l'industrie nucléaire française**, L'Harmattan, Paris, 1988, p.50; or : **The Military-civilian Nuclear Link. A Guide to the French Nuclear Industry**, Westview Press, Boulder, Col., 1988.

3.2. The New Notice to Importers and Exporters (June 1994)

The import and export of products subject to final destination control is governed by a special regime (Sections 36, 79 and 80 of the *Order of 30th January 1967* as amended), consisting of *Notices to Importers and Exporters* which specify their obligations and list the products concerned. According to the most recent notice, imports, exports and re-exports of the products listed in the annex, as well as commercial transactions with foreign countries involving purchase or sale of any such products without their import into French territory, are subject to final control. Thus, France extends its export control to extraterritorial trade transactions. The products subject to final destination control are those on the list published by the way of *Notice to Importers and Exporters*, whatever the origin or country of manufacture.[6] In June 1994 a new Notice was published[7] which proposes a new structure of lists. This new notice summarizes all recent lists published by different fora (COCOM, NSG, Australia Group and former Notice) in order to unify them and to propose a single list. This involves :

- NSG lists (especially Part 1 relating to nuclear and Part 2 relating to dual-use products - this list has never been published in France) ;
- Lisbon 1 List (European List, EEC) ;
- Lisbon 2 List (IAEA).

The consequence of this change is that some items which were not subject to authorization have now become so.

The structure of the lists is now as follows :

- First, the List of nuclear goods (*Liste des biens nucléaires*, LBN) covering materials, installations, equipment, blueprints and nuclear technologies.
- Second, the List of dual-use goods (*Liste des biens connexes au nucléaire*, LCN), covering equipment, materials and

---

[6] See "The regulation of nuclear trade", OECD, *Op.cit.*

[7] *Avis aux importateurs et aux exportateurs*, in : **Journal Officiel, Lois et Décrets**, 6 et 7/06/1994, No.130, pp.8218-8232.

technologies related to nuclear activities (such as equipment linked to isotope separation for uranium and components, or equipment for nuclear tests and components) ; it is the first time that this List has been rendered public in France. This is a very significant event.
- Last, the List of large nuclear units (research centres, research reactors, etc.)

This new Notice seems more effective and more complete than the last one. France is now in possession of a tool which should make it easier to prevent nuclear proliferation by means of improved control of nuclear exports.

In addition to the new structure of lists, the Notice presents the procedure for controlling nuclear exports, which has not been changed.

3.3. French Nuclear Export Control

The general characteristic of the French procedure, apart from the fact that it tries to follow the international regimes which France has joined (subject to the revitalization of the CNPE Document of Reference !), is that it combines political and administrative control.

For industrialists who want to export there are two national procedures :

The first concerns war materiel (*Arrêté of 20/11/1991*, which fixes the list of materials submitted to the export procedure and to the AEMG, *autorisation d'exportation de matériels de guerre*). This procedure does not concern us, as France does export neither nuclear weapons nor their parts. It is released by the Ministry of Defence.

The second which is of more interest for us concerns all goods appearing on the different lists : LBN, LCN, List of large nuclear units. This procedure is described in the new Notice to Importers and Exporters.

The procedures for exporting to all countries are laid down in the *Order of 30th January 1967* (Title II, Chapter II, Section II), which makes such exports conditional upon the granting of an export licence. For the export of large nuclear plants to any country an application for prior approval must be made first, following the procedure laid down in the *Order of 30th January 1967*. This particular rule is due to the high visibility, and thus political virulence, of all transfers of such items.

3.3.1. Control of nuclear material and equipment export (excluding large nuclear units and very sensitive materials)

If we first focus our attention on the procedure relating to nuclear material and equipment, we can say that these are governed by *Prime Ministerial Directive No.1337* (not published, dated 10th December 1979) for materials, and by *Directive No.1338* dated 10th December 1979 for equipment. According to the new Notice, all goods appearing on the LBN and LCN are subject to this procedure. Consultation is coordinated by the Ministry of Industry (*Direction Générale de l'Energie et des Matières Premières* [DGEMP] and *Direction Générale des Stratégies Industrielles* [DGSI]).

• The 02 Licence Procedure

The rules governing this procedure are stated in the *Order of 30th January 1967* (General Directorate for Customs). According to this last decree, exports require an 02 licence from the General Directorate for Customs, before which the Ministry of Industry must approve the application.

This export licence constitutes the basis of the French nuclear export control procedure.

Step 1 : Receipt of the application

An industrialist who wants to export must send his application to the SETICE, *Service des Titres du Commerce Extérieur*, Paris (ex-SAFICO ; *Service des autorisations financières et commerciales*), a department connected to the General Directorate for Customs and Indirect Taxation. This department only plays the role of manager of the procedure. It is a "mail-box" without political decision-making authority.

Step 2 : Technical examination of the application

SETICE acknowledges receipt of the application and transmits it to the Ministry of Industry, General Directorate of Industrial Strategies, Office of export controls. This office receives about twenty applications each day.

It is managed by a chief administrator. He is assisted by three graduate engineers - an electronics engineer, a chemical engineer, and a nuclear engineer who represents the General Directorate of Energy and Raw Materials - and by two assistants. The chief administrator distributes applications to be examined among these officials. At this stage of the procedure, the main problem is the need for fuller information.

Applications received are not very explicit. The controllers have to ask «What ? What for ? For whom ?». This is very precise work which involves collaboration with the intelligence service DST (*Défense et Sûreté du Territoire*) and which requires also direct contacts with exporters. Controllers work in shifts. They meet frequently to inform each other of their investigations, in order to ensure that they do not work by rule of thumb.

Applications are classified in two categories :

- When the product does not have a sensitive character, export authorization is given by way of a so-called "administrative licence".

-   When the product is sensitive, closer examination is required. Then an interministerial consultation begins. What is meant here by "sensitive" ? The classification is left to the judgement of these officials ; therefore it depends on the controller's experience. For some products he knows that there is no proliferation risk. He is absolutely sure of that. It is a question of routine and professionalism. In other cases he may have a doubt, perhaps a very small doubt. In this case he does not hesitate to undertake a fuller examination.

Nevertheless, in cases of doubt, the controller needs to be protected by his superiors and by the political authorities. A longer procedure is preferable to a mistake. For these sensitive procedures, a consensus of all controllers is required. The length of this procedure varies : from one or two days for straightforward applications up to several weeks for the most sensitive ones. At this stage, the quality of the French control system is clearly dependent on the professional qualities of the officials of SETICE.

Step 3 : Interministerial consultation (political control)

According to the 1994 Notice sensitive applications require interministerial consultation. The procedure is as follows : the chief administrator of the export control office makes six copies of each application, on which appears advice formulated by his department and countersigned by him :

-   one for the Ministry of External Affairs (*Sous-direction de la non-prolifération*) which provides political advice based on the state of political relations and cooperation with the country concerned, and an assessment of the international political climate and the risk of nuclear proliferation ;

-   one for the Ministry of Defence (*Direction Générale pour les Armements* (*DGA*), *mission Atome*), which provides military advice based on the military capacities of the country concerned, the state of development of its military programmes and the geopolitical situation in the area ;

- one for the Ministry of Economy (*Direction des Relations Extérieures*) which provides economic advice based on the financial situation of the country concerned ;

- one for the CEA (*Direction des Relations Internationales*) which gives technical advice in respect of the risk of nuclear proliferation with regard to the state of development of a nuclear programme ;

- one for the Ministry of Industry (*Direction Générale pour l'Energie et les Matières Premières*, DGEMP, *cellule nucléaire*).

A copy is also sent to the General Secretariat of National Defence (*Secrétariat Général de la Défense Nationale*, SGDN) for information.

Each ministry responds in the form of an advice, and the Export Control Office acknowledges receipt of these documents. We must note that, in the framework of this 02 Licence procedure, a minister who is member of the GIR (*Groupe Interministériel Restreint*, Interministerial Restricted Group) may well decide to refer an application to the GIR in cases where it appears particularly sensitive. This opens a predominantly **political** decision route under the guidance of the Foreign Ministry (see *infra*). As soon as the interministerial consultation is finished, the chief administrator presents the complete record to the Minister of Industry's departmental staff. The final decision concerning this application is then taken by the Minister himself. In reality, it usually turns out that the Minister of Industry delegates this final decision-making process to his own administration and that - in nearly all cases - this ministerial decision confirms advice formulated by the Export Control Office.

Step 4 : Permission is granted

As soon as the Minister of Industry has taken his decision, the application returns to the Export Control Office where it is countersigned. Thereafter it is sent to the SETICE, which returns it to the exporter.

3.3.2. Export control of large nuclear units and very sensitive materials

In cases where large nuclear units such as plants and some very sensitive materials (special fissile materials, heavy water, tritium in certain quantities) are concerned, the procedure is quite different and is carried out in the framework of GIR. GIR was instituted by a Prime Ministerial Directive in 1975. The GIR procedure is handled from start to finish by the Ministry of External Affairs (*Sous-direction de la non-prolifération*, formerly *Sous-direction des affaires atomiques et spatiales*). As a matter of fact the export of nuclear plants is heavily dependent on France's international commitments in the field of nuclear non-proliferation and on contacts that France maintains with international interlocutors (IAEA, NSG). The export of nuclear plants may also have important diplomatic and political implications for the countries concerned.

This procedure may be applied to all products appearing on the third List of the new Notice to importers and exporters (corresponding to the Atomic Energy List) and which are described in the annexes of the Directives relating to nuclear technology. The Notice to exporters states that «when fabrication or delivery of products or technologies submitted to an export licence require delays superior to the duration of the licence's validity (12 months) - which is always the case for nuclear plants - exports may form the subject of a prior approval» (Article 2, Sec.2.1, b). Prior approval is not an export authorization. It is not possible to present such a document to the customs as an export permit, a 02 Licence is always necessary. GIR work relates only to this prior approval.

GIR is entitled to demand access to all export projects of materials and equipment or all enrichment or reprocessing contract projects that one of its members would like to examine. Presently, GIR is no longer investigating large units (plants), due to the absence of new orders. It concentrates on enriched material, dealing with all that concerns higher than 20 % enriched materials. SETICE sends to the GIR all applications for prior approval relating to export of these types of products. A complementary technical slip must accompany such applications, showing the previous date of delivery and the estimated list of goods subject to export authorization necessary to build and to implement the nuclear unit concerned.

Members of GIR are the Minister of External Affairs, who acts as its chairman, the ministers of Defence, Economy and Industry (or their representatives), and the General Secretary of National Defence. CEA is also represented. Decisions are taken by consensus, or (when consensus cannot be reached) with the help of prime ministerial arbitration, either during plenary sessions (about one every two months) or in the form of written consultations by the Minister of External Affairs (*Sous-direction de la non-prolifération nucléaire*). The procedure for written consultations is very similar to the one we have described for the granting of 02 licences.

4. Control of the Application of the Law in the Field of Nuclear Export Control

4.1. Juridical or Legal Control

When a nuclear importer or exporter does not respect the procedure determined by the Notice and is caught by the customs, there are two levels of prosecution :

  1. administrative prosecution by the customs,
  2. legal prosecution before a court of justice.

1. Concerning the first level of prosecution, the customs' Disputed Claims Department imposes the sanction, which can be of three kinds :

  - fines ;
  - suspension of the special clearance procedures for nuclear materials ;

47

-   confiscation of the goods. This may mean considerable losses for the exporter, depending on the value of the goods.

All those sanctions - which are of an administrative nature - may be contested by the offender before the Administrative Tribunal (*Tribunal administratif*).

Prosecution remains at the administrative level if customs officials consider the breach of the procedure to have been the result of negligence. It is the case when the exporter has respected the 02 Licence procedure, but has made a mistake in informations given.

It is important to stress that it is dangerous for an exporter not to respect in the letter the procedure described above. In addition to the fact that there is a high probability of getting caught by the Customs, and that the financial costs could be high, the consequences of such a fraud could be disastrous for him and his company. We can cite as an example the case of an industrialist who wanted to export sensitive materials to Pakistan. Customs officials discovered a mistake : according to the documents, the destination was India. This "small" mistake (voluntary or involuntary ?) had major consequences : a customs fine amounting to about three times the value of the transaction, the opening of a DST investigation, the dismissal of the company president, and further measures.[8]

2. When customs officials estimate that the problem is more serious, involves a serious intent to evade the law and constitutes an offence, they bring an action against the offender before a court of justice (*Tribunal correctionnel*). Not to respect the procedure and to import or export without administrative authorization is considered by the law as a "first class customs offence" (Article 414 of the customs statute book). Those prosecuted may be condemned to 3 years' imprisonment (maximum), may have their goods and means of transport confiscated and may be fined one or two times the value of the goods not declared. Moreover, the tribunal may impose an additional sentence and ban the offender temporarily or permanently

---

[8] We were given the details of this case *viva voce* by the Head Clerk of the Export Control Office (Ministry of Industry).

from the direct or indirect carrying out of any industrial profession (Article 432 of the customs statute-book).

It is important to mention that no nuclear matter has ever been referred to a court by the customs. This means that there is no case-law in the matter.

Perhaps this is because industrialists have learnt how to export via safe channels which involve no risk of being caught. A customs officer has explained to us that it was very easy to export nuclear materials quite legally to South Africa via Switzerland.

4.2. Political Control

Nuclear export control is a very sensitive problem which determines the conditions of peace in the world. As a nuclear power and as an exporter of nuclear facilities, France has a great responsibility in this field. The French people, as represented in parliament, must be very attentive to all that concerns nuclear issues. It is in this spirit that we have interviewed the president of each parliamentary commission involved in export control matters.

We should also note the low level of parliamentary awareness of nuclear questions. The most probable explanation of this lies in the fact that parliament has traditionally only played a minor role in this field. From the beginning of the nuclear age, parliament has always suffered from "the legislation of Head Clerks".[9] Parliament has no nuclear culture and seems to censor itself very effectively.

Under these conditions it is not surprising that parliamentary control over nuclear policy appears weak.

4.2.1. The National Assembly

When we observe French legislation with regard to nuclear export control we notice that few texts of this legislation are parlia-

---

[9] Literally : «*la législation des chefs de bureaux*» (pejorative). See : Rapport de BOURJOL M. & LE LAMER C., *"Energie et démocratie"*, **La documentation française**, 1982, p.7.

mentary laws in the strict sense. Most of them are decrees, orders, or directives. They are regulations (*"textes réglementaires"*). Article 37 of the French Constitution states that all matters not covered by Article 34 of the Constitution have a "regular character" (*"un caractère réglementaire"*). The executive power (and especially the government) disposes of the real legislative competence for those matters. This is the case for all aspects of nuclear and non-proliferation policy. The consequence is a great proliferation of administrative regulations[10] in a matter which is only partially subject to parliamentary scrutiny. Regulation texts adopted under Article 37 are real laws. The executive power may use its own regular competence to make rules, and this is made even easier by the fact that nuclear trade is by its very nature international. As a matter of fact all texts which concern nuclear export may be qualified by government acts (*"Actes de gouvernement"*). According to the theory of government acts, acts of the executive power are not subject to judicial scrutiny. These texts escape the normal control by the Constitutional Court and are only subject to the Constitution itself and to general principles of law.[11]

President Giscard d'Estaing, former President of the French Republic and current president of the Commission for External Affairs of the National Assembly, refers to the debate on ratification of the NPT in order to illustrate the problem of export control.[12] He recalls France's decision to adopt the rule of "integral control" (full-scope safeguards) during the G-7 summit in London in July 1991. This declaration on "integral control" has the effect of banning French nuclear trade with such importing countries as India, Pakistan, Algeria, Cuba and Israel. Giscard d'Estaing also underlines that France decided to participate in the revision of the London Guidelines even though it had so far declared itself against reviving this body.

Concerning the technical implementation of the nuclear export control procedure, the Commission for External Affairs seems not

---

[10] *Op.cit.*

[11] See : BURDEAU G., **Droit constitutionnel et Institutions politiques**, LGDJ, Paris, 1976.

[12] In a letter dated March 30, 1994.

to be very well informed. No deputy seems to have precise knowledge of the procedural system of control, which is an administrative one and which is laid down in regulation texts.

4.2.2. The Senate

Senatorial examination of the problem of nuclear export control seems not to be any more effective than that of the National Assembly. The President of the Commission of External Affairs, Defence and Armed Forces, Senator de Villerin, is satisfied with citing the report written by his colleague,[13] Senator Cabanel,[14] on the draft law authorizing French adhesion to the NPT. Nevertheless this report is richer and better informed than the corresponding report produced by the National Assembly (Report of Deputy Crepeau[15]). The Cabanel report concludes that French adherence to the NPT does not require any modification of those internal regulations which already apply to non-proliferation policy. This shows that the Senate is not well informed. The fact that the *Document de Référence* which governs all French nuclear policy must be entirely re-written, proves that some modification in the internal legislation is necessary.

The publication of a new Notice to importers and exporters in June 1994 covering LCN (dual-use) demonstrates *a posteriori* that the Senate has not been very well informed on issues of nuclear export control policy.

5. Conclusion

An evaluation of the control procedure's efficacy is not very easy, since it is difficult to obtain information on the exact contents of

---

[13] in a letter dated March 8, 1994.

[14] Sénat, No.295, seconde session ordinaire de 1991-1992, Rapport fait au nom de la commission des affaires étrangères, de la défense et des forces armées sur le projet de loi autorisant l'adhésion au TNP, par M. Guy Cabanel, sénateur.

[15] Assemblée Nationale, No.2736, seconde session ordinaire de 1991-1992, Rapport fait au nom de la commission des affaires étrangères sur le projet de loi autorisant l'adhésion au TNP par M. Michel Crepeau, député.

different applications submitted to the administration in the frame-work of this procedure of control.

To be able to produce a satisfactory evaluation it would be necessary to examine all the applications received and stored by the administration. The administration always cultivates the principle of treating all information as confidential, a French tradition which is still observed in spite of some appreciable evolutions. As a matter of fact we must underline that we have been welcomed by the administration and that it has been willing to give us important information. For example, we have been permitted to consult some records.[16] Of course those records were not the most sensitive ones, but it was for the first time possible to have access to such documents.

Nevertheless, it has been possible to find out in the course of this investigation that nuclear export control is taken very seriously in France. This has been corroborated by exporters (FBFC, CERCA, etc.). Industrialists interviewed stress the severity of the procedure of control and supervision of which they are "victims". For example the person who is in charge of exports at the FBFC has explained that he has seen application returned up for additional information : the administration requested to obtain the three digits after the comma, of the planned transfer of material, when the weight was notified in grams !

This person has made an application for a 02 Licence relating to South Africa, which is currently going through the control process. Exporters consider that this severity is absolutely necessary.

Moreover, France is going to render its legislation more coherent and more solid. We hope that nuclear export control will be reinforced in France with the publication and the administrative and political implementation of the new Notice.

---

[16] The administration was ready to give us some records in order to illustrate our study. Of course, the agreement of the industrials concerned was a *sine qua non* condition and, interestingly, those exporters did not give their consent to publication.

PROCEDURE FOR NUCLEAR EXPORT CONTROL

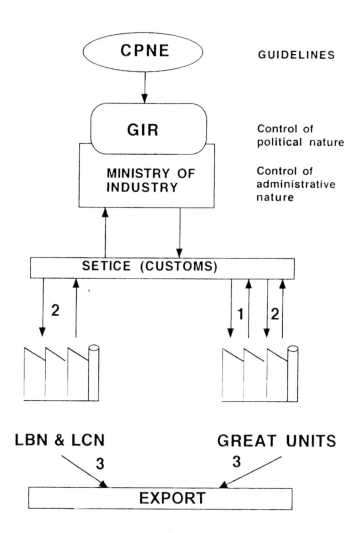

1 : PRIOR APPROVAL
2 : LICENCE 02
3 : EXPORT

Case 1: **Export of Materials from LBN or LCN**	Case 2: **Export of a Nuclear Plant** (third list)
Step 1:	**Step 1:** Prior Approval
- none -	1. The exporter contacts the ministry/ministries concerned. 2. He sends his application to the SENTICE for prior approval. 3. Political control by the GIR. 4. Prior approval given by the GIR. 5. The SETICE returns the record with the prior approval, valid for one year.
Step 2: Licence 02	**Step 2:** Licence 02
1. The exporter sends to the SETICE an application for a 02 Licence. 2. Administrative control of this record by the Ministry of Industry. 3. Authorization given by the Minister of Industry. 4. The SETICE returns the record with the authorization to the exporter.	6. The exporter sends to the SETICE an application for a 02 Licence for the 12 months. 7. Administrative control of this record by the Ministry of Industry. 8. Authorization given by the Minister of Industry. 9. The SETICE returns the record with the authorization to the exporter.
Step 3: Export	**Step 3:** Export
5. Export (subject to Final Destination Control).	10. Export (subject to Final Destination Control).

LBN: *Liste des biens nucléaires (List of nuclear goods)*
LCN: *Liste des biens à double usage connexes au nucléaire (List of dual-use goods)*
SETICE: *Service des Titres du Commerce Extérieur (Customs)*
GIR: *Groupe Interministériel restreint (Interministerial Restricted Group)*

UNITED KINGDOM

Darryl Howlett[1]

1. Introduction

The United Kingdom's (UK) export control policy has undergone radical change in the post-Cold War, post-Persian Gulf War world. Since 1990, there has been a marked shift away from controls governing technology exports from West to East during the Cold War, towards a system aimed at controlling technologies that could contribute to the proliferation of weapons of mass destruction and ballistic missile delivery systems.

This is not to suggest that global non-proliferation objectives were unimportant prior to 1990. Rather, priorities have changed. For the UK has traditionally held an image of itself as being at the forefront of global non-proliferation efforts. The UK is a Depositary State of both the Treaty on the Non-Proliferation of Nuclear Weapons (NPT) and the Convention on the Prohibition of the Development, Production and Stockpiling of Bacteriological (Biological) and Toxin Weapons and on their Destruction (BWC). The UK also tabled several papers during negotiations for the Chemical Weapons Convention (CWC) and became one of its first signatories when the Convention was opened for signature in January 1993. Finally, the UK was a founding member of the Missile Technology Control

[1] The author is grateful to Ben COLE for research assistance related to this chapter.

Regime (MTCR) in 1987 and has been participating in all the other export control groups, including the Zangger Committee and Nuclear Suppliers Group (NSG) governing nuclear exports, and the Australia Group concerning exports of chemical-related goods.

Until recently, however, the major emphasis in the UK's multilateral export control effort had been on implementing COCOM (Co-ordinating Committee for Multilateral Export Control) controls as part of the Cold War. Since 1950, when it was established, COCOM has served as an informal, non-treaty based method of controlling strategic exports (sensitive dual-use, military and nuclear technology) to the former Warsaw Pact and other communist states (commonly referred to as proscribed destinations). With the end of the Cold War, COCOM members decided, in November 1993, to terminate the system of controls based on the old East-West relationship and replace it with a system, still to be agreed, which is more appropriate for the post-Cold War world.

This transformation has been precipitated by two main factors. First, it is a reflection of the heightened concern surrounding the proliferation of weapons of mass destruction now that the Cold War has ended. Second, it is in response to a number of revelations that the UK and some of its companies may in the past have contributed, wittingly or unwittingly, to the development of weapons of mass destruction in other countries. The latter revelations have raised unprecedented public interest in export control issues, led to a series of trials and public inquiries to investigate the allegations, and provoked a concerted debate about the philosophy underlying the UK's approach to the control of strategic exports.

This chapter is divided into three sections. In the first and largest section, the conceptual and legal basis for UK export controls is outlined, focusing especially on those changes that have occurred since 1990. This is followed, in the second section, by an overview of those cases which have been brought to public prominence because of allegations that export control regulations have been breached. Finally, in the third section, an attempt is made to determine whether general lessons can be learned from the UK's past experience in implementing export controls. The chapter concludes by stressing the significance of the recent overhaul of UK export control procedures in reinforcing the country's commitment to non-proliferation, but contends that more changes will be required if UK policy is to meet the challenges of the new international environment.

2. The Conceptual and Legal Basis for UK Export Controls

The UK has applied export controls for several decades, but as a recent government publication points out, «export controls are the exception, not the rule. UK export controls administered by the DTI have an impact on just 5 % or so of UK exports overall».[2] As with several other industrialised countries, export controls affect certain manufacturing sectors in the UK more than others. Yet all sectors must apply for export licences if a good is on a control list and be aware of the procedures for making an application.

2.1. Why does the UK implement an export control policy ?

The underlying rationale for the UK's export control policy is defined as the following, «The purpose in controlling technology, as with export controls on goods themselves, is primarily to protect national security and strategic interests, and to limit the proliferation of weapons of mass destruction.»[3] The specific considerations which inform this underlying rationale are identified in official publications as :

- the UK's non-proliferation policy ;
- the collective security of the UK and its allies in NATO ;
- national security ;
- concerns about terrorism or internal repression ;

---

[2] *"How and Why Goods are Controlled"*, DTI ECO Annual Report 1992.

[3] *"Controls on the Export of Technology. Guidelines For Compliance"*, Department of Trade and Industry and the Central Office of Information, O/N 0801655 INDY J071075NJ, London, September 1993, p.2.

- foreign policy requirements ; and,
- international treaty obligations and commitments.[4]

2.2. Export control legislation

Prior to 1939, several pieces of legislation affected UK export controls.[5] At the beginning of the Second World War, all export legislation affecting the war effort was consolidated under the Import, Export and Customs Powers (Defence) Act (1 September 1939).[6] The Board of Trade was given primary responsibility for overseeing the new legislation due to its close relationship with commercial enterprise, the desire to ensure that exports of strategic goods did not reach the enemy, and to ensure that the regulations did not hinder too unduly the UK's international trading markets.

Although the 1939 Act was initiated to deal with an emergency situation, and therefore considered a temporary expedient, it remained in force after 1945 and throughout the Cold War period. But by the end of the 1980s, concern was increasing about the relevance of maintaining the 1939 Act in the perceived absence of an "emergency situation". Because the Department of Trade and Industry (DTI), the eventual successor to the Board of Trade, considered that the conceptual basis for the Act remained as relevant as it had always been, efforts were made to make it permanent. These efforts successfully culminated in the passing of the Import and Export Control Act in 1990. This repealed Section 9 (3) of the 1939 Act (which provides for the expiry of this Act when the emergency

---

[4] *"Export Control Compliance. Code of Practice"*, Department of Trade and Industry and the Central Office of Information, O/N 14470/A J1889NJ 10M, London, March 1993, p.2.

[5] The Customs and Inland Revenue Act of 1879 provided the central piece of legislation for exports related to «arms, ammunition and gunpowder, military and naval stores». This was later supplemented by additional legislation codifying further the prohibitions in this area.

[6] For text, see : *"Public General Acts and Measures 1938-39"*, Eyre and Spottiswoode, London, 1939, pp.1044-1049.

which was the occasion for its passing is declared by Order in Council to have come to an end).[7]

Although no other section was altered, the 1939 Act has provided the basis for the introduction of export control orders which specify the range of goods to be controlled via the provision of a licence. The 1939 Act is thus to be understood as enabling legislation : it allows for alterations to procedures ; additional items to be placed on the export control lists ; and changes to proscribed destinations to be made without requiring a substantive change to the Act itself.

In contrast to other subordinate legislation derived from a specific Act, the Export of Goods (Control) Order [EG(C)O] are regarded as Statutory Instruments made under the primary authority of the 1939 and 1990 Acts. Although as Statutory Instruments they are subject to oversight by the Joint Standing Committee on Statutory Instruments, they do not require prior Parliamentary consent and can normally be made by the Secretary of State for Trade and Industry or by an official of that department.

Amendments to EG(C)Os have occurred in 1990, 1991, 1992 and, more recently, in May 1994. The latter Order is now in force. The 1990 Order contained provision for three different export control lists : the Munitions List ; the Atomic Energy List ; and the Industrial List. The 1992 Order sought to simplify the three Lists by integrating them into a single format derived from a classification system developed by technical experts.

2.3. Export control classifications

The export control classification system divides the goods into three groups : Group 1 deals with "Military, Security and Para-Military Goods and Arms, Ammunition and Related Material" ; Group 2 with "Atomic Energy Minerals and Materials and Nuclear Facili-

---

[7] *"Import and Export Control Act 1990"*, HMSO, London, 1990. Section 9(3) of the 1939 Act had stated that the Act would «continue in force until such date as His Majesty may [...] declare to be the date on which the emergency that was the occasion of the passing of this Act came to an end, and shall then expire...».

ties, Equipment, Appliances and Software"; and Group 3 with "Dual-Use Industrial Goods and Technology not specified in Groups 1 and 2".[8] One significant feature of this classification is the identification of a range of goods in Group 3 considered to have a dual civilian-military use and which are therefore prohibited from export outside the UK without a licence. This inclusion followed a period of intense discussion within the technology supplier groups (COCOM, Australia Group, MTCR, and NSG) and within the European Community after it had been revealed that certain dual-use items had been used by Iraq prior to the Persian Gulf War to pursue weapons of mass destruction programmes.[9]

The 1990 and subsequent Orders also specifically include additional procedures, outlined in Schedule I, Part II of the Order, which are designed to prevent a manufacturer exporting goods that are known or suspected to be destined for use «in relation to chemical, biological or nuclear weapons and related missiles». Referred to as end-use control or "catch-all", an exporter must inform the relevant export licensing authorities if there are doubts concerning the final destination of a particular good. Any attempt to export that good without a licence is an offence.[10]

2.4. UK export licences

In the UK, export licences take several forms. An individual export licence (IEL) allows a manufacturer to export one or more shipments to one destination or consignee and is valid for up to two years. This is the most common licence issued in the UK.[11] An open

---

[8] *"The Export of Goods (Control) Order 1992"*, HMSO, **Statutory Instruments**, No.3092, London, 31 December 1992.

[9] For a detailed analysis of the debate concerning changes to dual-use nuclear export control guidelines see Harald Muller, *"Reform of the System of Nuclear Export Controls"*, in : MÜLLER H. & DUNN L.A., **Nuclear Export Controls and Supply Side Restraints : Options for Reform, PPNN Study Four**, Mountbatten centre for International Studies for the Programme for Promoting Nuclear Non-Proliferation (PPNN), Southampton (UK), October 1993.

[10] *"The End-Use Control. A Guide for Exporters"*, Department of Trade and Industry, DTI/Pub1280/5K/4/94/NP, London, April 1994, p.2.

[11] Bulk licences may also be issued to cover multiple shipments to several consignees, and not necessarily in the same country of destination. However, these licences are not allowed for proscribed destinations.

individual export licence (OIEL) covers situations where an exporter makes recurrent shipments of non-sensitive goods to several consignees or destinations (but not proscribed ones), and is usually valid for up to three years. An open general export licence (OGEL) allows shipments of certain goods to certain destinations without prior approval by the DTI, although Customs and Excise must be notified at the time the goods are being shipped that they are covered by a specific OGEL. A temporary licence covers goods that are being shipped from the UK on a temporary basis, such for an exhibition or repair and maintenance purposes, and must be returned within a specified time-period and remain at all times under the licensees control. Finally, an open general transshipment licence (OGTL) is granted in situations where a controlled good (although not certain proscribed goods, such as for use in weapons of mass destruction programmes) enters the UK *en route* to another country of destination.[12]

2.5. The Export Control Organisation (ECO)

The ECO, located within the DTI, has the main responsibility for the general administration of UK export controls. This Organisation is divided into several different units.[13]

The Export Licensing Unit is the largest unit in the Organisation and deals with the processing of export licence applications. This Unit is subdivided into sections dealing with particular areas of responsibility, such as licences for sensitive destinations, industrial dual-use goods, and goods with specific military or nuclear-related purposes.

The Sensitive Technologies Unit involves a multi-disciplinary team of engineers, scientists and administrators whose main function is to advise the other units in the Organisation on whether cer-

---

[12] For further details of these licences, see : THURLOW J., *"United Kingdom"*, in : **Worldwide Guide to Export Controls**, (updated June 1994), Export Control Publications, Chertsey, (UK), 1993/1994 Edition.

[13] *"Export Control Organisation. Annual Report 1992"*, Department of Trade and Industry, DTI/Pub1115/5K/7.93/NNNNNP, London, July 1993. The following brief outline of the Units within this Organisation are taken from this source.

tain technologies are subject to export control regulation and provides a direct link to Customs and Excise for similar information. Industry may also seek advice from this Unit on licensing requirements.

The task of the Policy Unit is to develop a coherent export control strategy which protects the UK's security interests while simultaneously allowing legitimate trade to flourish. This Unit has consequently been involved in the efforts to harmonise export policies within the Single European Market, controls on dual-use goods, and has been instrumental in recent years in developing measures to streamline export control procedures while at the same time strengthening those controls on sensitive technologies.

The Sanctions and Enforcement Unit was established specifically to handle the sanctions imposed by the United Nations on Iraq following its invasion of Kuwait in August 1990. The Unit does issue licences for the supply of essential medical equipment and foodstuffs to Iraq which are not covered by sanctions. It has also been tasked with overseeing UN sanctions on Montenegro and Serbia in 1992 and on a more selective basis, against Libya.

The European Community Special Export Licensing Unit was established in September 1992 as a result of a decision by the European Community to implement a dual licensing system for exports to Bosnia, Croatia and Macedonia in an effort to reinforce the UN sanctions against Montenegro and Serbia. The exports of food, medical and humanitarian items and certain goods destined for UN operations are excluded from this system.

In operation since August 1991, the Compliance Unit has responsibility for ensuring that exporters are aware of the UK's export control requirements and are implementing them rigorously. The Unit works closely with UK's exporting firms and has developed a "Code of Practice" on compliance in collaboration with this sector.

The ECO also includes : a Computer Services Unit responsible for the provision of information technology within the Organisation ; a Co-ordination Unit, which performs a management information role and also includes an Enquiry Unit as a first point of contact for the public on export control issues ; and finally, a Scott Inquiry Unit, established as a liaison point for issues related to the Inquiry concerned with UK trade with Iraq.

2.6. Who decides export control policy ?

Several governmental departments are involved in making judgments about export licence applications, especially the DTI, the Foreign and Commonwealth Office, the Ministry of Defence, Customs and Excise and the Department of Energy. All licence applications in the UK are considered on a case-by-case basis following standard procedures. Each case will be determined on its merits against a set of criteria, such as the specific kind of good to be exported and whether the country of destination is a party to relevant international arms control agreements. In the case of nuclear-related exports, for example, a crucial consideration would be whether a country is a party to the NPT.

Interdepartmental co-ordination is carried out under the umbrella of the Restricted Enforcement Unit (REU), in which officials from the DTI, MOD, Customs and Excise, and the FCO are represented. This Unit meets on a fortnightly basis and is tasked with assessing license applications for sensitive cases.[14]

There are also regular reviews of the goods to be controlled and of the list of countries for which a licence will be required before a good can be exported (referred to as the list of countries subject to special procedures or "proscribed destinations").[15]

---

[14] *"Exports to Iraq : Project Babylon and Long Range Guns"*, **Trade and Industry Committee, Session 1991-92, House of Commons**, (Second Report), HMSO, London, 13 March 1992, p.vii.

[15] For a recent list of these destinations, see : *"The End-Use Control. Guide for Exporters"*, *Op.cit.*, Annex B, p.11.

2.7. The manufacturer and export controls

The manufacturer also plays a critical role in ensuring that export controls are effectively implemented as, initially, it is the manufacturer who has to decide whether to apply for a licence.

To assist this process, the DTI has issued several pamphlets outlining the licence application procedure and has suggested that each company institute an 'Export Control Code of Practice'. This should involve a company implementing the following procedures : a basic "Commitment to Compliance", whereby each company makes a statement that it will abide by UK export controls ; the "Nomination of Responsible Personnel", whose task it is to oversee export control issues within the company ; a commitment by the company to "Information and Training" to ensure the workforce is well-informed about export controls ; the institution of "Internal Compliance Procedures", designed to ensure good export control practice within the company ; develop an awareness of "Suspicious Enquiries or Orders" ; undertake responsible "Record Keeping" to ensure that all records of transactions are in order and are kept in logical sequence for a minimum of four years ; make "Provision for Audits" so that an internal audit of the system for export control compliance can be conducted on a regular basis ; and, finally, companies should ensure that export control procedures are fully integrated with its "Quality Management Practices".[16]

As has been pointed out, the basic premise of the Code «is that the system of export controls is subject to much change and the burden of multiple individual licence applications is being reduced by the wider use of open licences but that an open licence approach has to be underpinned by consistent compliance with the licence conditions».[17] As an incentive for companies to implement the Code, the DTI has indicated it will treat companies that do so more favourably because they will be deemed to be pursuing good export control practise.

---

[16] *"Export Control Compliance. Code of Practice"*, *Op.cit.*

[17] THURLOW J., *"United Kingdom"*, *Op.cit.*

2.8. Non-compliance and penalties

Non-compliance with UK export controls risks considerable financial and legal penalties. While all government departments are involved in the co-ordination of enforcement, the main juridical enforcement power is granted to the Customs and Excise Service under the Customs and Excise Management Act of 1979. The principal offences covered by this Act are : false or fraudulent declarations (Section 167) ; attempts to knowingly evade export controls (Section 68/2) ; and presenting goods for export without a licence (Section 68/1). Illegal exports are subject to seizure, while suspect shipments may be detained for further investigation (Section 139).

Evasion of export controls is deemed a criminal offence in the UK. The penalties for this offence were increased in 1990 so that persons found guilty are liable «to a penalty of any amount, or to imprisonment for a term not exceeding (7 years), or to both».[18] Additional legislation has also been enacted which allows the relevant authorities to confiscate any profits made from previously successful crime.

There are also a range of offences connected with falsely obtaining an export licence under the EG(C)O. Persons found guilty are liable, on summary conviction, to a fine «not exceeding the statutory maximum», and «on conviction on indictment to a fine or imprisonment for not exceeding 2 years, or to both».

2.9. UK export controls and the European Union (EU)

The move to strengthen export control procedures within the various supplier groups (NSG, MTCR, Australia Group, etc.), has also had a marked effect on UK national export control policy. Potentially, the most significant development, however, concerns the attempt to develop a harmonised export control policy in the Single Market of the EU. Inevitably, there is a tension between the con-

---

[18] *"Offenses in relation to exportation of prohibited or restricted goods"*, Customs and Excise, **Halsbury's Statutes**, Vol.13, 1991 Re-issue, Butterworth's, London, 1991, pp.328-329.

cept of a single market and the continuation of export controls in any form. Since the Single Market was agreed by the member states of the EU, efforts have been made to reduce this tension.

In the UK, this has been expressed in the form of initiatives to reduce the need for export control licences to EU member states. However, a residue of export control within this framework is still maintained as a bulwark against a potential proliferator operating a highly sophisticated procurement network. On 31 December 1992, for example, a new OGEL was introduced to cover the export to the EU of most dual-use industrial goods on the EG(C)O.

3. Recent Cases Involving UK Export Controls

Devising and implementing a national export control policy is an essential component of the global non-proliferation effort designed to constrain the spread of weapons of mass destruction. This policy inevitably has many conflicting pressures for those government authorities responsible for ensuring its effectiveness. If the policy is deemed inadequate to meet the tasks demanded of it, changes may be necessary. In some countries, the debate which precipitates these changes is often a drawn out process and conducted primarily within government circles. In the UK, this debate has been undertaken within a relatively short time-frame and conducted, for the most part, in the glare of the public spotlight.

The period from the early 1990s has seen considerable media and judicial attention paid to export control procedures in the UK. Apart from exports of specifically defence-related goods, much attention has also been devoted to exports of dual-use goods which have a potential military or civilian application. What is noteworthy about all these cases is that they have all embraced issues which are both highly contentious and go to the very heart of UK export control policy.

3.1. Project Babylon

One of the first cases to gain a high public profile followed reports of the involvement of British companies in Iraq's so-called "supergun".[19] This was a project, code-named Babylon, designed to provide Iraq with a long-range gun capable of launching projectiles over vast distances.[20]

As the enforcers of UK export controls, Customs and Excise did bring charges related to export control offences against senior personnel in those companies involved in supplying components for the supergun, but the prosecutions were dropped on 15 November 1990.[21] Not long afterwards, the House of Commons Trade and Industry Committee began its own investigation into UK interest in this project.[22]

In the course of their investigation the Committee were informed that in 1988, UK exports to Iraq were valued at £412 million, a sum

---

[19] The main companies involved were the steel manufacturers Sheffield Forgemasters and Walter Somers who were contracted to supply large diameter steel tubes ostensibly for Iraq's petrochemicals industry but eventually destined for use in Project Babylon. For a summary of events, see : *"Exports to Iraq : Project Babylon and Long Range Guns"*, **Trade and Industry Committee, Second Report**, House of Commons, Session 1991-92, HMSO, London, 13 March 1992, pp.xv-xix. For a brief account of the background to the "supergun", see : SIMPSON J., *"Great Britain"*, in : MÜLLER H. (ed.), **European Non-Proliferation Policy 1988-1992**, European Interuniversity Press, Brussels, 1993, pp.106-107.

[20] However, it is considered unlikely that Iraq was capable of producing a miniaturised nuclear, chemical, or biological (NBC) warhead for use with these projectiles.

[21] Other personnel were arrested at the time the last consignment of steel tubes was seized at Teesport, and they «remained under threat of prosecution for several months, despite the fact that according to the DTI evidence they had supplied all the information requested and had received clearance for the export of the tubes». *"Exports to Iraq : Project Babylon and Long Range Guns"*, *Op.cit.*, p.xxxix.

[22] The broad terms of reference for this investigation were stated on 27 March 1991 to encompass :

«Defence-related exports to Iraq since 1984; government policy on the restriction of exports to Iraq; the criteria used in deciding whether to prohibit a certain export; liaison among government departments in the implementation of export control regulations; the work of the Export Control Organisation and its Export Licensing Branch; alleged examples of the export to Iraq of defence-related equipment and materials». *"Exports to Iraq : Project Babylon and Long Range Guns"*, *Op.cit.*, p.vi.

representing half of one per cent of total UK exports in that year, and that all UK defence exports to Iraq at this time were subject to a set of guidelines imposed in December 1984. These guidelines had been introduced as a result of the Iran-Iraq War, which had started in September 1980 and ended in August 1988.[23] A special Inter-Departmental Committee was also established to oversee defence-related licence applications to Iran and Iraq.

As a result of the Committee's inquiry several changes to UK export control procedures were introduced. A sensitive destinations section was established within the ECO to assess exports to these countries. New arrangements for the application of licences were also started, involving the requirement that all exports be subject to : comprehensive documentation ; detailed technical assessments ; and full disclosure of end use and end user.[24]

Efforts to improve both data management, by placing all industrial export licence applications on a central computer, and interdepartmental co-ordination, were also instituted. Similarly, the idea of "triggers", or key warning signals, has been implemented to «identify trends in licence applications that give cause for concern and to establish a matrix of information about which countries are seeking which technologies».[25]

In December 1990 a "catch all" clause was introduced. This made it a legal responsibility for exporting companies to take all reason-

---

[23] *Ibid.*, p.xi. The criteria for exports to Iraq were as follows :

(i) We should maintain our consistent refusal to supply any lethal equipment to either side.

(ii) Subject to that overriding consideration, we should attempt to fulfil existing contracts and obligations.

(iii) We should not, in future, approve orders for any defence equipment which, in our view, would significantly enhance the capability of either side to prolong or exacerbate the conflict.

(iv) In line with this policy, we should continue to scrutinise rigorously all applications for export licenses for the supply of defence equipment to Iran and Iraq.

[24] *Ibid.*, p.xxxix.

[25] *"Export to Iraq : Project Babylon and Long Range Guns"*, **Government's Response to the Second Report of the Trade and Industry Committee in Session 1991-92, Cmnd. 2019**, HMSO, London, July 1992, p.3.

able measures to ensure that their exports are not destined for a chemical or biological weapons programme. This provision was expanded in June 1991 to include missile delivery systems and nuclear weapons programmes.[26]

3.2. The "nuclear triggers" and Matrix Churchill cases

Two other incidents related to dual-use exports to Iraq surfaced during the early 1990s period. The first involved the alleged attempt to export forty electrical capacitors (devices which store and release electrical energy) to Iraq by the company, Euromac (London) Ltd. The arrest, in March 1990, of senior personnel from the company followed an eighteen month undercover operation, code-named Argus, by UK and American customs and intelligence officers. Charges of export law evasion were subsequently brought against these personnel under the Customs and Excise Management Act 1979 and the EG(C)O 1989.[27]

At the time of the arrests in the so-called "nuclear triggers" case, there were suspicions that Iraq was pursuing a nuclear weapons capability and that the electrical capacitors would have been vital components as trigger mechanisms for a nuclear warhead. This interpretation of the intended end-use was subsequently to become a key element during the two-month trial of the two people charged in late Spring 1991.[28]

On 12 June 1991, the managing director and export manager of Euromac were convicted of the offences and received custodial sentences of five years and eighteen months, respectively. However, on 23 May 1994 their convictions were quashed by the Court of

---

[26] "*Exports to Iraq : Project Babylon and Long Range Guns*", **Trade and Industry Committee, Second Report**, *Op.cit.*, p.xl.

[27] **PPNN Newsbrief**, No.9, Mountbatten Centre for International Studies for the Programme for Promoting Nuclear Non-Proliferation [PPNN], Southampton (UK), Spring 1990, p.7.

[28] **The Times**, 13 June 1991. In May 1990, President Saddam Hussein, the Iraq's leader, had stated that the capacitors were intended for use in a university laser project, not a nuclear weapon, and that Iraq was itself capable of manufacturing these devices. See : **The Washington Post, The New York Times, Financial Times**, all 9 May 1990.

Appeal on the grounds that there had been a "material misdirection" during the original trial relating to a «Confusion between two descriptions of prohibited exports for "military" use...».[29]

In giving reserved reasons for allowing the appeal, the Lord Chief Justice stated that no licence had been sought for the export of the capacitors, but in order to convict the appellants of the alleged attempt to evade export controls, the following had to be established :

1. That the capacitors were goods, the export of which without a licence was prohibited by the 1989 Order ;
2. That the appellants knew the goods fell into a prohibited category.[30]

The Lord Chief Justice stated that during the original trial the prosecution made its case concerning the first issue on narrowly-defined grounds, «that the capacitors were specifically designed for the firing set of a nuclear bomb ; that was much more limited than the general terms of the order, which under ML11 was widely "military use"». As to the second issue, it was incumbent on the prosecution to determine the appellants state of mind but «proof was sought only that they knew export of the capacitor was prohibited, that is, that they fell into the category of goods "specially designed for military use" in general, not necessarily military use in a nuclear weapon».[31]

The crucial aspect in this case, according to the Lord Chief Justice, came in the summing up provided by the judge in the original trial. Because the prosecution had to prove the more narrow case of military use, that the capacitors were intended specifically for nuclear weapons, the judge should have given clear direction to the jury that it was this intended use which had to be proven. Moreover, if the jury were not convinced of this beyond all reasonable doubt, they had no option but to acquit the defendants. Instead, the judge had indicated that the jury could convict if they were intended

---

[29] **The Times**, Report of Cases, 27 May 1994. The following account draws heavily on this report.

[30] *Idem.*

[31] *Idem.*

for "any military use", a broader definition than the one adopted by the prosecution. The Lord Chief Justice therefore considered that a material misdirection had occurred and quashed the original conviction.[32]

The second incident in the period to gain wide public interest concerned the alleged breaching of the UN arms embargo on Iraq by UK companies. These allegations centred on the machine tool maker, Matrix Churchill. Although it was discovered during the court case investigating the activities of the company that it had exported goods, the eventual end-use of which was in Iraq's armaments factories, no conviction was made and the trial collapsed in November 1992.

4. The Scott Inquiry : Lessons for UK Export Control Policy ?

The public disclosure of both the above incidents prompted a judicial inquiry, led by Lord Justice Scott, into the operation of UK export control procedures and the actions of the government in implementing them. On 30 March 1994, the Scott Inquiry closed following the most intensive examination of governmental export policy in UK history. The Inquiry sat in both public and private sessions for a total of over 450 hours and cost £940,000 of public money.[33] However, in the absence of the final report from the Scott Inquiry, which is not expected to be published until December 1994, it is not possible to give definitive consideration to the issues raised in the context of this Inquiry. What is possible is a preliminary sketch of the main issues which dominated the media's attention throughout the period that the Scott Inquiry was in session, and assess whether any general lessons may be gleaned. These issues were : the role of intelligence in export control policy ; the nature of the balance between the country's commercial interests and the need to implement non-proliferation guidelines, priorities and warnings ; the role of Customs authorities ; and the bureaucratic proc-

---

[32] *Idem.*

[33] **The Guardian**, 31 March 1994.

esses for the dissemination of information between those bodies responsible for exports procedures.

One theme which pervaded both the Scott Inquiry and the earlier Matrix Churchill trial is the role of intelligence in export control procedures. Because of the nature of the operation, the role of the intelligence services in the "arms to Iraq" issue will never be fully known. The indications from evidence given during the Matrix Churchill trial and the Scott Inquiry is that the need to gain reliable intelligence on weapons-related developments in Iraq was a primary reason for mounting an intelligence operation in 1988 and allowing the flow of potential dual-use goods to continue. By 1989, the Foreign Office and government intelligence agencies had become increasingly concerned about the supply of these goods and issued warnings that they were being used in Iraq's armaments factories.[34] However, it is unclear whether the government's decision to continue allowing exports to go to Iraq, and thereby ignore these warnings and its own guidelines on arms sales to Iraq, was determined by commercial expedient or the need to draw more conclusive evidence of their end-use.

Export control procedures inevitably require a careful balance between a country's commercial objectives and the desire to ensure its exports are not used in weapons of mass destruction or ballistic missile programmes. Unilateral and multilateral export guidelines are designed with this balance in mind. To complicate matters further, exports may also be geared to specific foreign policy goals, such as assistance to allies or to bolster one side's military forces in a regional situation.

The government's success in balancing these competing objectives has thus been another perennial theme of the Scott Inquiry and other investigations. Whatever view the Scott Report eventually takes of the government's position on this, one general lesson that does derive from the experience is the need for defence and security considerations to take priority over commercial ones. Another is the need for all export control procedures to be regularly subject

---

[34] *Idem.*

to extensive review and oversight. These considerations would ensure that export control legislation and guidelines remain credible and continue to reflect the central concerns of the post-Cold War world.

Because a potential lack of information flow within government has been identified as an important impediment by the Scott Inquiry to effective export control decision-making, there is also a need for all relevant personnel and government departments to be well informed of the nature of the exports, their destination, and whether there are national or multilateral restrictions applicable. Associated with this issue is the need for a clearer delineation of authority between officials and ministers concerning responsibility over export control-related decisions.

In the UK, the task of the Customs and Excise service in policing export control procedures is far from easy due to the sheer volume of trade conducted by the UK which needs to be scrutinized. The constitutional role of Customs in policing export control procedures was first brought to the fore during the Matrix Churchill trial and the spotlight on this role continued throughout the Scott Inquiry. Attention has focused on the system employed by Customs for investigating whether a breach of export controls has occurred : namely, that too much weight was given to information provided by the DTI while other departments involved in export control procedures, such as the Foreign Office and the Ministry of Defence, were not consulted. It has also been alleged that the manner in which intelligence information was used by Customs during their investigations into the activities of Matrix Churchill and the companies involved in the supergun was not as effective as it might have been.[35]

One issue that underlies the role of Customs as an enforcer of export controls concerns the nature of the evidence brought before a court in cases of alleged violation. For the cases discussed here, this has been a major problem for obtaining a conviction. The charges in the supergun affair were dropped because of inconclu-

---

[35] **The Independent**, 5 May 1994; **The Times**, 5 May 1994; and **The Guardian**, 10 May 1994.

sive evidence. The Matrix Churchill case also floundered due to similar problems, while, as pointed out, the convictions against the two personnel involved in the "nuclear triggers" case were quashed because the jury were "misdirected". These cases highlight to good effect the difficulties associated with prosecutions involving dual-use goods.[36] The lesson therefore seems to be, that in the future, it will be imperative for the prosecution authorities to establish as much accurate and reliable information as possible (and drawn from all sources), and attempt to ensure that the judge is well briefed on the nature of the good, especially its potential end-uses, and the implications of the specific charge that is being brought.

For those involved in the export business, the companies, the cases outlined above also raise another problem : how do they distinguish between what is a legitimate order and one that may have security-related implications ? As noted earlier, this affects some sectors of the UK's industry more than others. In the defence sector, for example, stringency is inevitably required to determine the country of destination and the end-use of the product. Yet, conversely, more stringency may actually be required in those economic sectors involving trade in dual-use goods but where there is no obvious direct linkage with defence or security interests. Recent changes to export control procedures in the UK have attempted to deal with this problem. However, as has been pointed out, the changes that have been implemented may have created a more complex and less satisfactory situation than the one they were designed to alleviate.[37]

Government moves towards deregulation have been designed for two ostensibly laudable objectives : first, to lighten the load on government departments tasked with overseeing export control licences and on exporters with a good record of compliance with licence procedures ; and second, to reduce the requirements for licences on those goods and destinations that give less cause for proliferation concern. The intention has therefore been to focus attention on those goods and destinations where there is a concern, and

---

[36] Electrical capacitors, for example, have uses other than in a nuclear weapon or a ballistic missile (e.g. in high-speed photography).

[37] This point has been made by John THURLOW.

to reward certain exporting companies for their past good behaviour. As part of this process, the DTI has been keen to reduce its role in export control procedures involving more routine exports and devote its resources to a case-by-case assessment of licence applications where a critical judgment may be needed. All well and good. In effect, however, this means that many of the routine applications are processed automatically by way of an "open licence" and that it then falls upon the company to ask the basic questions concerning the destination or the end-use of the good. The onus for export controls, and thence, the responsibility, consequently does not become a government prerogative but an exporting company one. In trading arrangements involving dual-use goods, this burden may be considerable and could have several unintended consequences. A company may not be qualified to interpret the guidelines (especially if they are new or technically complex), or have sufficient resources to devote to determining answers to the critical questions, or, in some cases, it could simply lead to abuses.

The understandable need to reduce where possible the cumbersome process of export control procedures has been at the heart of the recent deregulation effort. But unless emphasis is also placed on the provision of export control guidelines which can be understood by industry, and these are communicated by means of an intensive education process, the outcome may be less desirable in the long-term both for the competitiveness of UK companies and for maintaining non-proliferation objectives.

5. Conclusion

Since the early 1990s, considerable changes have occurred in the UK's export control policy. For the most part, these changes have seen a positive improvement in the focus of UK export controls and the procedures for their implementation.

First, there has been a noticeable shift in the focus of export controls away from the Cold War preoccupation with COCOM controls, governing exports to the former Soviet Union and its allies, towards one centred on preventing the proliferation of weapons of mass destruction and ballistic missile systems. Second, the role of UN sanctions as a determinant in the UK's national export control policy has been enhanced. Third, there has been a distinct increase in the attention paid to dual-use items and to resolving the dilemma of balancing the considerations of commercial trade in these items and non-proliferation objectives. Fourth, consideration has also been given to the difficulties of forging an harmonious export control policy within the EU. Finally, and probably the development of most significance for the UK, has been the attempts to foreclose the loopholes which allowed Iraq to establish a complex weapons procurement network so that other states cannot replicate a similar strategy.

While these developments are to be welcomed, as they are a distinct improvement on the policy of the 1980s, the issues identified in the third section of this chapter suggest that more will need to be done to ensure that the UK remains at the forefront of the global non-proliferation effort.

GERMANY

Alexander Kelle

1. Introduction

In late 1987 the German authorities received a rude awakening in the matter export controls : suspicions were voiced that German nuclear fuel had been shipped via the port of Lübeck to Libya and Pakistan. Politicians saw attack as the best means of defence and immediately informed the press - the Transnuklear scandal was born. Only a few days after the initial reports were circulated, a Bundestag investigating committee was established to look into the case. Paralyzed by the requirements of party politics, the commission did not make much progress during its first year of existence. It was only after revelations that German companies had substantially contributed to the construction of a poison gas plant in Rabta and the acknowledgement of the NTG case (see *infra*) that the mandate of the commission was broadened to enable it to review the whole of German export policy, and serious efforts were made to uncover the loopholes and weaknesses of the German export control system.[1]

To illustrate these weaknesses, three cases of illegal exports will be discussed. The cases of the *Hempel* group (brokerage and ship-

---

[1] MÜLLER H., *"After the Scandals"*, **PRIF Reports** No.9, PRIF, Frankfurt, 1989, p.31f.

ment of small quantities of heavy water), *Neue Technologien GmbH* (NTG) (export of tritium production equipment) and *H+H Metall-form* (export of dual-use equipment to Iraq) will be analysed in detail. Next, both reforms of law and regulations and concomitant reform steps such as changes in the administrative setting and staffing will be presented. Any successful export control policy needs the cooperation of the industries involved ; therefore changes in industry's export behaviour will be covered as well. The corporate export control policies reviewed here are those of *Leybold* and *Daimler Benz*. In addition, I shall discuss the efforts of the biggest German industrial association, the German Association of Industries (*Bundesverband der Deutschen Industrie*, BDI), to harmonize its members' export policies while protecting their interests. Finally, an evaluation of the performance of government and parliament during the reform process will be offered.

2. The Cases

The list of cases in which German companies have contributed with the transfer of nuclear know-how and hardware to the nuclear weapon programmes of threshold states seems endless. The first such cases were recorded in the late 1960s, when German industry began to conquer the world nuclear market.[2] Since then German companies have shipped - among other things - a uranium-conversion plant (*CES Kalthoff*) and a tritium extraction facility (*NTG/PTB*) to Pakistan, Beryllium (*Degussa*) and heavy water (*Hempel*) to India, and a variety of dual-use equipment to Libya (*Imhausen*) and Iraq (*H+H*).

2.1. *Hempel*'s Heavy Water Swaps

The case of the Düsseldorf-based *Hempel* company may serve to illustrate two of the four main weaknesses of the German export control system before 1989 : first, loopholes in the area of transit trade and the shipment of small quantities, and second, the lax atti-

---

[2] *Ibid.*, pp.2-7.

tude of export control operators in the responsible ministries, i.e. the Ministry of Economics (BMWi) and Ministry of Research and Technology (BMFT), together with a lack of political leadership from the top.

As far as sensitive commodities are concerned, the *Hempel* group traded mainly in heavy water and is reported to have supplied nuclear threshold countries like Israel, Argentina, Pakistan, and India with roughly 500 tons over a period of more than 15 years.[3] Most of these shipments exploited a loophole in German export legislation, which did not require a licence for the transit trade of nuclear or nuclear-related material and equipment as long as the shipment did not pass through German territory. Since *Hempel* obeyed this rule until 1983, the company's activities were not punishable under German law. In 1983, however, *Hempel* bought some 15 tons of heavy water of Norwegian origin. Since the company was able to produce an International Import Certificate (*Internationale Einfuhrbescheinigung*, IEB) issued by the Federal Export Licensing Office (*Bundesamt für gewerbliche Wirtschaft*, BAW) stating the Federal Republic as country of destination for the goods, the Norwegian authorities approved the export. Instead of being flown to Germany, the material was transported to Basel, Switzerland, where it was merged with a further 6.6 tons of Soviet heavy water. This shipment, however, had been brought to Basel on a truck which on its way crossed the inner-German border at Helmstedt and so did pass through German territory. To bring the deal into line with German law, *Hempel* would have had to apply for a transit licence, which the company did not do. This was therefore the first illegal and thus punishable shipment covered by the then existing German export control legislation and regulations. From Basel the heavy water was flown to Bombay, India, via the United Arab Emirates.

In 1985 a similar incident occurred. This time a Swiss *Hempel* subsidiary, ORDA, ordered nearly 6 tons of heavy water of Soviet origin. In order to circumvent IAEA safeguards the shipment was divided into seven parts slightly below the trigger amount for safe-

---

[3] *Ibid.*, p.5.

guards.[4] Six West European states plus Berlin were named as recipients of the heavy water, but once again the shipment never reached its declared destination. As before it was flown to Switzerland, this time to Zurich, from where it found its way into the Indian nuclear programme, again via the Middle East.

What is most striking about *Hempel*'s activities is that as early as 1980, one of *Hempel*'s legal advisers worked out the scheme according to which transit trade could be pursued without any application for a licence. He then sought confirmation from BMWi officials that his interpretation of the law was correct and that his plan could be implemented without interference with German export laws. As the work of the Bundestag investigative committee revealed, BMWi officials not only confirmed the existing loophole but, even worse, did not report it to their superiors in order to close it.[5]

2.2. NTG : New Technologies for Pakistan

Over the course of several years the illegal nuclear exports of *Neue Technologien GmbH* (NTG) and its subsidiary *Physikalisch Technische Beratung* (PTB) have contributed to the nuclear programmes of a variety of threshold countries. NTG/PTB shipped beryllium to India, measuring equipment for fuel elements to South Africa, and a whole panoply of nuclear-related items including containers for UF6, zircaloy for fuel fabrication, laser equipment, 8,000 Curie of tritium with a high degree of purity, and tritium extraction and storage equipment to Pakistan. Most of the supplied material was exported without any application for an export licence and without the knowledge of the export control authorities. But, ironically, in relation to the most "useful" equipment that NTG/PTB provided for the Pakistani nuclear weapon programme (a facility to

---

[4] INFCIRC/254 reprinted in : HOWLETT D. & SIMPSON J. (eds), **Nuclear Non-Proliferation. A Reference Handbook**, Longman, Harlow, 1992.

[5] Deutscher Bundestag, Beschlußempfehlung und Bericht des 2. Untersuchungsausschusses, Drucksache 11/7800, Bonn, 15.10.1990, pp.243ff and pp.746ff; in addition, see : KOPPE H. & KOCH E., **Bombengeschäfte. Tödliche Waffen für die Dritte Welt**, Knesebeck & Schuler, Munich, 1990, pp.159-220.

extract tritium from heavy water). The companies did contact both BMWi and BAW to check whether a "negative certificate" (*Negativbescheinigung*) could be obtained for the envisaged export. According to BMWi and BAW a tritium extraction facility was not covered by the list of items requiring an export licence. Therefore they had no reservation whatsoever about granting the desired certificate. Their view, however, was strongly contested by the Foreign Ministry (*Auswärtiges Amt*, AA) which also had to be heard in the case. AA officials argued that the "pollution" from which the heavy water was to be purified was tritium. Extracting tritium out of heavy water, however, the AA emphasized, is in fact a method of producing it, and tritium production facilities do require an export licence. In the ensuing debate between the AA on the one side and BMWi and BAW on the other, the latter followed the NTG/PTB line of argumentation according to which the subjective purpose of the facility, i.e. the purification of heavy water, should be the basis of decision, and so called the facility a "heavy water purification facility" instead of a "tritium production facility". The AA, on the other hand, maintained that the subjective purpose was of secondary importance ; from its point of view the objective capability of the plant to produce tritium made it impossible to grant a "negative certificate". Although BMWi eventually ordered BAW to approve the export in spite of the AA's reservations, the facility was never shipped to Pakistan.

Instead, NTG/PTB provided Pakistan with a tritium purification and storage facility - without applying for an export licence or checking whether a "negative certificate" could be obtained. In the judgement of the prosecutor in charge of the NTG case, the export of the heavy water purification facility was never intended and contacts with export control authorities were only initiated as diversionary measures.[6]

When the case came up for trial before the Hanau district court in early September 1990, the cases against the head of the air transporting company Crost and the middle-man Gutekunst were dis-

---

[6] BT Drucksache 11/7800, pp.251ff; KOPPE/KOCH, **Bombengeschäfte**, pp.121-129.

missed after they had paid fines of DM 50,000 each. Both were involved in the shipment of 8,000 Curie of tritium to Pakistan. The trial of the manager of NTG, Ortmayer, the "owner" of the letter-box company PTB, Finke, and a chemist from the Max-Planck-Institute for Plasma Physics, Weichselgartner, who was working as a consultant for NTG, lasted until the end of October. For Weichselgartner it ended with a sentence of 13 months imprisonment which was suspended. The court sentenced Ortmayer to five years and Finke to three years and nine months in prison. In the case of NTG manager Ortmayer 18 months were due to violations of the War Weapons Control Act (export of tritium to Pakistan), 12 months due to the breach of the Foreign Trade Act, and the rest due to tax fraud. Similarly, Finke received six months for assisting a violation of the War Weapons Control Act, and more than three years for tax fraud. Finke's violation of the Foreign Trade Act did not add to his term of imprisonment but instead was punished by a fine.[7]

2.3. *H+H*'s "Contribution" to the Iraqi Nuclear Programme[8]

When the court case against the two owner/managers of *H+H Metallform* was opened in October 1993, the state prosecutor in charge presented a 300-pages bill of indictment listing 22 breaches of German laws and regulations. The illegal exports involved more than 27,000 items for the production of SCUD-B missiles, artillery shells and gas ultra centrifuges worth more than DM 50 million. These criminal acts were committed between January 1988 and January 1992, i.e. at least some of them after the reform of German export controls was well under way.

Thirteen of these items deserve special attention : flow forming machines, of which *H+H* exported ten to Iraq and three more - via Poland - to Libya. Flow forming machines can be used to cold-press preforms into a centrifuge rotor tube or an outer missile casing.

---

[7] **Frankfurter Rundschau** (FR), 01.09., 05.09., 30.10.1990.

[8] The author would like to thank Bettina Goczol for very useful research assistance related to the H+H case.

When the rotor tubes or missile casings have the correct thickness, they must be cut to the right length - again, a flow forming machine is best suited to this task.

At the beginning of the trial the illegal export of the three flow forming machines to Libya was taken up first. It took until the end of January 1994, i.e. more than three months, to settle this issue. In the course of the trial it became evident that the *H+H* managers knew about the final destination of the shipment and had arranged the transit through Poland as camouflage from the very beginning. When the shipments to Iraq came up one of the *H+H* managers confessed to some of the violations, which included among other things his knowledge of the military end-use of the delivered machines and machine tools.[9]

Taken together the illegal exports violated *inter alia* § 34 (1) and (2), and § 33 (1), (7) and (2) *Außenwirtschaftsgesetz* (Foreign Trade and Payments Act, AWG) as of 24 April 1986 ; § 34 (1) and (3), and § 33 (1), (7) and (2) AWG as of 20 July 1990 and § 5c (1) *Außenwirtschaftsverordnung* (Foreign Trade and Payments Regulation, AWV) as of 11 March 1991 (see *infra*). However, since the majority of the criminal acts were committed before the tightening of German export controls, the two *H+H* managers received sentences of only two years and ten months and two years and six months, respectively.[10]

3. Reform of the Export Control System[11]

Since the Bundestag investigative committee was working at a snail's pace during its first year of existence, the loopholes and weaknesses of the German export control system came to light

---

[9] **Westfälische Nachrichten**, 12 January 1994.

[10] **FR**, 25 June 1994.

[11] For a more detailed analysis of the reform, see : MÜLLER H., DEMBINSKI M., KELLE A. & SCHAPER A., *"From Black Sheep To White Angel ? The New German Export Control Policy"*, **PRIF Reports** No.32, PRIF, Frankfurt, January 1994, esp. pp.13-49.

slowly and the committee's work did not exert much pressure on the federal government. Nevertheless, the initial shock over the possibility that German nuclear fuel might have been diverted led to some improvements concerning the position of the AA in the export control process. First, the "Nuclear Decree" of February 1988 added a "sensitive country list" to the already existing tools for export control. All exports to countries mentioned on that list as well as all exports of sensitive materials and technology to any country now required the consent of the AA. In addition, the 1988 "Guidelines for the Prevention of Illegal Technology Transfer" marked the government's first attempt to coordinate the activities of the agencies involved in the export control process.[12]

The reform steps initiated in 1989 concerned in the first place the two pieces of legislation regulating foreign trade in war weapons, the War Weapons Control Act (*Kriegswaffenkontrollgesetz*, KWKG) and in arms and dual-use goods, the Foreign Trade and Payments Act (AWG). In addition, the Foreign Trade and Payments Regulation (AWV) including the Export List (*Ausfuhrliste*, AL) was strongly revised and amended, and a new Federal Export Office (*Bundesausfuhramt*, BAFA) was set up. Government-industry relations were also reshaped substantially.

3.1. Reform of Laws and Regulations

3.1.1. The Foreign Trade and Payments Act

When discussing changes in or improvements of the AWG one has to keep in mind that all exports originating from German territory are in principle free. This iron rule was not touched upon during the reform process. What changed was the interpretation and application of the stipulations in the AWG that enable the German authorities to depart from that principle. As in the past, the legal basis for such a deviation is to be found in :

- Section 5 AWG, which allows restrictions in order to maintain conformity with international agreements, and

---

[12] MÜLLER H., *"After the Scandals", Op.cit.*, p.34f.

- Section 7 AWG, according to which exports may be restricted in order :
    a) to guarantee the security of the Federal Republic ;
    b) to prevent a disturbance of peaceful coexistence between nations, or ;
    c) to prevent a major disruption of the foreign relations of the Federal Republic.

The latter section of the AWG also forms the enabling provision for the rewritten Section 2(2) AWG, according to which the Minister of Economics has the authority to issue an "executive order" to stop any export threatening one of the legal values protected by Sec.7 AWG. Such an executive order can apply to a single export of commodities that are not mentioned on the export list or the war weapons list.

The first remarkable change in the AWG reversed the burden of proof, which had previously been placed on the plaintiff. Whereas in the unamended version of the AWG the damage had to be proven, Sections 34 (1) and (2) of the revised AWG of June 1990 made the danger of damaging the three above mentioned legal values sufficient grounds for prosecution.[13] The second major AWG reform in February 1992 went one step further. Now, all non-licensed exports of goods subject to licensing under the AWG (as well as the KWKG, see *infra*) are treated as a criminal rather than an administrative offence, regardless of whether they damage international peace and security, German foreign relations, or German security.[14]

In addition, many breaches of the law that before the reform qualified as mere administrative offences are now treated as criminal acts. In accordance with this change, and in order to increase the deterring effect of the law, penalties under the reformed AWG were stiffened. Following the 1990 and 1992 AWG amendments the maximum penalty for illegal exports of goods listed on Part I of the AL (see *infra*) is now five years imprisonment or a fine (Sec.34 (1)

---

[13] **BGBl**. 1990 I, pp.1457-1459.

[14] **BGBl**. 1992 I, p.374f.

and (2)), in serious cases ten years imprisonment (Sec.34 (6)). The latter provision applies to crimes committed by members of a criminal organisation, if the violation endangers German security, or if it constitutes a breach of a United Nations embargo (Sec.34 (4)). AWG violations by neglect are punished by terms of imprisonment of up to three years (Sec.34 (7)), unless the act of neglect amounted to assistance in breaching the AWG. According to Section 34 (3) such perpetrators go free in this case.

The remaining administrative offences under the reformed AWG are summed up in Section 33. Here the most important improvement is the doubling of fines for misdemeanours from DM 500,000 to DM 1 million.

Although the first reform package was basically worked out in 1989, the new legislation was not enacted until August 1990. The delay was largely caused by the attempts of some members of the CDU/CSU and FDP Bundestag caucuses to water down the government's proposals to tighten some provisions of the War Weapons Control Act.

Prompted by breaches of the UN embargo against Iraq by German companies, the BMWi initiated new legislation in early 1991 in order to tighten the export control law once more. The proposed measures, however, were highly contested between the CDU/CSU and the SPD opposition, while the Free Democrats took a middle position and were divided on some of the issues under discussion. In March 1991, however, the Bundestag adopted a draft law with a small majority and passed it to the second chamber of parliament, the Bundesrat, for approval. The Bundesrat, where the SPD had a majority, rejected the draft law and applied to the *"Vermittlungs- ausschuß"* - a joint commission of the two houses of parliament with the task of reconciling differences over draft legislation - and, after this attempt to get the legislation enacted had failed, sent it back to the Bundestag in early June.[15]

---

[15] For details of the debate, see : **Frankfurter Allgemeine Zeitung** (FAZ) 09.01., 24.01., 30.01., 01.02., 23.03., 20.04., 02.06., 04.06., 08.06.1991; MEIER-BERGFELD P., *"Spürhunde im Dienst. Zollfahndung in Deutschland"*, in : **Rheinischer Merkur**, 21.06.1991.

The dispute between the two houses of parliament focused mainly on the question of whether the Customs Criminal Institute (*Zollkriminalinstitut*, ZKI) should be empowered to open letters and intercept phone communications of companies or persons suspected of breaching the export law, even when a "sufficient initial suspicion" (*ausreichender Anfangsverdacht*) has not been established.

A joint hearing before the Bundestag's economics and judicial committee in November 1991 revealed the divergent principles and legal standards underlying the insistence of government and opposition on their respective positions, and showed that the dispute was not merely a matter of scoring points in the domestic political debate.

The issue at stake was whether or not the preparation of illegal exports which might contribute to the spread of weapons of mass destruction justifies the restriction of Article 10 of the German Basic Law. In addition, the competences given to the ZKI in the proposed legislation threatened, from the SPD point of view, to undermine an important principle of the German judicial system which provides for the strict separation between the state prosecutor's and the secret service's rights and competences.[16] In a revised draft law some minor adjustments were introduced which also made it unnecessary for the Bundesrat to approve of the legislation. Despite its successful attempt to exclude the Bundesrat from the legal process and thereby to circumvent the objections of the SPD opposition, the CDU/CSU and FDP Bundestag majority failed to enact the new legislation before February 1992.[17]

3.1.2. Foreign Trade and Payments Regulations

The AWV contains the details of AWG stipulations and regulates their practical application to day to day export control operations.

---

[16] See the compilation of the witnesses' statements in Deutscher Bundestag, Rechtsausschuß, Zusammenstellung der Stellungnahmen zur öffentlichen Anhörung des Ausschusses für Wirtschaft und des Rechtsausschusses am 13. November 1991, Bonn, 12.11.1991, esp. pp.16-21 and pp.33-47.

[17] **BGBl**. 1992 I, pp.372-375; it should be noted, however, that the new law empowers the ZKI only until the end of 1994 (§51). After that date a review will determine further developments.

Attached to the AWV is the export list (*Ausfuhrliste*, AL), which in turn consists of two parts. Part I specifies all goods and services whose exports are restricted on the basis of Sections 5 and 7 AWG. Before its reform Part I of the AL consisted of four sections (A to D). During the reform of the German export control system the already existing sections have been updated and streamlined, and a new section E was added in 1989.[18]

Table : The reformed export list

Section   Coverage

A   List of weapons, ammunition and armaments
B   Nuclear energy list
C   List of other goods and technologies of strategic significance
D   List of chemical plants and chemicals
E   List of plants for the production of biological substances

In addition to the various sections of the AL, exporters are referred to a set of country lists to assist their decision on whether to apply for an export licence. Country list A/B includes all countries with which trade has been liberalized. Country list C contains all (former) COCOM countries. Among the other country lists one is especially important, namely country list H which contained initially 33 sensitive countries to which particularly tight export controls apply. Countries included are involved in regional tensions, suspected of having dangerous arms programmes, believed to serve as transshipment points for the transferred goods and technologies, or refuse to accede to the NPT.

The provision in the AWV which explicitly refers to country list H was introduced in March 1991. The new Sec.5c requires a licence for the export of goods and their production documents **not**

---

[18] For more details of the evolution of the AL, see : GAYMANN W., *"Die Ausfuhrliste"*, in : BEBERMEYER (ed.), **Deutsche Ausfuhrkontrolle 1992**, Bernard & Graefe, Bonn, 1992, pp.89-98.

listed in the AL if they are «intended for the use in construction or operation of a plant used exclusively or partially for manufacturing, modernizing, or maintaining weapons, ammunition or armaments as defined in Part I, Section A of the AL [...] or intended for installation in such objects and if the purchasing country or country of destination/installation is [contained] in country list H and the exporter has knowledge of this situation».[19]

In other words : Sec.5c AWV introduces a project- and country group-related licensing requirement for goods and their production documents when exported to countries on list H if the exporter has knowledge about the intended end-use in a weapon or armament project.

Similarly, Section 5d AWV requires an export licence for goods and their production documents if they are listed on Part I Section B of the AL (nuclear list) and «if the country of purchase, of destination or of installation is Algeria, India, Iran, Iraq, Israel, Jordan, Libya, North Korea, South Africa, Syria, or Taiwan, and if the exporter has knowledge of this situation».[20]

Thus, both sections deviate from the time-honoured principle in German export controls that goods or technologies requiring an export licence have to be explicitly mentioned at some point in the AL. Instead, it is the combination of end-use of the commodities (for Sec.5c the usage in a weapon- or armament-programme, for Sec.5d usage in a nuclear programme), country of purchase, destination or of installation (either country list H or the countries named in Sec.5d), and the knowledge of the exporter.

With two AWV amendments of February and September 1989 another crucial loophole in the German export control system was closed. According to the new Sec.40 (1) AWV, transit trade and

---

[19] Section 5c AWV as reprinted in HADDEX, Section III.2 *"Scope of Export Licence Requirements"*. For the text of the 14th amendment of the AWV, see : **Federal Gazette** (Bundesanzeiger), No.50, 13 March 1991, p.1725.

[20] Sec.5d AWV as amended by the 27th ordinance amending the AWV of 31 March 1993; **Federal Gazette**, No.67, 7 April 1993.

brokerage in all materials and technologies listed on Part I of the AL is made subject to licensing unless the country of destination is an OECD member. This presents a twofold improvement. First, the licensing requirement exists even if the goods do not pass through German territory in the course of the transaction. Second, the items covered by this stipulation now include AL sections D and - with the 5th AWV amendment of September 1989 - E, i.e. goods and technologies for the construction of chemical and biological weapons production facilities.[21]

3.1.3. The War Weapons Control Act

German export legislation clearly distinguishes between "arms goods" and "war weapons". Whereas the first category is covered by the liberal AWG, in which any departure from the principle of free trade has to be justified (Sec.5 and 7 AWG), the second group of items is dealt with in the KWKG. Attached to the KWKG is the War Weapons List (*Kriegswaffenliste*, KWL) which further distinguishes between weapons of mass destruction (WMD) in its part A and all other war weapons in Part B.

Prior to its amendment in November 1990 the KWKG treated both parts of the KWL in the same way : actions related to either part of the KWL - including exports - were **not** forbidden but only subjected to a licensing procedure. However, in the light of the Federal Republic's renunciation of the right to produce WMD in Protocol III to the Brussels Treaty of October 1954, this theoretical possibility of producing WMD had no practical implications.

As one critic pointed out, in its unamended version the KWKG only applied to weapons exports but not to exports of weapons components or to the transfer of know-how. In addition, the old KWKG only covered the territory of the Federal Republic. Further, it mentioned nuclear weapons only in the annex and not in the main body of the law ; the minimum penalty for breaches was one year in

---

[21] **BGBl**. 1989 I, p.341, 1749.

prison.[22] Hence, the old KWKG was a rather unsuitable instrument for deterring illegal nuclear exports by German companies such as were uncovered at the end of the 1980s.

Following the KWKG reform of November 1990 the production of WMD is explicitly forbidden, regardless of whether the production takes place on German territory (Sec.17 and 18 KWKG) or abroad (Sec.21). However, nuclear weapons are privileged over biological and chemical weapons in two ways.

First, according to Sec.16 and 21 KWKG their production is prohibited only when they are not under the control of a NATO-nuclear weapon state and at the same time threaten the security of the Federal Republic, or international peace, or considerably threaten Germany's foreign relations.[23]

Second, in its amended form the KWKG differentiates between penalties for violations of the law involving nuclear weapons (Sec.19), biological and chemical weapons (Sec.20) and all other war weapons (Sec.22a). Sec.19(1) keeps the old minimum penalty of one year imprisonment and establishes a maximum of five years for the production, export, and transit trade of nuclear weapons, which also includes support and instigation of these criminal acts. For serious cases Sec.19(2) raises the minimum penalty to two years in prison, the maximum to 15 years. Under KWKG rules a violation qualifies as a serious one if it is conducted by a member of a criminal organization, endangers German security or international peace, or considerably threatens Germany's foreign interests. According to Sec.19(3) minor violations of Sec. 19(1) can be punished with periods of imprisonment of up to three years or a fine, minor violations of Sec.19(2) with terms of imprisonment between three months and five years. Sec.19(4) and (5) establish penalties of up to three years or a fine for KWKG violations caused by negligence or carelessness.

---

[22] CHAUVISTRE E., *"Germany and Proliferation : The Nuclear Export Policy"*, in : **Arbeitspapiere der Berghof-Stiftung für Konfliktforschung** Nr.43, Berlin 1991, p.38f.

[23] **BGBl.** 1990 I, pp.2428ff; reprinted in HADDEX, Section D.

In contrast, Sec.20(1) provides for penalties of between two and 15 years imprisonment for the production, export and transit trade of biological and chemical weapons, again including support and instigation. According to Sec.20(2) minor violations can lead to penalties of between three months and five years, and for violations caused by negligence or carelessness penalties of up to three years or a fine (Sec.20(3)).

One can easily see the discrepancy between the stipulations for nuclear weapons on the one hand, and for biological and chemical weapons on the other. Criminal acts related to nuclear weapons carry penalties of between one and five years unless they qualify as serious cases. In contrast, all crimes and not only the ones that qualify as serious with respect to B- and C-weapons lead to terms of imprisonment of between two and 15 years. Similarly, punishment for minor violations related to nuclear weapons is less severe than for B- and C-weapons. What is more, criminal acts involving dual-use parts of nuclear weapons are punishable only under the general rule of Sec.22a. Accordingly, violations that fall under the category of serious cases are restricted to those conducted by members of criminal organisations and carry only a penalty in the range of one to ten years. This unequal treatment is justified by the government with the claim that nuclear weapons are still an essential part of NATO strategy and are not banned internationally.[24]

As has been indicated above, the implementation of the revised version of the KWKG - and with it the implementation of the new AWG - had been subject to an endless controversy between the CDU/CSU/FDP government and members of its Bundestag caucuses. In this debate one point of contention was the minimum sentence for assistance in the production of nuclear weapons. The Bundestag majority's change of the government's draft legislation re-established the *status quo ante* with a minimum prison sentence of only one year for all types of WMD. This change derives its importance from the fact that sentences of up to one year are usu-

---

[24] **BT Drucksache** 11/4609, 30.05.1989, p.9; cf. also SPOHN H.-D., *Die neuen Bestimmungen des Kriegswaffenkontrollgesetzes*, in : BEBERMEYER (ed.), *Op.cit.*, pp.13-20.

ally suspended. In practical terms the change proposed by the Bundestag majority would have meant that violations could have been fined but would not necessarily have led to imprisonment. The second substantial change was the introduction of a so-called "scientists clause." According to this amendment, violations of the KWKG taking the form of scientific cooperation would have been treated as violations by neglect, for which the sentences are much shorter. This, however, would hardly have reflected to the growing importance of scientific and/or technical advice provided to assist the procurement strategies of potential proliferators. In addition, it would have placed in question the seriousness of Germany's efforts to set up a new export control regime credibly deterring future violations. The problem was eventually papered over by the KWL definition of what is a war weapon, and thus subjected to KWKG rules. A clause in the introduction to the KWL exempts from the WMD-definition components and substances that are exclusively used for «civilian purposes or scientific, medical, or industrial research for pure and applied science».[25]

The delay in passing KWKG- and AWG-amendments caused by this debate even induced some US senators to address the Bundestag directly, urging a quick decision on the legislation.[26] Obviously, the senators feared that because of the upcoming all-German election campaign the issue might be put on the shelf for some additional months. In response to this American pressure the Bundestag finally transmitted its watered-down draft legislation to the Bundesrat in June 1990. Ironically, the conflict between the government and its Bundestag caucuses was solved by the SPD majority in the Bundesrat, which reversed the changes made by the Bundestag and thus was instrumental in pushing the executive's original proposal through.

3.2. Concomitant Reform Steps

In addition to the changes in administrative setting and the reshaping of government-industry relations - which will be dealt with

---

[25] KWL is reprinted in HADDEX, Section D.

[26] **FAZ**, 17.05.1990.

in detail below - the second reform of German export control legislation of February 1992 contained changes in laws other than KWKG/AWG that deserve mention. First, the "Law on Breaches of Administrative Regulations" (*Gesetz über Ordnungswidrigkeiten*) was changed. In its old form it allowed only the confiscation of profits gained from illegal exports violating an administrative regulation. With the introduction of the new Sec.29a of the law, the complete turnover of an illegal export can be confiscated. Since the potential loss in case the violation is detected is now much higher, it can also be assumed that the deterrent effect of the provision has increased.

The second change concerns the criminal code. Its Sec.73 was changed so that violations of the AWG are now explicitly mentioned. This measure is obviously an attempt to make it clear that AWG violations are something more than minor misdemeanours.[27]

3.2.1. Changes in Administrative Setting

Changes in administrative setting and staffing prompted by the revelations of the weaknesses of the German export control system have mainly involved the old Federal Export Licensing Office (*Bundesamt für gewerbliche Wirtschaft*, BAW) which is subordinated to the BMWi, and the ZKI, subordinated to the Ministry of Finance (BMF). In a first reform step the BAW department with responsibility for (among other things) sensitive exports was subdivided into three departments. In addition, the staff of the newly created departments has been substantially increased. These measures could not, however, solve the basic dilemma inherent in the structure of and the tasks assigned to the BAW : besides controlling sensitive exports it was in charge of energy safety measures, the supervision of imports, and the promotion of trade. In other words, both the promotion and the control of exports were assigned to the same government agency. This contradiction, inherent in the BAW structure, was aggravated by the fact that the task of controlling

---

[27] **BGBl**. 1992 I, pp. 374f.

sensitive exports was still only assigned marginal importance by the BAW's leadership.[28]

Following the revelations in early 1991 that German companies had contributed to the Iraqi nuclear programme and thereby violated the UN embargo against Iraq repeatedly, the then minister of economics Möllemann proposed for the first time the idea of separating the tasks of export promotion and export control by setting up a new export control agency.[29] Möllemann's idea received a mixed response, and so it was not until April 1, 1992 that the new *Bundesausfuhramt* (BAFA) opened its doors and took over the task of controlling the exports of sensitive material.[30] In practice, the core of the new BAFA consisted of the BAW Division VI in charge of export controls. The three departments actually issuing licences had a staff of 35 employees, only eight of which (including secretarial staff) belonged to Department 5, which was responsible for the nuclear sector.[31] In addition, the Subdivision *"War Weapons Control"* was removed from BAW Department II, i.e. export promotion, and transferred to the new BAFA.

Before the creation of the BAFA, however, the number of BAW staff in charge of issuing export licences rose to some 250 employees in 17 departments. In April 1992 the entire BAW licensing division was transferred to the BAFA, which will have some 400 persons on its payroll when completely staffed. Even if one takes into consideration the fact, that part of the staff is dealing with bureaucratic matters, this represents a dramatic increase. In addition, BAFA does not have to cope with the competing and at times contradictory tasks of export promotion and export control, as did the old BAW.

---

[28] See the statement of the then BAW head Rummer before the Bundestag investigative committee.

[29] **FR**, 30.01.1991; **FAZ**, 30.01.1991.

[30] Among the critics was also BAW head Rummer; see his interview in **FR**, 11.03.1991; for the text of the law setting up the new BAFA, see : *"Gesetz über die Errichtung eines Bundesausfuhramtes"*, in : **BGBl.** 1992 I, pp.376-378.

[31] **BT-Drucksache** 11/7800, pp.181ff.

A similar development took place in the customs agencies. The Customs Criminal Institute (*Zollkriminalinstitut*, ZKI) which is in charge of detecting illegal exports, had a total staff of eleven officers in its two relevant departments, one in charge of exports related to the Atomic Energy Law, the Radiation Protection Regulation and the KWKG, the other for AWG/AWV violations and embargo cases.[32] During the reform process the ZKI staff has been increased to some 370 employees. What is more, its status has been upgraded and it is now a federal authority (*Zollkriminalamt*, ZKA). Some 50 persons are now in charge of detecting illegal exports, with another 100 engaged in communication surveillance operations.[33]

In addition to the increase in staff, export control agencies - mainly BAFA and ZKA - have been strengthened with respect to the equipment available to them. A considerable portion of the newly allocated personnel and material resources has been used to equip BAFA and the customs agencies with efficient computer systems. BAFA has established a computerized database which contains information that originates in the agency itself (mainly from applications for export licences) as well as information obtained from the ZKA, the Ministry of the Environment and Nuclear Safety, the AA, and German and foreign intelligence services. The legal basis for this exchange of information is provided by the new Sec.45 of the AWG introduced with the 6th amendment to the AWG of 20 July 1990. Sec.45(2) explicitly authorizes the establishment of an electronic data link to connect BAFA and ZKA.[34]

3.2.2. Government-Industry Relations

As the case studies presented earlier in this chapter show, prior to the reform of the export control system the relationship between government officials in charge of issuing export licences and industrialists applying for those licences could best be described as a symbiosis aimed at furthering export promotion rather than export control.

---

[32] CHAUVISTRE, *Op.cit.*, p.44.

[33] MÜLLER *et al.*, *Op.cit.*, p.40.

[34] **BGBl.** 1990 I, p.1460f.

The central part of the new framework regulating the government-industry relationship is to be found in the "Principles on the Reliability of Exporters of War Weapons and Related Goods".[35] The principles have to be applied to all exports under the KWKG and AWG if the commodities fall under the purview of sections A, B, D, and E of the AL. Exports of goods listed in section C of the AL are covered only if the country of destination is mentioned on country list H.

Paragraph 2 of the government's principles obliges companies to name a member of the governing board or a manager of the company who will serve as the "export responsible" (*Ausfuhr-verantwortlicher*) and as such be held personally responsible for all breaches of export laws and regulations.[36] In case the BAFA suspects or has evidence of a breach of either KWKG or AWG, it is empowered to respond in three stages :

- In a first step, the processing of any application by that company is stopped until it has been clarified whether a violation has actually occurred ;

- If the exporter is deemed unreliable at the end of the investigation, in the second step the company will be informed of that judgement and that future applications for export licences will not be processed ;[37]

- For the third step of BAFA action the company itself has to take action. Paragraph 5 of the principles offers the company a way of lifting the verdict of being unreliable and thus deprived of the right to export. The company has to take adequate steps to ensure that in future it will comply with the export laws. One possibility explicitly mentioned is the

---

[35] Grundsätze der Bundesregierung zur Prüfung der Zuverlässigkeit von Exporteuren von Kriegswaffen und rüstungsrelevanten Gütern, Bonn, November 28, 1990.

[36] SINNWELL W.A., *Die Aufgaben des Ausfuhrverantwortlichen im Unternehmen*, in : BEBERMEYER (ed.), *Op.cit.*, pp.121-127.

[37] Paras.3 and 4 of the *"Principles Governing ..."*.

removal of the export responsible, who can both be taken to court and forbidden to take up this post with another company in the future.[38]

In January 1991 the BAFA issued its "Recommendations Concerning the Handling of Exports Requiring an Export Licence", supplementing the government's principles. The BAFA recommendations include suggestions on the shape of corporate structures related to export controls and on the procedure a company should follow if it wishes to apply for an export licence.[39]

In addition, the BAFA continuously issues announcements and circular directives related to developments in export controls, thereby offering advice on and interpretations of export requirements, general licences and the like. Last but not least, BAFA publishes and updates a handbook containing and explaining the quickly changing rules of the game.[40]

4. Changes in Industry's Export Behaviour

4.1. *Leybold/Degussa*

The new policy of the *Degussa* subsidiary *Leybold AG* found its expression in the formulation of the "Corporate Principles Governing Internal Export Controls on Nuclear Non-Proliferation" of March 1992. Starting from the assumption that «certain types of state-of-the-art equipment and advanced technology developed and produced by the company may be regarded as so-called "dual-use" items»[41] and «as a consequence of the possible misemployment of

---

[38] See SINNWELL, *Op.cit.*, p.125.

[39] *"Empfehlungen für die betriebliche Behandlung genehmigungspflichtiger Exporte"*, reprinted in : BEBERMEYER (ed.), *Op.cit.*, Anlage 4, pp.185-189.

[40] BAFA (ed.), **The Export of Embargo Goods. Handbook of German Export Control** (HADDEX), Bundesanzeiger, Köln 1993f; Section K of the HADDEX contains a selection of the above-mentioned BAFA announcements.

[41] All quotes are from the "Corporate Principles Governing Internal Export Controls on Nuclear Nonproliferation", issued by the Executive Board of Leybold AG on March 17, 1992.

so-called "dual-use" items», *Leybold*'s Executive Board felt compelled to issue these corporate principles. In them *Leybold* attributes «clear-cut and unambiguous priority to the goal of nuclear non-proliferation of nuclear weapons [*sic* !] and their delivery vehicles over commercial interests». To achieve this goal all employees involved in export deals shall be familiarized with and abide by the stipulations of national and foreign (!) export control laws and regulations. According to the principles, Leybold will supply commodities, technologies and services to customers and end-users in a non-nuclear weapon country if that country :

a) has signed the NPT, or
b) has renounced the possession, production, and acquisition of nuclear weapons by other legally binding acts, or
c) has its nuclear facilities under full-scope safeguards (FSS) and is not suspected of not fully implementing these FSS, or
d) is to be regarded as sensitive for any other reason.

Besides the "catch-all clause" in point d), the fact that these criteria are to be applied to domestic contracts as well, «if *Leybold* knows or has reason to believe that its products are to be diverted to such countries for sensitive projects», deserves special mention. To implement this corporate policy, contacts with all relevant federal agencies shall be established and maintained and in cases in which an item under consideration for export is subject to US jurisdiction, the company even intends to approach the US Department of Commerce.

4.2. *Daimler Benz AG*

The *Daimler Benz AG* (DB) issued as early as December 1989 an internal "Guideline on Export Controls"[42] which went beyond the stipulations of the German export control system in place at that time. The guideline was binding for all divisions and subsidiaries of the DB group. The preamble of the guideline acknowledges the dual-use capability of some commodities and services supplied by

---

[42] Richtlinie zur Exportkontrolle, **Konzern-Richtlinie** 2/90.

DB companies, and deduces from this the need to establish a group-wide information and control system covering exports of these commodities and services. The first guideline then states that no company of the DB group or any employee of such a company will either participate in the development, construction, production or trade of nuclear, biological, or chemical weapons or parts thereof, or contribute to the build-up of facilities to produce those weapons. Accordingly, not only have all related legal provisions to be obeyed, but, in addition, it has to be checked on a case by case basis whether "circumstances of overriding importance" forbid the export of the commodities or services. Following the second guideline such circumstances can be deduced from the security interests of the Federal Republic, agreements on EC- or UN-level, the political conditions in the recipient country, or from specific provisions of a single contract. These two guidelines also apply to exports that a DB company may undertake jointly with another company. In these cases the consequences of the collaboration for DB's corporate export policy have to be assessed "in time".

4.3. The Federation of German Industries (BDI)[43]

At the beginning of the reform of export control legislation, the BDI was opposed to any governmental interference in the trade in either dual-use or military goods. This initial resistance gave way to a general acceptance of export controls as an unwelcome but unavoidable "evil" one has to live with. BDI criticism then changed its focus, addressing specific points in the ever more complicated web of legislation and regulations.

As to the policy goals formulated by the BDI, four main issues can be distinguished. First, the BDI tried to have the language of legislation and regulation systematized and standardized. Second, the BDI argued that the interrelation of issues or issue areas had to be laid out more clearly, especially when these issues were covered by different laws and regulations. Third, the BDI demanded a more

---

[43] The following section is based on research work done by Christian SCHLUPP for the PRIF Non-Proliferation Project, March 1992.

detailed explanation of certain issues. Finally, it requested fourthly, a consistent interpretation of the new regulations.

On the institutional level the BDI set up in 1989 an expert group for export controls which is conceptualized as a counterpart to the interagency group on foreign trade (*Ressortkreis Außenwirtschaft*) of the federal government. This expert group was complemented by a BDI working group on export controls set up in March 1992, whose aim is to work out a strategy for members on how to deal with the new legislation and regulations. The working group is subdivided into four smaller groups dealing with i) export lists, ii) applications for licences, iii) declarations, and iv) procedural issues related to these declarations. The third and final level of BDI activities is related to achieving a harmonization of export controls on the European level in order to minimize problems for its members in competition with companies from other European states. To this end, the BDI has increased its lobbying activities in Brussels considerably, for example by taking over the leadership of the UNICE working group on export controls.

5. Government and Parliament in the Reform Process

5.1. The Executive Branch

The past attitudes of the German political leadership concerning export control were characterized by a preference for promoting exports over controls, and negligence with respect to the proliferation problem. In the late 1980s this attitude began to change considerably. Non-proliferation came to be accorded a much higher priority on the political agenda of the then former Foreign Minister Genscher and of the foreign policy bureaucracy as a whole.[44] The Kohl government is on record with a statement by Staatsminister Schäfer stating that non-proliferation is «the most urgent objective

---

[44] For a thorough analysis of the bureaucratic decision-making process, see : MÜLLER H./SCHLUPP C., *Nuclear Decision-making in the Federal Republic of Germany*, in : MÜLLER (Ed.), **How Western European Nuclear Policy is Made ? Deciding on the Atom**, Macmillan, Houndmills, 1991, pp.74-98.

of our disarmament policy» ; the strengthening of export controls is deemed "extraordinarily important".[45]

This shift in priorities found its expression in a reshuffling of the competences and foci of the work of several offices in the Foreign Ministry and in the Ministry of Economics (BMWi). In the Foreign Ministry three offices have non-proliferation as the control focus of their work, while three other offices devote many of their resources to the topic.[46]

In the BMWi the main changes have occurred in Department V B, which has been divided into more subdepartments with a higher degree of specialization in export controls. V B4 oversees the new BAFA and is also in charge of handling the interagency decision-making procedures. With BMWi also now prioritizing export control over export promotion, relations with the Foreign Ministry have become much smoother.

5.2. Parliament

If the emphasis of past parliamentary debates on nuclear non-proliferation was placed mainly on the question of full-scope safe-guards, the interest of parliamentarians has recently been extended to a variety of issues. In addition, there is now a broad consensus among parliamentarians of the governing parties and the SPD opposition on the desirability of nuclear non-proliferation and the need to apply strict export controls.[47] Of course, differences still remain,

---

[45] Protokolle des Deutschen Bundestages, 12. Wahlperiode, 165. Sitzung, 23 June 1993, p.14182.

[46] These offices are 424, 424.9 and 431 in the Economics Department of the Foreign Ministry and offices 240, 242, 250, and 252 in the Disarmament Department. For more details, see MÜLLER et al., "From Black Sheep to White Angel ?", **PRIF-Report** No.32, Frankfurt, 1994, p.45f.

[47] The convergence of arguments in the parliamentary debates from 1989 is covered in Das Parlament, No.30/31, 21/28 June 1989, pp.5-7 to 1991 (Das Parlament, No.16, 12 April 1991, pp.2-4) and 1992 (Das Parlament, No.6, 31 January 1992, pp.1-5).

related to the assessment of past export practices and to the question of how strict the new rules should be.[48]

Despite the remaining differences, the Bundestag was able in June 1993 to adopt a resolution on non-proliferation with a unanimous vote. This resolution was based on a SPD draft submitted to parliament in summer 1992 and then passed to the Subcommittee on Disarmament of the Bundestag Foreign Relations Committee. Unlike past resolutions on the topic, the June 1993 resolution was not the usual type of self-congratulatory statement, endorsing what the government was doing anyway. It contained several requests that are so far-reaching that the government is simply not able to implement them. It demands full-scope safeguards for all exports related to civilian nuclear activities, including activities in nuclear weapon states. In addition, it demands that IAEA safeguards in NPT member states should be supposed to include challenge inspection as a regular feature and should be applied to facilities as well as to fissionable material. On top of that, the IAEA should also be authorized to safeguard waste disposal. With respect to export controls, the resolution calls for the creation of an international export control agency whose main task would be the collection of all export related data, including requests for supplies. Data collected would cover not only nuclear technologies and items but also nuclear-relevant dual-use items. As regards sanctions, the resolution requests that they be applied both against individual companies and against supplier and recipient countries in violation of transfer rules.[49]

6. Conclusion : Watch Out ! The Pendulum Might Swing Back

The reformed German export control system certainly represents a huge improvement compared with the situation as it was in 1989. Reforms have affected legislation, regulation and administration.

---

[48] Indicative of divergences on the latter question is the parliamentary debate on the impact of the harmonization of export controls in the European Union on the German export control system, cf. Das Parlament, No.3, 21 January 1994, p.8.

[49] Deutscher Bundestag, 12. Wahlperiode, Drucksache 12/5116, 15 June 1993.

But no matter how appreciable these changes are, there is still some room for improvement in all three fields of reform activities.[50]

First, concerning German export laws, it hardly makes any sense to have two definitions of what constitutes an "Atomic Weapon" included in the KWKG. Second, the differentiation in Section 19 of the KWKG between those who assist "pro-Western" and those who contribute to the programmes of "other" nuclear proliferators is indefensible. It establishes a double standard that should be abolished as soon as possible. Third, all exports of dual-use goods listed in Section C of the AL should be treated as criminal acts. The differentiation included in the AWV does not reflect the increasing importance of dual-use goods in the procurement strategies of potential proliferators. Fourth, the conditionality of the punishment in Section 34(6) AWG suggests that a threat to international peace is not rated as high on the political agenda as a threat to German security. This impression should be avoided. Thus, the threat to international peace should also be regarded as sufficient to qualify an illegal export as a "serious case".

As regards the reformed German export control regulation, problems related to the two "catch-all" clauses, i.e. Sec.5c and 5d AWV deserve closer attention. The intra-German problem with this type of regulation is to find a sensible balance between what is desirable and what is manageable. The situation becomes still more complicated when the regulation has to be harmonized in the context of the European Union. So, regardless of the suggestions for improvement of Sec.5c and 5d that have been floating around, with the new EU regulation in place changes in national regulations have to be made anyway. This means that Section 5d AWV will contain only regulations concerning civil nuclear power, as this aspect is not covered in Section 4 of the EU regulation. This will apply to all countries originally mentioned in Section 5d minus South Africa and Taiwan. As regards Section 5c AWV, the part of the section dealing with non-listed items for the production of weapons of mass destruction and missiles will be taken over by the EU regulation, which

---

[50] For a more detailed treatment of these deficiencies, see : MÜLLER *et al.*, **From Black Sheep to White Angel ?**, pp.57-60.

requests the application of this rule *erga omnes*. Again, as contributions to conventional weapon programmes are not covered by the EU regulation, they will be dealt with in the remainder of Section 5c AWV. Country list H, which spells out the countries to which the stipulations of 5c AWV apply, will be cut down in size and renamed country list K. It will contain the following countries : Angola, Afghanistan, Cuba, Libya, Lebanon, Iran, Iraq, Mozambique, Myanmar, North Korea, Somalia, Syria, and all Yugoslav successor states. The control of technology transfer and services will not be touched by the EU regulation as its focus is on dual-use goods. Consequently this issue will remain covered by legislation.[51]

Finally, we have seen that changes in administration procedures have been accompanied by a dramatic increase in staff members. Fears that because these people were recruited in a relatively short period of time they might not be adequately qualified and might thus not be up to their job do not seem to have been borne out. However, some doubts still exist with respect to the efficacy of the ZKA's computer based KOBRA system.

So, all things considered, the conclusion can only be that Germany, but also the non-proliferation regime, is far better off with the reformed German export control system than with the old one. All export control systems have their inherent limitations. Eliminating the remaining weaknesses outlined above would bring the German system very close to these inherent limits.

However, there is also a contradictory development. Efforts to bring European export controls up to the German level have been successfully resisted by Germany's European partners. It might well be that these countries will find themselves in a strange alliance with those - admittedly very small and marginalized - forces in Germany who dug in during the "export control years" and waited for the pendulum to swing back towards later export controls.

---

[51] **Süddeutsche Zeitung**, 9 February 1995; additional information obtained from government officials.

ITALY

Alessandro Politi

1. Introduction

The findings of this paper are based on several interviews with politicians and governmental officials of the cabinet and the Foreign, Defence and Foreign Trade ministries. A more extensive reference can be found in the research paper *"Sistemi di controllo sulle esportazioni di armamenti e di alte tecnologie dopo la Guerra del Golfo"*, scheduled to be published this year by the Rome-based CeMiSS (the Military Centre for Strategic Studies of the Defence Staff).

2. The Case of the Brazilian Reactor

The case under consideration was first mentioned in the official report on the activities of the intelligence services which is issued every six months by the Italian government. This report provides for a certain degree of public control over intelligence operations, in addition to the activity of a parliamentary committee with responsibility for this policy area. According to law 801, which regulates the tasks and composition of the Italian intelligence services, the battle against proliferation is entrusted to SISMI, the military intelligence branch.

On August 9, 1991 the *Fucine SpA Terni* shareholding company presented to the Foreign Trade Ministry a request for an export licence for a 1 billion lire (approx. $1 million) nuclear reactor vessel whose final destination was Brazil. *Terni* is a specialized foundry located in Central Italy, with a long-standing tradition in the treatment of special steels. *Terni* was also contacted by Iraq in connection with the forging of pipeline components later discovered to belong to the Babylon project for the construction of a 1,000 mm super-gun. Up until now no representative of the company has been proven to have been knowingly involved in this project.

The reactor vessel, whose function is to hold the core of a nuclear reactor, had been ordered by the Austrian *Voest-Alpine* company. *Voest-Alpine* is also a highly specialized metallurgical company with a solid tradition of direct and indirect arms exports. The final client was the Brazilian COPESP agency (*Coordenadora para Projectos Especiais*), at the University of Sao Paulo.

At that time there were two export lists in operation : one for weapons and the other for dual-use goods, which includes the lists agreed through membership of the NPT and the NSG. An export licence was necessary and the request was supported by an end-user statement from the University of Sao Paulo.

During 1991, although Brazilian President Ferdinando Collor de Mello and his government were discussing a full-scope safeguards agreement with the IAEA, the military had secretly provided some $60 million to the IPEN (Institute for Energy and Nuclear Research) at the University of Sao Paulo.

Moreover, the construction of a centrifuge at Ipero, a facility controlled by the Brazilian navy, continued throughout 1990 and 1991 despite a parliamentary funding moratorium and in spite of Collor's shelving of a request from the military to fund the development of nuclear technology. The military-sponsored plan, worth hundreds of millions of dollars, was frozen by the President pending an executive review of a long-term nuclear development plan that had been completed by a special commission in 1990.

The Navy sought during 1990 to exempt the entire nuclear fuel cycle from IAEA safeguards. Although this attempt failed, in 1991 the navy did succeed in exempting the production of HEU for submarine reactor fuel from IAEA safeguards. The US government was inclined to concede the exemption of the navy fuel, as long as an accounting system could be established to ensure that the HEU was immediately manufactured and loaded into the reactor of a future SSN (nuclear attack submarine). However, the SSN program has now been abandoned by the Brazilian navy because of budget constraints.

Western intelligence agencies had begun to collect information about this SSN programme in 1980. The project was a joint venture between the IPEN (University of Sao Paulo) and the navy for the construction of a 2,700-3,000 ton SSN called NUC-1. It was intended to be the first submarine of a class of three boats to be completed by the year 2000 as a replacement for three conventional attack submarines (SS) of the British-built Oberon class already in service. The replacement project could have followed the trend of building a national SS (called NAC-2), which would have been employed as test-bed for an SSN, possibly with a nuclear propulsion system.

By 1986 Argentina and Brazil, notwithstanding their regional strategic competition, had signed an economic cooperation and a nuclear cooperation agreement which raised the possibility of cooperation in the SSN domain as well.

In 1989 IPEN was commissioned to construct a first experimental reactor (the IPEN-MB-01). A further PWR reactor (Pressurized Water Reactor), especially designed for submarine propulsion, was to be completed by 1996.

Naturally the navy tried to obtain foreign technical assistance from various countries ; France and Canada were particularly interested. France had a good track record with SSNs because it had been the first and only Western nation to build a small 3,000 ton SSN called RUBIS. RUBIS was particularly suitable for the Brazilian navy because, unlike US, UK, Soviet and Chinese SSNs, it had a small displacement and a shorter logistic tail.

Canada was interested because the ECS Group Inc. (Energy Conversion Systems) had designed a small reactor which could be plugged into an SS with the addition of a special section and could provide a hybrid nuclear/diesel electric propulsion. The advantage of this technology was that it eased the upgrading of an existing SS, offering the same autonomy as an SSN. The drawback was that maximum speed, typical of an SSN and useful in evading enemy ASW (Anti-Submarine Warfare) measures, could not be obtained. Canada also had some politicians pushing for a national navy capable of asserting sovereignty over territorial waters covered by the polar ice cap through patrols conducted by SSNs. There was therefore a market for the AMPS-N 400 (Autonomous Marine Power Source) developed by ECS.

Against this background the special Italian governmental committee given the task of considering whether an export licence should be granted to *Fucine Terni* decided not to deny the export but to grant it on the condition that an EUC (End-User Certificate) was obtained directly by the Brazilian government. An EUC would have entailed the acceptance by the Brazilian government of full-scope safeguards as a condition of the export.

The intelligence services had concluded that the reactor had a military rather than a scientific use. This meant the export licence had to be processed under the newly established control system devised by law 185/1990, which had been drawn up to deal with military exports and passed by parliament in 1990. The licence request was waived by the company.

From a strategic point of view the export of a small reactor, possibly for an experimental military programme, would not have represented a threat to national security. Provided that EUC and full-scope safeguards were granted by the Brazilian government, the reactor could have been exported, but the Italian Foreign Ministry did not pursue the deal.

There are two lessons to be drawn from this case study concerning the control of nuclear technology exports :

1) In 1991 the legal system was incomplete because while a specific law existed for military exports, dual-use goods were still controlled by the old Formica decree (passed in 1986). Before 1990 the so-called Formica decree (named after the then Foreign Trade minister, Mr. Rino Formica) regulated both military and dual-use exports. The bureaucratic machinery for processing licences still existed, but it was in a critical transition phase due to the transfer of responsibility for military exports from the Foreign Trade Ministry to the Foreign Ministry. One year later the new law 222/1992 was passed by parliament.

2) Investigations by military intelligence were essential in establishing the real destination of the small reactor. We will see that this is still true today.

Because it occurred before the enforcement of the new law, this case does not help us to identify all the loopholes in the law. This will be discussed further under (4) *infra*.

3. The New Law 222/1992

The law 222/1992 (hereafter referred to as law 222) is in several respects similar to the above mentioned law 185. The main similarity lies in the history of the parliamentary debate on the arms export bill.

At a certain stage parliament envisaged passing a single bill in two parts, one dedicated to arms exports and the other to dual-use exports. The idea was abandoned - officially because Parliament did not want to send the wrong signal to the Soviet Union during the period of Gorbachev's reforms, but in fact because the civil industry lobby wanted to avoid an association with arms exports and because it was privately dissatisfied with the double standards adopted by the USA in managing COCOM (the Coordinating Committee for multilateral export control).

Another proposal quietly shelved was the idea of giving a single ministry (the Foreign Ministry) responsibility for processing all export licences. This idea was strongly supported by the military community and by other bodies directly involved in the control of exports. It was believed that sensitive exports formed a unity, and splitting them up would be illogical. Political lobbying succeeded in maintaining a competence for the Foreign Trade Ministry, which had recently been deprived of its responsibility for arms export control.

Despite the fact that the US government had pressured Italy several times to adopt clear legislation on the issue, the Italian government relied on the *de facto* guarantee against technology leaks provided by its military intelligence services. Only the spate of scandals around illegal transactions with Iraq before the Gulf War brought about sufficient political pressure for such a bill to be passed.

Law 222 provides for export control on the basis of a list of materiel for which licences are required. Exports to EC, former EFTA and NATO countries enjoy easier licensing. The Foreign Trade Ministry, in collaboration with the Foreign Ministry, is responsible for the licensing process. Before formal approval by the Foreign Trade Minister a consultative committee must give an opinion on the export request. A negative opinion can be overridden by the minister, but generally the committee's opinion is followed.

An important point of the new law is that sanctions are harsher than in the past ; fines range from 50 to 500 mio lire (ca. 30,000 to 300,000 US$). Jail sentences of between two and six years are possible. Funds belonging to offenders can be frozen at the request of the prosecutor ; the prosecutor is also authorized to ask for the co-operation of other countries to seize assets belonging to defendants charged with a crime. Under the Italian penal code the full scope of participation can be prosecuted ; in practice, support of illegal exports has been punished in Italian courts.

Before December 1993 a high level governmental committee was responsible for updating the lists and formulating an export policy. After that date a reform of the public administration, aimed at simplifying the governmental machinery, led to the dissolution of this committee, the CISD (Interministerial Committee for Defence Exports). The Berlusconi government did absolutely nothing to fill this void. The current government led by Mr. Lamberto Dini is trying to modify the function of an existing governmental committee in order to include the functions of the disbanded CISD.

Following the model established by law 185, law 222 also requires that the government present to parliament a yearly report on the licences granted and on the effectiveness of the control system. In 1993, for the first time, the government provided some data, including them in the yearly report stipulated by law 185. There was no political reaction, despite the fact that the data provided were generic, and controls evidently relied only on export documents, not on checks in the field or end-use controls. Only one company was listed as an unreliable applicant.

But even this law cannot be fully enforced because it lacks several executive regulations. Most of these regulations have now been drafted, but they have not yet been approved by the different governmental and legislative organs. The staffing of the foreign trade bodies is also far from complete, because until May 1994 only personnel of the ministry were employed and no external experts called in. Only at the beginning of 1994 did the then minister, Mr. Paolo Baratta, appoint the experts foreseen by the law to the consultative committee.

The SISMI, although able to conduct appropriate operations, is involved in an ongoing political debate on the reform of the intelligence services. This debate could have disruptive effects on the service's capabilities if the transition is not managed carefully. The fight against NBC proliferation is seen as an important undertaking and the success of the anti-proliferation branch stimulates predictable turf battles.

4. The Change in the Business Environment

The effects of the Gulf War for the business community can be summed up in the words "business as usual".

Interviews inside the export control community reveal that only one company had an internal export control policy, but it had been established before the Gulf War. The Rome-based Selenia company (now merged in the *Alenia* group) was prompted by the Formica decree to set up an internal procedure for controlling export licences. While the Formica decree set precise requirements for the documents to be presented with each export request, the fragmentation of competences between different ministries dictated the logic of a coordinating action inside the commercial direction of Selenia. One year later this internal procedure was fully established and disseminated among Selenia's divisions.

A further evolution of the system was stimulated by the issuing of law 185. Since the list of controlled items was being continuously revised, Selenia needed to establish in advance which items could be freely exported and which needed a licence. Selenia is a leading company in civil and military electronics. ATC (Air Traffic Control) radar can have hi-tech characteristics that fall within military specifications. In 1990 the CAE (Exportability Analysis Committee) was created within the commercial direction with the goal of separating normal from licensed exports. Since June 1990 the CAE, through its experts, has prevented potentially illegal deals that would have breached the agreements concluded by Italy on hi-tech and military exports.

The internal procedure has been adapted to the new law 185 and the fact that law 222 has still not been fully enforced is a minor problem for the *Alenia* group, because the commercial network can track all the customs operations and control the final delivery to the client.

However, the CAE has been seriously affected by the loss of relevant institutions (COCOM and CISD) and by commercial developments. COCOM was important because it had established procedures and because it was a strong reference point for national control authorities. The end of the CISD and the arrival of a new government have added further elements of uncertainty to the Italian control system. Moreover, the shrinking of the military market, coupled with another company shake-up, may render this specialized committee less necessary than before.

If the CAE disappears and pressures for restoring the balance of the company increase, grey or black deals could present a temptation that would be hard to resist. In Italy few companies have the will and the means to complement governmental controls, and even the few successful attempts in this field do not look very permanent.

5. The Problems of the Italian Control System

There are three critical areas in the present Italian export control system : juridical, operational, banks and intelligence.

On the juridical level difficulties arise from the fact that law 222 was largely modelled on the earlier law 185. The definition of military items does not mark clear boundaries between these and dual-use items, making it difficult to coordinate the application of the two pieces of legislation. A draft paper from the UCPMA (Coordinating Office for the Production of Military Materiel), still unpublished, is an attempt to address this problem.

While law 185 limits transactions to foreign countries or companies authorized by those countries, the law on hi-tech exports does not limit the range of clients that can import these goods.

Finally, law 222 foresees the possibility of conducting inspections at the importer's office or where the imported good is employed, after prior consent. This poses the delicate question of whether extraterritorial inspections are lawful or violations of national sovereignty.

Bodies with responsibility for preventing NBC proliferation face even worse problems. Law 222 proceeds from a distinction between the regimes governing arms exports and hi-tech exports. Arms were considered subject to political considerations, while dual-use technologies were considered in the light of country risk evaluations. In fact the Iraqi case showed clearly that technology exports are much more sensitive and dangerous than arms sales. Moreover, the range of technologies considered attractive by proliferating countries belongs to the low-medium bracket rather than the hi-tech domain. This implies that a stronger coordination between the two control systems is needed ; appropriate solutions are currently being studied by the UCPMA.

The demise of the CISD has stimulated significant discussion inside the export control community. A number of ideas are being debated, among them a proposal to assign the competences of the dissolved committee either to the Prime Minister or to the Foreign Trade Ministry, or to the CIPE (Interministerial Committee for Economic Programming). Another proposal, advanced by the author of this paper, is to unify all the export control competences under the Foreign Ministry, since all these sales have strategic and political significance. In the background looms the already mentioned reform of the public administration, partially carried out by the former government led by Mr. Carlo Azeglio Ciampi. This reform also considered the disbandment of the Foreign Trade Ministry. The UCPMA is once again the main focus of the debate here, but it is very cautious in opening a public debate on the matter since it fears the possible negative political consequences of such a debate.

It is very difficult to evaluate the strength of the agencies engaged in the fight against proliferation. Theoretically the Customs should be fully engaged, but in reality their contribution is limited simply to the seizure of goods already tracked by the SISMI. Almost the same can be said of the three major police agencies in Italy. Although better equipped and with better intelligence networks, the Police, the *Carabinieri* (gendarmerie) and the Finance Guards (a militarized police under the control of the Finance Ministry) are not very active in the field of anti-proliferation except as official arm of the intelligence services. Obviously the strength and equipment of the SISMI are classified.

Until the 1st of March 1995 a fundamental loophole in the control system was the absence of a catch-all clause. After this date Italy can integrate a catch-all clause into her regulations. Since Italy is a country whose laws derive from the Roman juridical system, there are two possible ways to frame a catch-all clause.

  a) If the government knows that a certain dual-use export could help potential proliferators, it can ask the company concerned to submit a request for an export licence.

  b) If a company suspects that an export could have proliferating effects, it is obliged to inform the authorities.

In countries with an Anglo-Saxon juridical system the government, after having passed a catch-all clause, can block the goods without much difficulty.

A catch-all clause must be complemented by : a good information campaign with the companies concerned ; provision for compensation if an application is rejected ; preventive precautions taken by the exporters themselves.

But a catch-all clause also entails a fundamental reform of the customs system, because only real-time knowledge of export flows from Italy will make feasible a selective use of the clause against specific proliferators. At present the customs authorities only have the power to collect taxes and to draw up commercial statistics. Without more effective customs and the institution of a computer network linking different administrations (called the CIN project,

National Information Circle) it will be difficult to combat future proliferation attempts.

Another consequence of the catch-all clause will be the need to issue a warning list. Actually no official warning lists are issued, but the situation has been improved by a decision to add to the lists of controlled items the international agreements that influence the composition criteria of the lists themselves. This simple measure has ended or at least strongly eroded a long-standing undeclared principle of the Foreign Ministry : the *erga omnes* dogma.

The *erga omnes* (towards everybody) principle states that Italian foreign policy does not discriminate against any state except where binding international agreements are involved. This dogma was a consequence of the international and internal conditions of the Cold War, which dictated that any high-profile foreign policy should be avoided. Now Italy declares openly, albeit indirectly, which countries it considers undesirable as trading partners.

One curious aspect of proliferation is the export of so-called immaterial items (manuals, software, plans, microchips, etc.). It is very difficult to control this type of export and the only way to keep track of these transactions is again through intelligence and through the UIC (Italian Exchanges Office). The Italian anti-proliferation community takes the view that immaterial items alone are not enough to transfer a technology effectively. To integrate a technology takes a multifaceted effort, as countries acquiring technology legally also know, and this implies that other more tangible aspects can be tracked.

Italy has no specific provisions for extraterritorial actions, except for controls on the effective arrival of dual-use goods in declared countries of final destination (law 222).

Finally, the possibility of parliamentary control must be significantly enhanced by an annual report that must be complete and accurate, although harmonized with the standards of Italy's major European partners.

The BNL Atlanta case, still under examination by the courts, has shown beyond any doubt the central role that the international banking systems plays in the illegal technology trade. Nevertheless the case did not result in any new measures to improve controls over the flow of money involved in these operations. Intelligence activity remains the best way of penetrating the banking side of illegal sales, but cooperative steps could also be undertaken. For instance a yearly seminar involving governmental officials and medium-high level bank management could disseminate useful information for the prevention of or early warning about suspect transactions. The banks' major interest is to avoid the negative image projected by scandals, although it has been a time-honoured policy to pursue any deal provided that a plausible denial can be issued in order to disclaim any responsibility for the true goal of the transaction.

The military intelligence service is still a mainstay of the fight against proliferation, especially when law 222 is enforced. The critical stage will be reached when a new, more stable government puts the reform of the intelligence services on its agenda.

The scandals emerging from the trials of several top officials of SISDE (the Italian civil intelligence) will induce the government to draft a new bill on the matter, but it is unclear what measures will be taken.

The risk is that anti-proliferation operations may be paralysed by turf battles between different bureaucracies. There is, however, now an opportunity to introduce new working methods concerning the use of open sources and to establish a relationship with public opinion through more transparency on the services' operations in the field of international security.

6. Conclusion

In conclusion it is difficult to predict how future Italian non-proliferation policy will evolve. The Berlusconi government, despite its numerous promises, achieved little. The Dini government could continue to maintain basic Italian commitments to non-proliferation, but the duration of its political survival is difficult to predict. At the same time governmental agencies are trying to improve the effectiveness of the control system. Starting from the beginning of 1995, customs officials are undergoing specialized training in order to be able to monitor more effectively the trade in dual-use goods.

SPAIN

Vicente Garrido Rebolledo

1. Introduction

It is no exaggeration to say that after Spain joined the European Community in 1986 it moved very rapidly to adopt both its legislation and its practice in matters of nuclear and dual-use materials trade (export-import) to the norms of the rest of the EC countries. This process has had many difficulties, as we will see, due to the fact that when Spain joined the EC it was a non-NPT country, with incomplete - if not deficient - legislation in the sphere of nuclear trade. At that time Spain was also seen as being a potential "Emerging Nuclear Supplier".[1]

The present paper's conclusion is that both Spanish nuclear export control legislation, - now fully consistent with the requirements of the international fora in which Spain participates - and Spanish practices, are quite satisfactory. Nevertheless, this fact does not exclude some observations on intrinsic deficiencies of the legislation, or the suggestion of some scenarios involving more or less controlled nuclear exports. My research is based on open sources.

---

[1] See : ELLIOTT ZOPPO C., *"Spain as an Emerging Nuclear Supplier"*, in : POTTER W. (ed.), **International Nuclear Trade and Non-Proliferation. The Challenge of Emerging Nuclear Suppliers**, Lexington Books, Lexington, Mass./ Toronto, 1990, pp.331-358.

The following study has primarily been based on a detailed analysis of Spanish nuclear and dual-use export control legislation, including analysis of parliamentary debates on this legislation. Secondly it draws on a number of interviews (ten) with persons whose professional activity is directly related to Spanish nuclear export control policy : officials of the ministries of Foreign Affairs, Defence, and Commerce and Tourism (former Industry and Commerce Ministry) ; parliamentarians of the principal Spanish political parties *Partido Socialista Obrero Español* (PSOE) and *Partido Popular* (PP) ; and representatives of governmental organisations in the defence sector and also a private defence company. As on previous occasions, the nuclear industry adopted a no-interview policy.[2] Thirdly, open sources such as newspapers, information from agencies and institutes, and articles published in books and reviews have been consulted in order to identify possible loopholes in the control of nuclear and dual-use materials during the last six years (1988-1993). Sometimes comparisons have been drawn with earlier periods, but only as a reference. The sources consulted are not necessarily the best tools for discovering possible loopholes, but they are the only ones available.

2. Spanish Nuclear Export Control Legislation

2.1. Background

The decisive factors which obliged the Spanish government to adopt legislation on trade in nuclear and dual-use products and technologies even before Spain's membership of the EC were its accession to NATO in 1982, and to a considerable extent its membership of COCOM from 1985. This commitment was stressed when Spain signed the NPT in 1987.

During the early years of the Franco regime, two instruments to be applied in this field were set up. The first (Order of 4th October

---

[2] See : MÜLLER H., *"European Nuclear Elites and Non-Proliferation : A Comparative Survey"*, in : MÜLLER H. (ed.), **European Non-Proliferation Policy 1988-1992**, European Interuniversity Press, Brussels, 1993, pp.23-24.

1945) established a monopoly situation in which the state retained, temporarily, the exclusive right to mine the uranium deposits in 40 Spanish provinces in which such deposits were known to exist. This exclusive right was extended in 1948 (Decree of 23rd December 1948, Section 2) to all of metropolitan Spain and in 1951 it was conferred on the *Junta de Energia Nuclear* upon its creation (JEN, today CIEMAT-JEN).[3] This system was abolished in 1958 by the Freedom of Mining Act (Act of 17th July 1958 amending the Decree of 22nd October 1951). Other firms were allowed to mine deposits outside the areas reserved for the JEN, but they had to obtain authorisation from the Ministry of Industry.

The first disposition which regulates foreign trade in nuclear material dates from June 1985. But this fact does not mean that Spain had not previously been subject to any international control, since the Cooperation Agreement between Spain and the United States referring to the civil uses of nuclear energy (dated March 20, 1974) determined the supply conditions and utilisation guarantees of radioactive material from the USA. Before transferring to other EC countries Spain needed the American "prior consent" over trade in radioactive materials, and a special safeguard regime based on the application of the "Three Party Agreement" between the IAEA, Spain and the USA from December 9, 1966 (amended June 6, 1974) to all the materials supplied by the USA was established.[4] This agreement, also known as "Safeguards Transfer Agreement", transferred to the IAEA the responsibility for administering the safeguards provided for in successive peaceful nuclear cooperation agreements between Spain and the USA.

When Spain ratified the Non-Proliferation Treaty in 1987, the provisions of the Tripartite (Verification) Agreement of 1973 between the IAEA, EURATOM and the non-nuclear weapon member states of the Community which are party to the Non-Proliferation Treaty (INFCIRC/193) also became applicable to it. At the time, all

---

[3] OECD, **The Regulation of Nuclear Trade. Non-Proliferation, Supply, Safety**, Vol.II, *"National Legislations"*, Paris, 1988, pp.210-212.

[4] For this question, see : VINAS A., **Los Pactos Secretos de Franco con los Estados Unidos**, Edit. Grijalbo, Barcelona, 1981.

Spanish nuclear facilities were already subject to IAEA safeguards of the INFCIRC/66 type. Nevertheless, the Safeguards Transfer Agreement had been operative until 21 January, 1994, when a protocol (signed in Vienna on March 23 and entered into force on October 15, 1993) was published. The 1994 protocol is very confusing when it says "suspension" and not "repeal" of the 1966 Safeguard Agreement. The non-application of the USA-Spanish Agreement depends on two conditions : a) the application to Spain of the safeguards system established in the INFCIRC/153 document, and b) the application to the USA of the Safeguard Agreement between the USA and the IAEA (INFCIRC/288).

2.2. The Royal Decree 480/1988 and its consequences

Spain joined COCOM in 1985 at a time when this body was rapidly losing its significance. In the same year, Spain published the Ministerial Order of June 5, which regulated the imports of dual-use technology and incorporated the document used by COCOM to control exports (the International Certificate of Imports). But the scope of this order (today repealed) was limited since it focused only on the re-export of goods previously imported, without specifying any regulation on the export of those products which, according to COCOM's lists, were to be submitted to controls.[5] This law, clearly insufficient, remained in force until May 30, 1990, when the Royal Decree 480/1988 of March 25, 1988, finally took effect.[6]

The Royal Decree's principal innovation was the creation of the "Interministerial Committee for Trade Regulation of Defence Material, Dual-Use Goods and Technologies" or JIMDDU (the Spanish acronym). This committee was charged with controlling the trade in so-called "sensitive materials". JIMDDU's origins can be traced

---

[5] AVILA A.M. & PORTILLO J.M., *"Nueva normativa de comercio exterior de material de defensa y tecnologías de doble uso"*, in : **Boletín de Información Comercial Española**, No.2.240, Ministerio de Industria, Comercio y Turismo, 2-8 July 1990, pp.2603-2608.

[6] Royal Decree 480/1988, published in the **B.O.E. (Offical Bulletin of the Spanish Government)** May 21, 1988.

back to the Decree 3.150/1978 dated 15th December.[7] The Ministries represented in the Interministerial Committee remain the same - Economy and Finance, Foreign Affairs, Defence, and Industry and Commerce - but its precise composition varies.

In 1988 JIMDDU was established as follows :

- the General Secretary for Trade (Ministry of Economy and State Finance) as its chairman (under the earlier decree this position was occupied by the General Director of Trade Policy, Ministry of Trade and Tourism) ;

- the Deputy Secretary from the Foreign Ministry as vice chairman (previously the General Director of International Economic Relations from the same Ministry, but without the functions of vice chairman).

Further members are :

- the General Director for Armaments and Materials from the Defence Ministry,

- both the General Director for Foreign Trade (instead of the General Secretary for Defence Policy Affairs from the Defence Ministry), and

- the General Director of Customs (instead of the General Director of Iron, Steel and Shipping Industries from the Ministry of Industry and Energy) from the Industry, Commerce and Tourism Ministry, and

- the General Technical Secretary (previously the General Deputy Director of Industrial Goods Exports, Ministry of Trade and Tourism) from the Industry and Energy Ministry. According to the Royal Decree 480/1988, the Secretary of the

---

[7] **B.O.E.** January 17, 1979. This Decree, which was repealed by the Royal Decree 480/1988 dated 25th March, regulated the functions of the Interministerial Committee for Trade Regulation of Arms and Explosives, Spanish acronym JIRCAEA.

Interministerial Committee will be the General Deputy Director of Foreign Trade from the Ministry of Economy and State Finance.

In this way, the Royal Decree apparently gives priority to the Ministry of Trade, but the department that has the final say in questionable cases is the Ministry of Foreign Affairs.[8] The inclusion in the JIMDDU of the Director General of Customs (now integrated into the Commerce and Tourism Ministry) was due to his responsibility for customs free zones and warehouses, a domain in which the General Director of Foreign Trade had no competence.

The law of 1988 also established that the responsibility for fixing the list of products covered by the Decree would lie with the Spanish government. The Ministerial Cabinet acts on the initiative of the ministers of Foreign Affairs, Defence, Industry and Energy before the Interministerial Committee will be informed.[9] Another of the novelties of this law is the creation for the first time of a special register for exporters of defence material and dual-use products and technologies (*"Registro Especial de Exportadores de Material de Defensa Productos y Tecnologia de Doble-Uso"*). These exporters require a licence given by the JIMDDU. Previously, nothing more than inscription in the General Register of Exporters was required.

In the matter of imports, the Royal Decree 480/1988 required importers to obtain an Entrance Verification Certificate for the product drawn up by the Customs Services, and a Final Destination Certificate which should be drawn up by the General Director of Armaments and Material with the approval of the Defence Secretary of State.[10] In the same way, the presentation of an International Certificate of Import issued by the authorities in charge of examining the imported goods is compulsory, although this certificate is

---

[8] Interviews with Ministry of Foreign Affairs officials.

[9] First final disposition from Royal Decree 480/1988 dated March 25.

[10] RUIZ-GALLEGOS M., **Industria y Defensa Nacional. Estudio Jurídico-Administrativo**, Ministerio de Defensa, 1989, pp.250-260.

only needed for goods from a certain group of countries specified by the government (the former COCOM countries).

Although published, the Royal Decree 480/1988 only took effect with the approval and official publication in the BOE (*Boletin Oficial del Estado*) of the lists of "sensitive goods" (dual-use armaments, equipment, products and technologies) subject to control by the JIMDDU.[11] These lists, the *Relacion de Material de Defensa y Relacion de Productos y Tecnologias de Doble-Uso* (List of Defence Material and List of Dual-Use Products and Technologies) were approved on June 23, 1989, and May 29, 1989, and were published on 7th and 8th February, 1990, respectively.[12] This procedure established a period of 90 days before the lists entered into force on May 30, 1990.[13] In this way, the Royal Decree 480/1988 can be described as the first step since 1985 towards controlling exports of so-called "sensitive goods".

The system of rules established in the Royal Decree 480/1988 was completed by three further laws. The Order dated January 23, 1990 lists the defence and nuclear material submitted to import control (modified by the Order of July 31, 1990)[14] ; the Order of January 31, 1990[15] regulates the special Register of Exporters of defence material, dual-use goods and technologies ; and the Order of May 28, 1990[16] regulates the foreign trade procedures for defence material, dual-use goods and technologies. The Order of January 31, 1990 did not enter into force until June 1990, when exporters had to be listed in a Special Register of Exporters. This requires the exporters to fill in a form with specific information including the name of the firm or corporate body, address, tax identity number,

---

[11] Article 1 of the "Real Decreto 480/1988".

[12] Ministerial Order dated 23rd January, 1990.

[13] See also my study on Spain in : MÜLLER H. (ed.), **European Non-Proliferation Policy, 1988-1992**, *Op.cit.*, pp.165-168.

[14] **B.O.E.** September 1, 1990 and December 19, 1990.

[15] **B.O.E.** February 9, 1990.

[16] **B.O.E.** May 29, 1990.

legal status, constitutive document and later amendments, certificate of inscription in the Trade Register, composition of the firm, participation - if any - in foreign firms. The Order also demands from the exporter such details as :

1. Goods exported in the last three years, divided into goods entirely produced by the exporter and goods produced in part by the same exporter.

2. Technology or technologies associated with goods exported during the last three years.

3. The exporter's participation in research and development projects with the Ministry of Defence or the Ministry of Industry.

4. International experience in the export of engineering projects.

The order of May 28, 1990 also specifies the different kinds of licence to be drawn up by the General Direction of Foreign Trade which affect the products covered by the Order dated 23rd January 1990 - all exports from the Iberian Peninsula, the Balearic and Canary Islands, Ceuta and Melilla are included.[17]

a) Export licences for single transactions (for defence material and dual-use goods and technologies). The licence, once approved, allows one or more consignments up to the fixed amount authorized, to a named addressee and country, through a specified customs office and within a time limit of six months. This time limit can be extended to one year.

b) Distribution export licences (for dual-use materials and technologies). There are several compulsory conditions and the time limit is 12 months, without possibility of extension. This licence was only granted for COCOM countries and to those companies that had demonstrated good conduct from the administrative point of view. The exporter must present quarterly reports of consignments to each

---

[17] Order dated 28 May 1990 (**B.O.E.** 29 May 1990), chapter II.

country of destination ; all the information referring to these operations must be made available to the General Direction of Foreign Trade.

c) Open export licences (for dual-use materials and technologies), for material included in Annexe III of the Order of January 23, 1990. The end-use of the exported technology or material must be unrelated to defence, the aerospace industry or nuclear energy.

The Order of May 28, 1990 also establishes the Preliminary Export Authorisation, which does not constitute a formal licence for exports. This authorisation is required by the exporter to cover the period when the trade contract for long-term deliveries (up to 5 years) is under negotiation.

2.3. The New Legislation

As a consequence of Spain's accession to the different international fora dealing with nuclear exports and products and dual-use technology control (such as the MTCR in 1989), as well as the modification of the Nuclear Suppliers Group lists from 1991 onwards (Spain joined this group in 1987), the country has also been obliged to update its legislation in order to harmonize its lists with those drawn up by the rest of the participating countries.

The most important measure is the Organic Law of 30th April 1992[18] (Law 3/1992), which establishes criteria for identifying smuggling of defence and dual-use materials. The new legislation is completed by the Royal Decree of Development from the Law 9/92 (Royal Decree 824/1993, dated 28th May)[19] by which the Foreign Trade of Defence and Dual-Use Regulations are approved. This new law modifies the Royal Decree 480/1988 and sets out updated lists which replace the ones published in 1990. The new legislation provides for the total harmonisation of the Spanish lists with those

---

[18] **B.O.E.** May 1, 1992.

[19] **B.O.E.** September 21, 1993 (as corrected by **B.O.E.** January 4, 1994).

of the COCOM, NSG, MTCR and Australian Group (for chemical agents).

The main changes introduced by the new legislation are as follows :

1. For the first time the illegal export of defence or dual-use material is considered as a crime of smuggling. It is very important to say that before this Organic Act was approved, the only punishment foreseen by the Spanish authorities in case of infringement of the law, falsification of information or illegal export of dual-use materials was exclusion from the Special Register of Exporters, which could be easily evaded by setting up a new company with a different name. After the Organic Law 7/1982 dated 13th July, the crime of smuggling defence and dual-use materials without authorisation, or obtaining authorisation by means of a false declaration, can be punished by a maximum of six years in jail and fines of up to twice the value of the exported goods.

2. The "catch-all" clause (in Spanish also known as the "broom clause") has been introduced for the first time in the Spanish legislation. In this way, products which are not included in any list can be submitted for authorisation. The Spanish version of the "catch-all" clause is less strict than the German one : it is required that the Spanish authorities inform the exporter of the necessity to obtain authorisation before exporting a product to specific destinations. Without such information, no requirement for an export licence exists. The Spanish version of the "catch-all" clause, unlike the German one, does not consider, like the German one, the necessity for the exporters to obtain authorisation only because they suspect that the material could be used for military purposes.[20]

---

[20] On this question and the novelties introduced into the new law, see : *El Control del Comercio Exterior de Material de Defensa y Material de Doble Uso en España*, in : **Boletín de Información Comercial Española**, No.2409, Ministerio de Comercio y Turismo,18-24 April, 1994. See especially the article of GIMENEZ de CORDOBA E., *"El Control del Comercio Exterior de Material de Defensa y Material de Doble Uso en España"*, pp.6-15.

3. The Lists of Defence and Dual-Use Materials which harmonise the Spanish lists with those of the NSG, MTCR and Australian Group have been drawn up.

4. The general authorisation in order to go ahead with the Communitary Regulations on nuclear export control has been established.[21] In this way, the export of dual-use material is authorized whenever (in addition to being included in Annexe II) the goods have a final destination in an EU country, the material is not on the exclusion list covered by the law (Annexe V of the Royal Decree) and finally, a special notification is made to the General Direction of Foreign Trade at least a fortnight before the transfer ; this notification must declare that the product will not have a non-EU country as final destination. Furthermore, it is necessary to deal with all the documentation individually ; i.e. to provide all the above-mentioned documentation to the General Direction of Foreign Trade and to the Customs and Special Taxes Department whenever required ; to make a declaration to the General Direction of Foreign Trade every six months on the exported material ; and finally, to demonstrate in the invoices and in the transport documents that the merchandise will not be exported out of EU territory.

5. The regulation of the Special Register of Defence Material and Dual-Use Products and Technologies Exporters has been modified. Inclusion on this register will not be necessary whenever the government gives a general authorisation, i.e. for EU countries. The army and the security services of the state have to ask the Interministerial Committee (JIMDDU) directly for authorisation.

6. The JIMDDU's composition and power have once again been modified. It is now called *"Junta Interministerial del Comercio Exterior de Material de Defensa y Material de Doble-Uso"* (JIMDDU). The Interministerial Committee is for the first time assigned to the Ministry of Commerce and Tourism, which increases its membership to seven. In addition, to those who took part before, the General Director of the Superior Centre of Defence Information

---

[21] Article 12 from the Royal Decree 824/1993.

(CSID) from the Defence Ministry and the General Police Director of the Home Affairs Ministry are also now represented. The General Deputy of Trade continues as the secretary of the JIMDDU, who is entitled to speak but not to vote. It is also established that the Foreign Affairs Ministry should inform JIMDDU periodically on all transits of defence material through national territory which are authorized.

The JIMDDU's decisions on trade authorisations and rejections are both obligatory and binding. Since no exception is admitted, the government cannot override the JIMDDU. The President of the Committee can, depending on the issues to be discussed, invite other representatives of the administration and relevant experts to meetings of the JIMDDU. With this legislation, it is established for the first time that working groups consist of representatives of all the committee's members with a status of Deputy General, who will elaborate the proposals to be discussed in the meetings.

Nevertheless, this legislation seems to be quite confusing where it deals with the criteria by which the JIMDDU is to be guided when drawing up the licenses, for which general guidelines had already been established in the law 3/1992.[22] Criteria mentioned include :

a. Any indications that the defence and dual-use material may be employed for purposes that disturb international or regional peace, stability and security, or exported in ways that may be in conflict with Spain's international obligations ;

b. The general interests of national defence and Spanish foreign policy.

In the preliminary discussions of the Organic Law in the Spanish parliament, the Conservative Party (PP) was against the inclusion of these criteria in the law, and considers that the criteria of "national defence and foreign policy interests" allow the government

---

[22] Organic Law 3/1992, dated April 30, 1992, Article 2.a and 2.b; this criterion appears again in the Royal Decree 824/1993, dated May 28, 1993 (**B.O.E.** 21st September) in Articles 13 and 19.3.a.

to manipulate the authorisations according to its own political interests.[23] Some of the non-published governmental criteria forbid sales that may be in breach of international agreements already signed by Spain ; that would jeopardize friendly relations with third parties, whose destinations are countries subject to UN or EU sanctions or to countries in conflict or which violate human rights or even to former communist countries on the former COCOM list.

7. The regulation of imports according to Royal Decree 480/1988 has revised in order to establish tighter control of import and of collaborative activities with other countries. In this way, a list of weapons is created (Annexe VI), after the import of which Spain should comply with certain conditions. Should the exporting country ask for it, an International Import Certificate for Defence Material or Dual-Use Products and Technology could be issued or a Final Destination Certificate if it is war material. These certificates will not be granted to third countries and they will be valid for six months.

Finally, on January 1, 1993 a Royal Decree (*Real Decreto* 1631/ 1992 dated December 29, 1992) on restrictions to the circulation of some goods was published. This covers dual-use technologies, defence material and explosives. With this Royal Decree the Spanish government intends to harmonize Spanish legislation on exports of these materials and goods with the legislation of the rest of the EU countries, and to control trade in products not covered by previous legislation. But the requirement that a license is needed to export a product or dual-use technology to an EU country is removed by the already mentioned Royal Decree 824/1993.

3. Spain's Participation in International Fora for Nuclear Export Control

Since signing the NPT on November 5, 1987, Spain has been progressively incorporated into all the fora for controlling the ex-

---

[23] Interviews with parliamentarians of this political party.

port and import of nuclear and dual-use materials. Spain has also tried to play a more active role. Two facts should be underlined :

1. Spain's joining the Zangger Committee completes the Spanish participation in this kind of forum. On 27th May 1993 Spain formally became a member of the Zangger Committee (before it was only an observer). Nevertheless it should be remembered that before this Spain had considered the Zangger Committee list as discriminatory for Spanish industry, and stricter than the NSG list. This was the main (but not openly admitted) reason why Spain had previously refused to join the Zangger Committee.[24]

2. During the year 1994, Spain had taken over the Nuclear Suppliers Group presidency which, in the opinion of some Spanish officials, will help to increase Spanish prestige within the International Non-Proliferation Fora (taking into consideration the fact that Spain has only been a member of this group since 1988). The Plenary Meeting of the NSG took place in Madrid from 12th to 14th April 1994 under the chairmanship of the Spanish Ambassador to the IAEA in Vienna, José Antonio de Yturriaga. Spain welcomed the accession of Argentina as the 29th member of the Group, and deems the meeting in Madrid to have been very successful ; it also recognizes that the main obstacle for implementing the NSG export controls is China.[25] Another important step of the Plenary was the request to the chairman to conduct a series of briefings for non-members on the outcome of the Madrid meeting.[26]

Spain is also working actively to adapt Spanish nuclear export control legislation to future European regulations in this area, which Spain considers will not present any problems for the controls al-

---

[24] Interviews with officials from the Industry and Foreign Affairs Ministry.

[25] Interviews with officials from the Ministry of Commerce and Tourism.

[26] Press Statement of the Nuclear Suppliers Group Plenary Meeting in Madrid, April 12-14, 1994.

ready being applied. The principal difficulty is translation. Spanish officials point to technical problems here, and to the fact that EU definitions and parameters for sensitive products are sometimes not the same in Spanish.

Referring to Spain's participation in the New Forum, which will replace the COCOM, Madrid does not think it will play an important role within this new organization. One subject of concern is the question of China's inclusion in the new forum, since some officials believe that it is too risky to supply advanced dual-use technology to this country, and others believe that the inclusion of China could help Madrid to improve its commercial relations with Beijing.[27]

Another aspect to be stressed is the shortage of officials in the Spanish administration who are competent to attend these fora. As a consequence, the officials who are in charge of Spanish export control policy formulation at a domestic level are the same ones who attend the meetings in the NSG, MTCR, Zangger Committee and EPC, which makes their position difficult.

4. The Practice : Spain's Nuclear Trade Activities

In order to study Spanish practice regarding nuclear exports we have to establish a dividing line between before and after Spain's long-awaited accession to the NPT in 1987.[28] As Elliott Zoppo has already said : «There is a direct co-relation between domestic nuclear industry capacity and technology transfer as a nuclear supplier...».[29]

Currently, and after the extension of the Spanish nuclear moratorium, all the sources consulted agree that there is no research reac-

[27] **El Pais**, May 8, 1994, p.22.

[28] For this issue see for example SABA K., *"Spain and the Non-Proliferation Treaty"*, in : MÜLLER H. (ed.), **A Survey of European Nuclear Policy, 1985-1987**, Macmillan, London, 1989, pp.111-130.

[29] ELLIOTT ZOPPO C., *"Spain : An Emerging Nuclear Supplier"*, *Op.cit.*, p.347.

tor operating in Spain at the moment, and that all research projects have been cancelled. This means that the Spanish nuclear industry has lost its capacity and consequently Spain imports more nuclear materials than it exports. In the opinion of several officials, the nuclear industry is no longer profitable for Spain.[30]

In the 1970s and 80s, Spain was able to provide assistance for the establishment of research laboratories, research reactors, hot fuel facilities, research reactor fuel fabrication and research reactor re-processing facilities. We can identify contracts between the Spanish Junta de Energia Nuclear (JEN-CIEMAT today) and Chile, for supplying fuel and building a research reactor in Santiago in the 1970s, and the participation of several Spanish companies (SENER, TECHNATOM) in consulting contracts with Pakistan (Pakistan's Atomic Energy Commission) for plant design criteria, updating main component specifications, basic engineering system design, quality assurance and costs for the Chashma nuclear power plant.[31] On several occasions since 1986, Spain has also been accused of collaboration with Iran. Criticism arose in February 1990 when an agreement between Teheran and Madrid was signed to complete, with the participation of INI enterprises (National Institute of Industry), ENSA and ENUSA (National Uranium Company), two nuclear power plants started (and later abandoned) by German companies near the Iranian town of Busher. In 1987, Spain had already exported to Iran (through EMA) equipment for light-water reactors and technology for BWRs and PWRs, and in 1990, for heavy-water reactors.[32] In September 1990, Bonn urged Madrid to end its construction work in Iran.

In 1985, a Spanish journal specializing in nuclear issues wrote : «The penury of the domestic market has obliged our engineering and equipment manufacturing companies to make a very beneficial

---

[30] Interviews with officials of the Commerce and Tourism Ministry.

[31] ELLIOTT ZOPPO C., *"Spain : An Emerging Nuclear Supplier"*, *Op.cit.*

[32] **Eye on Supply**, No.2, Fall 1990, p.25 and No.3, Winter 1990/1991, pp.41-49. Monterey Institute of International Studies, Monterey, Cal./USA. For further information about this period, see : GARRIDO REBOLLEDO V., *"Spain"*, in : MÜLLER H. (ed.), **European Non-Proliferation Policy, 1988-1992**, *Op.cit.*, pp.167-168.

foreign opening, but with lots of risks ; due to the lack of big investments in Spain and the general economic crisis, the companies have been looking for work abroad. The first results have been very beneficial contracts both in the construction of finished power plants and in technological assistance to these countries.»[33]

In the same article, Algeria and China were identified as the two most promising markets for exports of Spanish nuclear technology.

The application of the already mentioned Royal Decree 480/1988 meant, according to some of the mass media, a loss of competitivity on the part of the Spanish nuclear and dual-use material export companies, since something like a third of the Spanish exports of these materials (Pts. 1.35 billion in 1988) required an authorisation from that year.[34] Although the Royal Decree was not very welcome to Spanish managers, the Economy Ministry recognized that it was the only way to guarantee the supply to Spain of some advanced technologies from those countries which demanded these controls. A lot of managers considered that the new regime represented the return of a controlled, bureaucratic trade regime. This was clearly a reference to JIMDDU's powers to deny or concede an export licence. Other managers interviewed saw in the new legislation the political price that had to be paid for Spain's joining NATO and conditions imposed by countries with more advanced military technology.

Three years after the law's application, the managers interviewed for this study took the view that Spanish government policy on exports of defence and dual-use material is today very demanding, and that the companies have very limited export opportunities due to the restrictiveness of the procedure.[35]

On the other hand, representatives of the Spanish opposition party (PP) said that the recently approved sanctions law was irrelevant, since Spain exports neither nuclear nor dual-use products with mili-

[33] **Luz y Fuerza**, May-June 1985, pp.38-43.

[34] **Actualidad Economica**, May 9, 1988, pp.102-108.

[35] Interviews with managers of two Spanish defence companies.

tary purposes, and that this legislation had been drawn up in order to meet international obligations acquired by Spain after its signing of the NPT.

In the last four years various accusations have been made in the media to the effect that Spain has been selling to several "nuclear suspect" countries. But none of this has been confirmed by official sources, which have pointed out that Spain has never exported anything of importance and that the exports have always been regulated in a more or less efficient manner.[36] The same sources stress that controls over the export of nuclear and dual-use materials have become far stricter since 1990, when Spain published its nuclear material lists. At present, Spain states that the only product being exported is uranium to be enriched abroad (France, Russia, USA) and the exported material is in any case for nuclear states or OECD countries. The characteristics of the Spanish market have also led the German company Siemens to declare «not being ready for fuel contracts in Spain because Spain's market is essentially closed».[37]

One of the most controversial incidents of the recent years took place in 1989, when the Spanish government denied permission to build two nuclear power plants in the Negev desert (Israel), a project which would have meant some US$ 4,000 million for Spanish industry. This operation, dated from 1983, could initially have been backed by the Spanish President[38] who for five years discussed with Israel the idea of building two nuclear power plants of 982 MW each, and a generation system which included a reactor of the PWR type. In 1987 Spain signed the NPT and a year later international pressures (the United States knew about the plan) forced Spain to withdraw from the undertaking.

Spain, according to officials of the Industry and Commerce Ministry, has contributed together with other EU countries to the prevention of cases of illegal nuclear export. In March 1992 the Spanish

---

[36] Interviews with officials of the Commerce and Tourism Ministry.

[37] **Nuclear Fuel**, August 31, 1992, p.12.

[38] **El Pais**, October 28, 1990, pp.6-7 (Sunday Report).

police arrested six members of an arms smuggling ring engaged in purchasing high technology equipment, including "Klystron" 200 amplificators whose final destination was to have been the Iranian F-4 Phantom aircraft.[39] The Spanish Commerce Ministry claimed that it never had any knowledge of this matter. According to the Ministry, in the last five years no concession of a dual-use export licence has ever been refused to any company which had asked for one ; that means, in the opinion of some officials, that there have never been any suspicions of dual-use illegal exports.

The Ministry of Commerce and Tourism has never admitted the involvement of Spanish companies in the manufacturing of the Iraqi "supergun". In the middle of May 1990, the Spanish General Direction of Customs discovered a plan to export "metallic structures" to Iraq, according to a Spanish newspaper.[40] One of the companies involved could have been Trebelan, which had already aroused suspicions in 1989, since it could have transported to Iraq a cannon of 210 mm diameter with base-bleed munition, using a Soviet Antonov 124 aircraft which landed in Vitoria, in the north of Spain (where the company has its headquarters). The material was declared as material for public works, and therefore no application was made for the corresponding licence for defence and dual-use material. Although the Royal Decree 480/1988 had already been approved, it did not come into force until a couple of days after the company investigation began, i.e. at the end of May 1990. At that time the lists of defence and dual-use materials had not yet been approved. In July 1988 the Spanish government had also investigated an application by Trebelan to sell 500 "munition glasses" to the Iraqi Hutteen General Establishment state company. This operation was very controversial since the Spanish Defence Ministry established that it was technically possible to fill the cartridges with chemical armaments already used by Iraq. The then manager of Trebelan said that the cartridges were for testing a new type of large-calibre and long-range artillery. And should the tests be successful, Trebelan could build a complete plant which would cost Iraq several million

---

[39] **El Mundo**, March 22, 1992.

[40] **El Pais**, May 23 and 24, 1990. See also : **Financial Times**, May 26, 1990.

dollars. Both representatives of Trebelan and the Spanish Commerce and Tourism Ministry and the Defence Ministry have avoided making any declaration referring to this question and have played the matter down, saying that Spain has never manufactured anything of importance in this field for Iraq. The then manager of the company and a number of its directors then left Trebelan and founded another company, MARTEC, which was registered in the category of "Industrial Engineering Services". The Trebelan company had been founded in 1983 and in 1988 its annual turnover was already pts 800 million.

According to a report prepared by the US Senate Foreign Relations Committee from open sources on March 25, 1991, a total of 17 companies were involved in the sale of dual-use and defence material to Iraq. In addition to Trebelan at least two more Spanish companies, FOREX and Space Research Corporation Española (which was in charge of the design and construction of Dr Bull's gun) could have participated in the "supergun" design.[41] Spain has never had a significant domestic debate on this question, and public opinion is not informed about it. This case definitely showed that the legislation had many loopholes, and lacked clear differentiation on the criteria to be followed for the export of defence and dual-use materials to Third World countries. This situation was to change, as already mentioned, in 1990 with the application of the new law.

A very different matter was the speculation about the possibility that relevant components of the Argentinian missile programme Condor II could have been sent to Spain in order to be used in a Spanish military programme[42] - the Capricornio Programme. This possibility was denied by the INTA (National Aerospacial Institute), which said that there was only a co-operation programme with Argentina in connection with launch vehicles (satellites) for the Spanish Capricornio space missile programme. Furthermore, all the sensitive elements of this missile, including its 14 rotors, were sent

---

[41] *"Saddam's Foreign Legion. Corporations Marching to Saddam's Call"*. Compilation prepared by the US Senate Foreign Relations Committee Republican Staff from open sources, March 25, 1991, pp.20-22.

[42] **EFE Agency**, November 16, 1992; December 14, 1992 and January 5, 1993.

back to the USA, and all that remained in Spain were metal parts described by Spanish officials as "scrap".[43] The Ministry of Commerce and Tourism and the Spanish Defence Ministry declared that Spain had merely done Argentina a favour by means of the agreement between the Spanish INTA and the Argentinian CONAE (*Comision Nacional de Actividades Espaciales*) which served as the legal basis for the operation, which was designed to improve the Argentinian international image by eliminating its missiles, when the other EC countries had turned their back on Argentina. Spain had always good relations with Argentina and the topic was brought up by the Argentinian President Menem in 1992 on the occasion of the Ibero-american summit in Madrid. This Spanish effort, according to the INTA, was also highly appreciated by Argentina.

5. Conclusion

The process of harmonising Spanish legislation in nuclear and dual-use export control issues was a consequence of Spain joining the COCOM in 1985. With the entry into force of the Sanctions Law (Organic Law 3/1992) which provides for jail of up to six years for offenders and the Royal Decree 824/1993 which approves the Foreign Trade Regulations on defence and dual-use material updating the Spanish list of defence and dual-use materials to the former COCOM, the NSG, the Zangger Committee and the MTCR lists, we can say that the process of adaptation of Spanish legislation to that of the other EU countries has been completed. This places Spain in a more favourable position with respect to other countries which have belonged to these fora for longer, but whose lists do not yet include all the changes. The new Spanish legislation even includes the controversial "catch-all" clause, not recognized by many countries.

This paper has shown that the Spanish government has made a remarkable effort to update its legislation in only five years. The same happened with Spain's participation in international fora for

---

[43] **El Pais**, March 2, 1993.

nuclear export control, which has concluded with Spain joining the Zangger Committee. The 1994 Spanish NSG presidency was treated very seriously by the Spanish authorities as an opportunity to demonstrate a clear nuclear non-proliferation policy. Spain also continues to work on the updating of its lists for the future European regulations which are now under discussion, and to assess the changes which the disappearance of COCOM as an administrative procedure will necessitate for national export controls. Therefore, it is possible that in 1995 modifications in the Spanish regulation will be necessary ; nevertheless, these modifications will only affect the Spanish product list and not the control procedures which have already been clearly established.

Finally, and because of the change of attitude on the role played by the nuclear industry in Spain (the decision not to build any further nuclear power plants), it is quite possible that the pressure from private industry regarding nuclear exports will decrease, and as a consequence Spain will cease to be an "emerging nuclear supplier". As has been shown, the participation of Spanish companies in nuclear programmes abroad has decreased in recent years, and in any case it goes no further than civil cooperation programmes.

ANNEX 1

Spanish Legislation on Nuclear and
Dual-Use Export Control
(Rules currently operative and main contents)

Order of May 28, 1990 (entry into force on May 29)

Regulates the procedures on foreign trade in defence material, dual-use goods and technologies.

Organic Law 3/1992 of April 30, 1992 (entry into force May 2, 1992)

Establishes the assumptions relating to smuggling of defence and dual-use material.

Royal Decree 1631/1992 of December 29, 1992 (entry into force January 2, 1993)

Restricts the circulation of special goods and materials, including the export of defence materials and dual-use goods and technologies (also explosives). This is a harmonization law.

Royal Decree 824/1993 of May 28, 1993 (entry into force September 22, 1993)

Errors corrected January 4, 1994. Approves the Defence and Dual-Use Materials Foreign Trade Regulation. Modifies the composition, attributions, assignments and functioning of the Interministerial Committee for Trade Regulation of Defence Material, Dual-Use Goods and Technologies (JIMDDU). Approves and updates the defence and dual-use material lists submitted for purposes of export control by the JIMDDU and defines the different kinds of export licences and the control documents. This is a Development Law of the Organic Law 3/1992 and repeals the Royal Decree 480/1988.

ANNEX 2

NUCLEAR AND DUAL-USE EXPORT CONTROL PROCEDURE

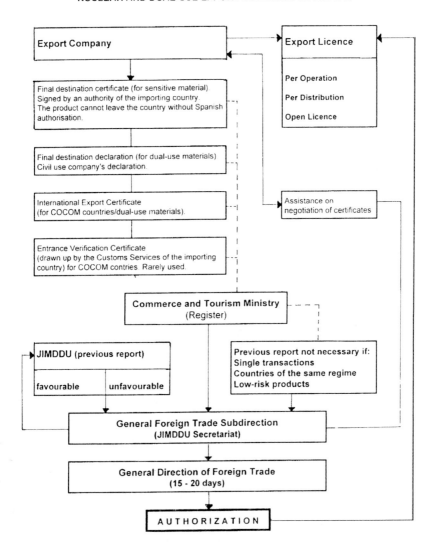

BELGIUM

Quentin Michel

1. Introduction

Nuclear weapons non-proliferation in Belgium does not seem to have been a political priority over the last decade. Everything has been done to respect and implement Belgium's international commitments, but most Belgian politicians have not shown much interest in the issue. When the draft law on controlling and monitoring transfers of nuclear material and equipment and relevant technological data was submitted to Parliament in 1978,[1] it did not stir up any great debate. The draft was shelved for approximately two years, and when the law was finally put to the vote in January 1980, it was adopted unanimously without any real discussion.[2] This situation may seem surprising in view of the number of heated parliamentary debates on nuclear energy generation that have taken place.[3]

Neither Parliament nor the Belgian government shows much interest in nuclear non-proliferation export control. For example, the

---

[1] Chambre des représentants (CDR), Session 1977-78, document No.358-1

[2] Sénat, Minutes of the plenary session, November 27th, 1989; Parliament, Minutes of the plenary session, January 31st, 1980

[3] See, for example, the debate on nuclear energy generation where the Parliament had to choose between reprocessing burned up fuel and the once through cycle process (CDR, Minutes of the plenary session, Wednesday December 22nd, 1993).

law on controlling and monitoring nuclear transfers was enacted eight years later, when the *Official Journal* published the "Royal Decree on transfers of nuclear material, equipment and relevant technological data to non-nuclear weapon states".

This situation appeared to have changed a little when, only two years after the meeting of signatories to the "Nuclear Suppliers Guidelines" in Warsaw (April 1992), the *Official Journal* published the list annexed to the guidelines for transfers of nuclear-related dual-use equipment, material and related technology, as adopted at this meeting.

To understand the Belgian export control regime properly, it is important to know that almost 60 % of Belgium's electricity is produced from nuclear energy.[4] As a consequence, Belgian manufacturers and designers, engineering and consulting offices and research organisations involved in nuclear activities supported by national programmes have developed considerable expertise. Due to this particular nuclear structure, Belgium's industries are able to design and supply, for example, mixed-oxide fuel facilities and more than 90 % of the country's large nuclear power stations.

2. State Organisation

With the revision of its Constitution in May 1993, Belgium became a federal state. It is divided into three Regions and three Communities.[5] Each has specific competences defined by the Constitution and by a so-called special law.[6]

---

[4] In 1993, the OECD's estimate was 59 % (**Nuclear energy data**, Nuclear Energy Agency, Paris, 1994, p.10)

[5] The Regions are : The Flemish Region, the Walloon Region and the Brussels Region. The Communities are : the Dutch-speaking community, the French-speaking community and the German-speaking community. The communities are mainly concerned by matters pertaining to language issues (culture, education, audiovisual issues). The regions have competences in economic and geographical issues (housing, environment, water policy).

[6] A special law must be adopted by a special majority in Parliament (two thirds of the valid votes and the majority of each linguistic group with the majority of the members of each group present at the vote).

Export control legislation is drawn up by the federal Parliament and implemented by the federal government, in other words : by the Ministry of Foreign Affairs and the Ministry of Economic Affairs. Although nuclear export control legislation and organisation was not modified directly by the last constitutional reform, some amendments like the regionalizations of the *attachés commerciaux* and the possible division of the National Export Assurance organisation between the three regions could influence nuclear export control policy indirectly.

3. Belgium's Legislation on Nuclear Non-Proliferation

The nuclear export control regime is governed primarily by two laws : the law of August 1962 which has been amended several times,[7] and monitors exports, imports, and the transit of goods and technology ; and the law of February 9th, 1981, on the control and monitoring of all transfers of nuclear material and equipment and of relevant technological data.[8]

These two laws organise the nuclear export control system in two stages : authorisation and licensing. In short, authorisation is the political control in line with government policy and Belgium's nuclear non-proliferation commitments. And secondly the licence itself is a physical means for customs officers to control transfers.

The difference between these two laws is that the authorisation law is tailored specifically to nuclear non-proliferation, and this is not the case with the licence law. The licensing process is applicable to any kind of goods and technology which could be involved in international trade in nuclear-related materials.

---

[7] This law was amended respectively by laws of July 19th, 1968, July 6th, 1978 and August 3rd, 1992. *"Licence law"* is the abbreviated form used in the text.

[8] *"Authorisation law"* is the abbreviated form used in the text.

3.1. The law of February 9th 1981 on the control and monitoring of all transfers of nuclear material and equipment and of relevant technological data

The principle established by Article 1 of the law obliges any transfer of nuclear material, equipment and related technology to a non-nuclear weapons state to be destined exclusively for peaceful purposes, and to be in accordance with any special controls required. To meet these conditions all transfers must have an authorisation.

The authorisation procedure is laid down by law and by the Royal Decree of May 12, 1989 on transfers of nuclear material, equipment, technology and relevant by-products to a non-nuclear weapon state.[9]

Application for authorisation must be submitted and signed by the company representative dealing with the transaction, following the procedure defined by the Minister.[10]

Authorisation is granted by the Minister for Energy. Before the decision is taken, advice is sought from the Nuclear Non-Proliferation Committee (better known as CANPAN). This is composed of Ministries' cabinet representatives from the ministries of Economic Affairs, Defence, Justice, Foreign Trade, Foreign Affairs, Public Health, the Environment and Scientific Policy. CANPAN members are appointed for a three year term. In terms of its composition, CANPAN should be considered as a means of co-ordination between the different government bodies involved in the export control regime.

It is an advisory committee on the non-proliferation of nuclear weapons with the task of advising the Minister for Energy on each transaction requiring authorisation. It ensures that requests for transfers comply with all the regulations and with government policy.

---

[9] This Royal Decree was modified by the Royal Decree of July 16th, 1993.

[10] Ministerial Decree of September 12th, 1989, applying Article 2 of the Royal Decree of May 12th, 1989, related to the transfers to a non-nuclear weapon state of nuclear material, equipment, technology and relevant by-products.

This committee is more concerned with political aspects of non-proliferation than technical ones. When necessary, it seeks technical advice from nuclear research centres and university experts.

Normally, authorisation may not be granted unless the following conditions are satisfied :

- the material, installations or technology to be transferred must not be used for manufacturing nuclear weapons ;
- they must be covered by International Atomic Energy Agency (IAEA) safeguards or by an equivalent system in the recipient country ;
- they must be subject to effective physical protection to prevent any non-authorised access, use or handling.

Moreover, the facilities where the item will be used must also be covered by IAEA safeguards, as should the other items produced by those facilities.

Finally, the state to which the item is to be transferred must undertake to guarantee that these conditions will be respected, and in the case of transfer or retransfer to another country, prior consent is required from the Belgian government.

As Belgium has adopted guidelines for transferring nuclear-related dual-use equipment, material and related technology,[11] the transfer of nuclear items should not be authorised unless the recipient state has concluded a so-called full-scope safeguards agreement with the IAEA. This condition has not so far been incorporated into the legislation itself, but it seems to be the policy followed by CANPAN.

After advice from CANPAN, the Minister has to inform the Central Office for Quotas and Licences (OCCL), an administrative department of the Ministry of Economic Affairs, of the decision on whether to grant or refuse authorisation. CANPAN's advice to the

---

[11] Decision adopted March-April 1992 in Warsaw, at the meeting of the Nuclear Suppliers Group.

Minister has to be well founded[12] and is strictly confidential. Moreover, it seems that ultimately the Minister is not bound by CANPAN's advice.

On the other hand, the grounds for the Minister's decision to grant or refuse authorisation are not always given to the applicant which might seem to run counter to the legal specification that the administration's decision must be "justified".[13] The fact that in some cases the Minister does not give reasons for his decision could be explained in part by the dispensation, proved by Article 4 of the above-mentioned law, permitting this in very specific case such as when state security could be jeopardised.

If authorisation is denied, the legislation does not establish any kind of appeal process for the applicant. The only possibility is to appeal to an administrative jurisdiction, the *Conseil d'Etat*. This procedure is not tailored specifically to nuclear items, could last as long as a year, and ultimately could only annul the decision to reject authorisation. This procedure has never been used by an applicant. One explanation could be the political and economic pressure placed on enterprises, either deliberately or by circumstances.

Enforcement measures in case of violation and attempted violation of nuclear export control regulations are established by Article 6 of this law. The period of imprisonment ranges from one month to five years and can be accompanied by a fine of between 15,000 and 150 million Belgian francs.[14]

3.2. The Law of August 27th 1962 on monitoring exports, imports and transit of goods and technology

Once the applicant is informed of the Minister's decision to grant authorisation, the export licence permitting transfer of the item may be issued. The licence is granted by the OCCL which verifies that

---

[12] Article 9 of the above-mentioned Royal Decree.

[13] Law of July 29th, 1991, relating to the grounds for the administration's decision.

[14] As updated by the Programme law of December 24th, 1993.

the export regulations have been applied correctly and in full. Under this authorisation procedure, the licence may not usually be issued until the applicant has submitted an end-user certificate and a written non-retransfer guarantee. If the end-user is a private company, the certificate has to be countersigned by the relevant authorities (which could be the government of the state concerned).

Other specific requirements may be established regarding the decision to grant the licence, for instance a short period of validity.[15]

The Law and its Royal Decree[16] give the authorities broad powers to make inquiries to check the accuracy of the information given by the applicant. The person applying for the licence, as well as anyone in possession of relevant information, is obliged to place this information at the disposal of the authorities. This provision covers all employees and workers of the firm to which the licence is granted. Moreover, any government body which might have information about a breach of the law has to inform the OCCL if requested to do so.

Normally, once the licence is granted, the authorities may not withdraw or suspend it except under exceptional circumstances and by a joined founded decision of the Ministers concerned by the transfers.[17]

Any breach or attempted violation of the law is punishable by severe sanctions.[18]

Firstly, the applicant, whether an individual or a legal entity, could be banned from obtaining licences for a period of up to six months.

---

[15] Normally a licence is valid for six months.

[16] Royal Decree of December 30, 1993, monitoring the import, export and transit of goods and related technology.

[17] Usually this decision will be taken by the ministers for Foreign Trade, Economy, Foreign Affairs and Energy.

[18] Article 10 and 10*bis* of the law, related to Article 231 of the general law on customs and excise duties.

Secondly, the items could be seized and a fine equivalent to the transfer value could be imposed.

Finally, a prison sentence of between four months and a year could be imposed and this could be doubled in the case of a second offence.

Graphic of the Procedure

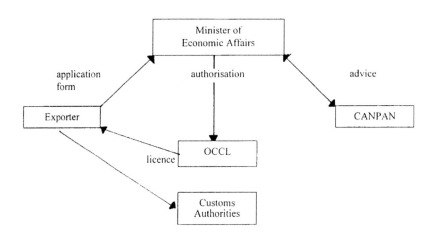

3.3. Export Control Lists

The Belgian nuclear export control regime is, as described above, made up of two laws which have somewhat different fields of application.

The authorisation law is tailored specifically to nuclear items, and in the Royal Decree which implemented this law the list of items covered is mainly made up of nuclear and dual-use items with possible nuclear applications.

The list is divided into two parts : the first contains nuclear material, equipment and technology and includes all items specified by the Zangger Committee and by the Nuclear Suppliers Group.[19] The second is made up of nuclear-related dual-use equipment, material, and related technology.[20]

The definitions of technology applied in the two parts of the list are quite different. The first part of the list limits control to technical data in physical form, while the second part is more comprehensive and includes so-called intangible technology which could be, for instance, the supply of technical assistance. This distinction, amazing as it might seem, conforms with international requirements, in particular with the commitments undertaken in the different meetings of the Nuclear Suppliers Group.

Contrary to the authorisation law, the licence law is not tailored specifically to nuclear items, as it concerns all categories of goods which could be subject to export control. The licence regime could be imposed on a specific category of goods for any destination or on all exports destined for a given country. The reasons for imposing this regime could be :

- To safeguard state interests of a sector of the Belgian economy.

---

[19] Respectively INFCIRC/109, INFCIRC/254.

[20] As defined by the arrangements adopted in March-April 1992 in Warsaw at the meeting of the Nuclear Suppliers Group.

- To safeguard state security.

- As a way of applying pressure on states which do not respect the fundamental rights and duties of nations and of human beings. Such a decision was taken in May 1993 in respect of the Federal Republic of Yugoslavia, the Republic of Croatia and the Republic of Bosnia in the shape of a requirement to license all imports, exports and transfers.[21]

- To assist the integration and transcription of international a-greements or commitments into the Belgian federal legis-lation system. These were the reasons behind the Ministerial Act of November 20, 1989, subjecting the export of so-called strategic items to the licence regime, which contains a list of nuclear items. This list is based on the COCOM list.

Before a nuclear item is exported an export licence must be sought, and this is the only document recognised by the customs authorities. Normally, one of the main conditions for obtaining a licence is prior authorisation. Therefore, the licence procedure guar-antees that the authorisation procedure has been respected. Thus, if the export control regime is to be effective, the lists for authorisa-tion and licensing must be identical. If the authorisation list is longer than the licence list, there is no guarantee that the authorisation law will be respected, and nuclear items could be exported without au-thorisation and without encountering any problems with customs controls.

Unfortunately, the authorisation list is more precise than the li-cence list. The nuclear dual-use items and some nuclear items have been left off the licence law list.[22]

---

[21] Ministerial Act of May 13, submitted to license, the import, export and transit of goods.

[22] For example, reactor fuel assemblies are not mentioned in the licence list. Only Plutonium, Uranium, and Zirconium are specified as material, and the technology of other reactor fuel assemblies seems free for transfer or export.

Where definitions are concerned, the licence law appears on occasions to be more complete than the authorisation law. For example, the definition of technology as applied to the licence list includes intangible technology.[23]

Interviews with the different actors have revealed that the industries concerned, in order to avoid unnecessary difficulties, almost always ask the OCCL when they start to negotiate a contract if this activity will be subject to the export control regime. However, this is less likely to be true of black sheep companies, and these are the reason why the export control regime is needed in the first place.

Since the beginning of the Belgian nuclear research programme and its industrialisation, interaction between industry and the public authorities has always been important. Where nuclear safety and security are concerned, the different advisory committees always include representatives of industry. However, in the nuclear export control regime no formal interfaces or information programmes have been organised. Some informal contacts are arranged from time to time between those in charge of the export control system and representatives of industry, but that is all.

The new European Union export control system[24] should in part close the Belgian export control legislation loophole as described

---

[23] The definition of technology in the licence law is similar to the one use in the authorisation law list for dual-use technology. Compare the annex (Article 1000) of Ministerial Act of November 20, 1989, where the following require a licence : the import, export and transit of goods (strategic goods), with annex II of the Royal Decree of May 12th, 1989, on transfers to a non-nuclear weapons State of nuclear material, equipment, technology and relevant by-products.

[24] The European export control system is based on two legal instruments, a Regulation and a Joint Action, which together form an integrated system. Whereas the regulation contains the substantive provisions governing the export of dual-use goods, the Joint Action provides the necessary annexes which are subject to the provisions of the Regulation. These annexes contain a list of dual-use goods which are subject to control when exported from the European Union, a list of countries for which simplified formalities could be applied, a list of items which should be, temporarily or permanently, be excluded from the provisions for free circulation between Member States, and finally the guidelines for authorisation of the export of dual-use goods.

above.[25] To the extent that such a regulation is binding in its entirety and is directly applicable in all member states,[26] the export control of dual-use goods and technology in the European Union will from now on be governed by this regulation. In short, the regulation submits the export of dual-use goods and technology to authorisation which is granted by the member state's competent authorities. The authorisation is valid in all European Union member states. When the exporter completes the formalities at the customs office, it must be proved that export has been duly authorised.

Unfortunately, this regulation covers only dual-use goods and technical data[27] and not intangible technology, which remains the exclusive responsibility of the member state.

The Belgian export control system has drawn up no systematic lists of countries for which all or some exports must be submitted to special formalities, except a simplified one for items destined for a European Union member state. Presently, the Minister is authorised to impose some special requirements on the applicant for each transaction for any kind of destination, if this is considered necessary.

However, when the new European Community Council Regulation on export control of dual-use goods and technology is enacted, its list of countries subject to simplified formalities will be applied by the Belgian export control authorities.[28]

---

[25] The regulation applies to dual-use goods and technology which could be utilised, entirely or in part, for use in connection with the development, production, maintenance, detection, identification or dissemination of, on the one hand, chemical, biological and nuclear weapons and, on other hand, missiles capable of delivering such weapons.

[26] Article 189 of the Treaty establishing the European Community (signed in Rome on 25th March, 1957).

[27] Plans, blueprints, diagrams, formulae, engineering designs and specifications, etc.

[28] The Regulation and its related Joint Action have been adopted by the Council of Ministers on 19th December 1994. It is important to point out that the list of countries to which simplified formalities should be applied is a non-exhaustive list, so European Member States could apply simplified formalities to other countries. In this case they should inform the other Member States and the European Commission.

3.4. The Possible Catch-All Clause

The two laws which govern the Belgian export control system do not contain a specific catch-all clause. However, the licence law contains some provisions which could function as a soft version of a catch-all clause. Once the Minister for Economic Affairs has granted the licence, it may not normally be withdrawn.[29] Only under exceptional circumstances and in an emergency may the licence be suspended for up to sixty days. During this time the licence could be withdrawn by a joint decision of the ministers concerned. No definition of the terms **"exceptional"** and **"emergency"** is provided by the law, and the interpretation is left to the minister concerned. So if the minister is informed that certain items are to be used in a nuclear weapons research programme, a previously issued licence may be suspended.

A more efficient catch-all clause is established by the so-called weapons law[30] which does not concern the nuclear export control regime directly but could be applied to a certain degree. In the Annex to the Royal Decree[31] which implemented the weapons law the words «**other equipment, goods and technology which could support military action**» have been added. This sentence has to be interpreted in the light of King's Report on the Royal Decree, as placing an obligation on suppliers, exporters and transferrers to apply for a licence if they know that the items will be used for military purposes.

Enforcement measures for violation of this provision are quite similar to the sanctions established by the licence law. However, the prison sentence and fine are more severe : they go up to a maxi-

---

[29] Only under exceptional circumstances, by a founded joint decision of the different ministers concerned by the transfers (see *infra*).

[30] Law of August 5, 1991, relating to the import, export and transfer of weapons, munitions, goods and technology which could be used specifically for military purposes.

[31] Royal Decree of March 1993 regulating the import, export and transfer of weapons, munitions, goods and technology which could be used specifically for military purpose.

mum of five years' imprisonment and 150 million Belgian francs respectively.

It would seem that this very equivocal catch-all clause has not yet been used, and it is unclear how it could be applied in the absence of clearly defined provisions.[32]

Finally, the new European Community Council Regulation on the export control of dual-use goods and technology has established two kinds of catch-all clause, one obligatory and one optional on dual-use items.[33] The obligatory clause obliges exporters to apply for authorisation once they have been informed by the authorities that items which are not subject to the authorisation procedure are intended for use in connection with an ABC weapons or missile research or manufacturing programme. Moreover, if the exporter knows that the items could be used in such a programme, the authorities should be informed and they will decide whether or not to submit the exports to an authorisation procedure.

The optional provision, left at the discretion of the individual member state, goes a little further and obliges the exporter to inform the authorities if it is known that the items could be used in ABC weapons or a missile research or manufacturing programme. This regime is applied in Belgium as the catch-all clause of the weapons law is also valid for dual-use items.

4. Export Control Verification

The system set up to ensure that the export control regime is observed involves several administrative authorities, primarily the OCCL, the Customs authorities and the *Inspection générale économique*.

---

[32] The liabilities procedure, the definition of when and how the exporter is aware of the military purpose of the export, who is required to prove the knowledge of this military purpose (the exporter, the administration), are all very unclear.

[33] Article 4.

Before granting the licence, the OCCL requires an end-user certificate and a no-retransfer guarantee from the exporter. Once the items have reached the end-user, the exporter should provide the OCCL with an International Delivery to Destination Certificate issued by the customs authorities of the end-user's country.

As there is a shortage of qualified personnel, the OCCL can only verify the existence and the accuracy of this certificate from time to time by means of random inspection. Moreover, the submission of this certificate is not a legal obligation, and hence infringements are not liable to prosecution.

The *Inspection générale économique* is in charge of investigations of and keeping records on violations of the export control regime. It checks the accuracy of licence data, and on the basis of trade documents verifies the destination and the nature of the items. This control is carried out once the items have left the country, usually at the request of the Minister of Economic Affairs, Minister of Foreign Affairs, or the OCCL.

The role of the customs authorities is to control the use of the licences before export and to check whether they conform with the trade documents. Due to insufficient personnel and the amount of international trade (more than 74 % of Belgium's GNP is made up of exports), it is no longer possible for customs officials to check the accuracy of all customs declarations. Only from time to time can they check whether shipments correspond to the licences granted. Before the Single European Market came into force, the percentage of physical controls was estimated at about 2 %.[34] So it would be possible for containers filled with weapons items, but declared as porcelain, to pass through customs without being intercepted. Actually, this situation is not new, as for a long time the customs authorities have been warning about the difficulty of organising physical inspections and identifying strategic items, includ-

---

[34] Chambre des représentants (CDR), Session 1988-89, document No.137/6 on parliamentary survey on weapons and munitions deliveries to countries involved in an armed conflict or under embargo (Report), p.541.

ing nuclear items.[35] But since the government has frozen the federal administration budget for several years, this situation will not change in the near future.

5. Influences on Belgium's Export Control System

The authorisation and licence system which governs Belgian export control is applied to all exports to non-nuclear weapon states. Normally authorisation is not required for exports to a nuclear weapons state[36] and the licence is granted automatically. In this case, the OCCL should notify CANPAN of the list of items on the licence.

A similar procedure is applied within the European Union for transactions between member states.[37] However, transfers of nuclear materials from a member state within the Union, as well as transfers to non-members, must be registered with the European Commission.

Another important exception to this system is the export control procedure applied in the Benelux states (Belgium, the Netherlands and Luxembourg), where there is a high level of integration between the countries. Between this group an export licence to any destination issued by one of the three countries' authorities is valid and recognised by all three customs services.

6. Conclusions

Just after the Gulf war, when the scale of the huge Iraqi military research programme became known, questions were asked about the

---

[35] See, for example, Chambre des représentants (CDR), Session 1988-89, document No.137/6, *Op.cit.*, p.539.

[36] As defined by Article IX §3 of the Treaty on the Non-Proliferation of nuclear weapons.

[37] Moreover, for dual-use items transactions, a licence is no longer required. The system is organised by the European Union export control system (the Regulation based on Article 113 of the Treaty establishing the European Community and the Common Foreign and Security Policy Joint Action).

efficiency of the export control regime in Belgium. Some important changes have now been made to the system to improve its efficiency. However, the different reforms introduced during the last three years should be seen within the framework of policies defined by the NSG and by the European Union rather than as consequences of the discovery of the Iraqi military research programme.

The description and analysis of the Belgian nuclear export control system given above might give the impression that the whole system is rather weak, but this impression should be qualified a little. Since the legislation discussed here came into force, no case of fraud or violation has been discovered. We do not think that this is due merely to inefficient application of the law. Furthermore, the high level of expertise needed to design and manufacture nuclear and nuclear-related items requires huge financial and research capacity that only a few large Belgian companies possess. Most of these companies are more or less involved in the production of equipment for nuclear utilities on which the public authorities have considerable influence, either directly or indirectly.

DENMARK

Lars van Dassen

1. Small States and Their Perception of Carrots and Sticks

Although the nuclear non-proliferation norms are gaining ground as more and more states sign the Non-Proliferation Treaty (NPT), it must not be forgotten that behind the signatures, much disagreement remains concerning the policies that will best serve the adherent states and the goal of non-proliferation. The regime is, therefore, an immensely complicated system of pillars that have to fit together, be counterbalanced and observe various national interests.[1]

Probably the most fundamental but also very troublesome balancing-act the regime has to perform is the one between carrots and sticks. On the one hand, every country has the right to develop and

---

[1] Danish nuclear export controls have to the best of this author's knowledge not received any attention in scholarly work. Because of the paucity of written sources, this chapter is almost exclusively based on interviews with selected Members and academic staff of Parliament, officials from the Ministry of Foreign Affairs, The Ministry of Industry, The Confederation of Danish Industries, Risø National Laboratory and the European Commission. The author wishes to thank the interviewed persons for their cooperation and kindness. Because of the lack of previous attention given to this issue and the almost exclusive reliance on interviews, the interviewed persons have been asked to comment on an earlier version of this article. Also, presentations of an earlier draft of the study at PRIF briefings with the Baltic and Bulgarian governments have produced most valuable comments.

use nuclear energy and may receive the necessary materials, equipment and know-how from the adherents to the NPT, if it itself submits to the regime norms. On the other hand, if a country stays outside the Treaty and does not abide by the regime norms, it will ideally receive no such assistance and will also on other accounts suffer the sticks of condemnation and restriction that the "good society" places on it.

Nuclear export controls play a pivotal role as specification and regulation of articles III and IV of the NPT, where this basic relation is stated. But although the effectiveness of nuclear export controls is frequently discussed, very little attention is paid to how they are implemented and regarded by the smaller members of the Nuclear Suppliers Guidelines (NSG). Denmark is one of these small countries, and is moreover one with a very low status with respect to nuclear infrastructure. At the Risø National Laboratory, there are two research reactors, one fuel fabrication plant, a storage area for fuel fabrication and scrap material from the fabrication process, a waste facility for storing irradiated fuel, a decommissioned hot cell plant and a decommissioned ore processing plant. In addition, there is nuclear material at eighteen installations in other parts of Denmark, mainly in the shape of depleted uranium that is used as radiation shields. Last but not least, there is a large quantity of uranium ore in Greenland, but there are for political reasons no plans for utilizing this material. The nuclear material in Denmark is under Euratom and IAEA safeguards, with the exception of any nuclear material on the Faroe Islands and Greenland. The latter are not members of the EU, but these materials are still covered by the Danish NPT safeguards agreement with the IAEA.[2] Although the primary nuclear goods and equipment are therefore few and well safeguarded, there are other reasons why a proliferator might find Denmark attractive as a source of technology and know-how, as there are considerable engineering and dual-use capabilities in Denmark as in other industrialized countries.

---

[2] According to Section 7 of INFCIRC/153, a National System of Accounting and Control (NSAC) must exist in all signatory States. Although this is not implemented uniformly in all States, in Denmark the location of all nuclear materials is known at all times. On top of this, the comprehensiveness of the material balances is stressed by the fact that the provisions of INFCIRC/153 that allow for exemptions from safeguards have not been used for many years.

But this does not explain how a country like Denmark perceives the importance of nuclear export controls and what role she herself seeks to play. One might think that the entire system of international cooperation on nuclear export controls contains a mixture of carrots and sticks, depending on a given country's vested interests and importance in the nuclear field. One hypothesis might be that Denmark follows suit when "the nuclear establishment" sets the pace as adherence to the common export control guidelines has advantages for the general Danish export situation. Alternatively, it could be the case that Denmark sees nuclear export controls more idealistically as an integral part of non-proliferation and disarmament efforts, issues which Denmark has a long and undisputed tradition of supporting. A further hypothesis might be that there is fierce resistance from industry as the nuclear issue is not directly a Danish problem but it nevertheless also places restrictions on Danish business. As will become evident, this last hypothesis can be ruled out, and the first two provide an accurate description of Danish nuclear export control policy.

2. Something Rotten in the State of Denmark ?

In February 1993, it was revealed that a Danish company was on the International Atomic Energy Agency and UNSCOM's list of exporters to the Iraqi nuclear weapons programme. There was for a short period some discussion of the case in the press but it soon emerged that the whistle had been blown too loudly. First of all, the equipment that had been found was a quite unsophisticated tool for straightening out damaged vehicle axles. It was a product that had never been on any of the export control lists, and moreover the company, Stenhøj Hydraulik A/S, seemed never to have exported anything to Iraq.[3]

---

[3] This information is based on information from the Danish press, e.g. *"Dansk udstyr på atomanlaeg"*, **Information**, 9th February 1993, and a telephone conversation of March 3rd 1993 with the export manager of Stenhøj Hydraulik A/S.

This is in fact the closest one gets to a case of detected illegal Danish nuclear or dual-use exports.[4] Nor is it likely that this clean record can be explained by inadequate detection. Denmark is closely associated with the intelligence and police networks of its allies and partners in NATO and the EU. So even if the Danish telescope were held to the blind eye, it is likely that others would have identified breaches of the rules. Moreover, a peripheral relation to the nuclear industry is also unlikely to be the explanation for this "success story". A sizeable part of Denmark's exports consists of machinery, engineering and computer technology applicable for many purposes, and this is reflected in the attention that Danish companies receive from time to time from more or less dubious companies especially in the Middle East. As will become apparent, the absence of Danish exports for such purposes owes more to consensus and cooperation between the authorities and companies than to strict regulation and law enforcement.

3. The Origins and Evolution of Danish Export Controls

The best confirmation that export controls in Denmark have been quite successful can be obtained by testing the standard assumption that export control failures lead to changes in the regulations in order to plug the gaps. The Danish export control system, both general and nuclear, has remained practically unaltered since its introduction around 1950.

The Western attempt to control the export of technology to the Eastern Bloc grew out of the Cold War. The West, under US leadership, wanted to place an embargo on the East in order to ensure that no assistance was unintentionally provided to the qualitative development of the arms industries in the socialist countries. As a close ally of the USA and as a NATO member from 1949, Denmark participated in this cooperation which was formalized in the shape

---

[4] Another more remote case relates to smuggling. In 1992 a 3 gr plutonium sample was smuggled from Lund in Sweden through Denmark to Hamburg. The sample was supposedly the "appetizer" for a bigger deal, but it was discovered by the press and German authorities.

of the Coordinating Committee for Multilateral Export Controls (COCOM), founded in 1950.

Despite this institutionalization, COCOM was not discussed openly - either in Denmark or elsewhere. But the regulation of exports could not be so tacit or secret that business and industry would not know of its existence or be obliged to comply with it.[5] Therefore a solution had to be found, providing both for an effective export control system and for an absence of too much public and maybe even parliamentary debate on the issue.

The Danish Currency Act states in its § 6 and 15 that the Minister of Industry is authorized to regulate exports if overall trade policies, the general supply situation, or Denmark's agreements with other states define such needs. Other parts of this Act have been changed, but the authorization to provide an export control regulation without the involvement of Parliament still stands. This has been done by the establishment of an "Ordinance on exports of certain goods".[6] And though the situation that led to all the secrecy has vanished, export control regulation has remained outside the political limelight. This, however, has not hampered the overall objectives and implementation of effective export controls.

In early 1995, a new Danish export control legislation will be implemented. Its purpose is twofold. First, it is intended to facilitate the transition to the common EU dual-use regulation which will

---

[5] The matter was sensitive for domestic as well as external reasons. First of all, American assistance for Europe's recovery from World War II was tied to compliance with certain restrictions concerning exports to the East. This might lead to mixed feelings in a population which felt that the peoples of Eastern Europe endured sufficient hardships already, and where at the national level, the Communist Party enjoyed considerable sympathy in the post-war years, mainly due to the important role the communists had played during World War II in the Danish anti-Nazi resistance movement. Secondly, there were at times disagreements between the USA and the other Western countries over the extent of the embargo. Whereas the former at times saw the strategic embargo as a component of a general economic warfare with the goal of crippling the socialist East, the latter were mainly concerned with the security implications of exports; ROODBEEN H., **Trading the Jewel of Great Value : The Participation of The Netherlands, Belgium, Switzerland and Austria in the Western Embargo**, Ph.D. Dissertation, University of Leiden, 1992, p.12.

[6] **Bekendtgørelse om udførsel af visse varer**, 12 November 1993.

probably enter into force on 1 March 1995. The common regulation leaves very little to be regulated through national legislation. Secondly, the new Danish legislation will facilitate a swift implementation of internationally decided economic embargoes of third countries. Hitherto, such cases (most recently, Iraq and Serbia) had to be dealt with separately, under individual pieces of legislation.

3.1. The Danish Export Control Regulation

In the following, the main instruments of nuclear export control will be outlined. Organizational changes have occurred from time to time, but instead of tracing these mostly small and insignificant alterations, a general portrayal of the system will be attempted.

The Ordinance on exports of certain goods consists of two parts : a preamble where the general legal provisions are stated, and a second part that includes the lists from the various export control regimes. In general, the **licence authority** rests with the Ministries of Industry and Justice. The latter is in charge of weapon exports and some goods from the MTCR list, while for all other listed goods, including the NSG list 1 and 2, the Ministry of Industry is the appropriate authority. The ministries have the authority to demand any kind of information they consider appropriate for decisions on issuing an export licence.

All Danish, foreign, new, second hand, re-exported and in-transit listed goods are covered by the **licence requirement**. If a listed product constitutes a part of another unlisted product, it nevertheless falls under the regulation. Whereas the definition of single (military) use, civil use or dual-use refers to the Guidelines definition of each term, there are no provisions that stand in the way of exports of **intangible knowledge** (for instance, a computer programme, a fax transmission etc.), unless it is a part of another listed item. This means that there is no barrier to trade in intangible knowledge as a separate export item.[7]

---

[7] If such cases were to arise, they might to some extent be covered by other regulations, for instance in relation to high treason or industrial espionage.

How to deal with exports that are not listed but nevertheless known to contribute to nuclear weapons programmes is a tricky matter. Theoretically, there is a possibility that § 6 of the Weapons Export Act could provide the **catch-all clause**. However, there is a general recognition that this provision would not apply as a general catch-all clause because it only encompasses specific categories of weapons, and weapons of mass destruction are not among them.[8] Neither of these possible weaknesses in the legislation has so far given rise to serious practical concern.[9]

The legal measures regarding **extraterritorial** actions are minimal. There is no provision that can prevent a company from trading abroad goods which cannot be exported without a licence from Danish territory. Equally troublesome is the question of **end-use control**. A general requirement for exports of licensed goods is a certificate from the recipient country or company confirming peaceful uses and stating that re-export will not take place without the prior consent of the Danish authorities. However, these certificates are not accompanied by concrete measures to establish that they correspond to reality.

The **penalties** for violations of the Ordinance are the following. In cases of general violations of the Ordinance, the sentence may vary between fines and two years imprisonment. Unintentional breaches are only subject to fines. Violations of the procedural requirements (documentation, presentation of documents to the Customs and other state authorities, the obligation to return unused licences etc.) can similarly only be punished with fines. Profits from illegal transfers cannot be confiscated under the Ordinance.

Although it was stated earlier that export controls have remained virtually unaltered over the years, this only holds true for the provi-

---

[8] This means that the clause only has relevance if a Danish company were, for example to export, hunting riffles in the knowledge or with the suspicion that they were to be used as sniper rifles.

[9] I deal later with the reasons why there have been no problems in these areas, and under heading on Denmark and the EU, I explain how Denmark sees the establishment of a common EU regulation.

sions outlined above. The content of the adherent lists changes regularly in accordance with the agreements Denmark reaches with other states. In short, there are two lists, A and B. List A contains eight appendices, of which the first three are COCOM related. The fourth establishes the essential definitions, the fifth deals with the products applicable to chemical weapons (Australian Group), the sixth relates to the Nuclear Suppliers Guidelines, the seventh lists the MTCR products and the eighth is the dual-use list of the NSG. List B contains only one appendix on waste products.[10]

4. The Implementation of Nuclear Export Controls

Beyond the legal provisions stated above and despite the absence of interesting cases of export control failure, much still remains to be said about the administration of nuclear export controls and the Danish role in negotiations on these issues. One thing that may be striking to many is the intertwined or cooperative nature of the agencies involved. This is also a reason why it is slightly inaccurate to describe one agency as responsible for a particular task, as such sharp lines do not reflect reality. Instead, attention must be paid to the various steps concerning the implementation of the regulation. The important private and governmental agencies are : the Parliamentary Commission on Currency Issues, the Ministry of Foreign Affairs, the Ministry of Industry, the Confederation of Danish Industries, Risø National Laboratory and the Customs Services.

4.1. Political Attention ?

It was stated earlier that the Currency Act was the instrument used tacitly to establish an export control regulation. This legal peculiarity has led to a situation in which issues related to nuclear export controls, or any other export controls for that matter, are the concern of the Parliamentary Commission on Currency Issues. In other words, it is not the parliamentary commissions on industry, foreign

---

[10] On 12 November 1993 and 22 April 1994 this system of lists underwent minor alterations. The order and composition of the appendices has changed and a ninth appendix has been added to list A.

affairs or defence that supervise and discuss the issue. The representation of the political parties on these commissions corresponds to their representation in Parliament and they play an important role in parliamentary debates on new laws and regulations. In these fora, the responsible minister is obliged to answer relevant questions.

However, changes concerning export controls were, as stated earlier, virtually confined to the adherent lists, and the Secretary of the Parliamentary Commission on Currency Issues and a member of Parliament who has been on the Commission for almost a decade, do not recall any situation where nuclear export controls have appeared on the Commission's agenda.[11] In fact, export controls on the whole have only been discussed very rarely in Parliament. What little discussion has taken place has been largely restricted to questions to the Minister of Industry, regarding COCOM and the unnecessary restrictions it was thought to place on Eastern Europe after the end of the Cold War.

4.2. The Day-to-day Implementation of Export Controls

The lack of political attention has by no means led to a situation where the implementation of nuclear export controls is administratively "a no man's land". In fact, the situation may, when measured against the standards of most other states, be unique in the way it rests upon very close cooperation among all the parties involved : companies, the business organization and governmental agencies. The figure below depicts this relationship and shows that the political level is of very little importance. The arrows, on the other hand, indicate where interaction takes place.

---

[11] The main reason why there are no political discussions on the implementations of new lists is that the Minister of Industry has delegated this authority to the Division Head of Export Controls. A revised list only needs the Minister's and the Division Head's signature to be implemented.

Figure 1

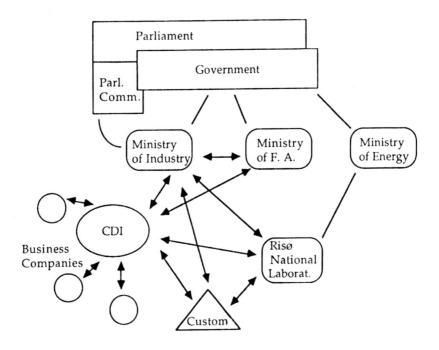

4.2.1. Export licences and the control of exports

The Ministry of Industry is the agency responsible for exports of nuclear and dual-use products, but it cooperates with other authorities in order to carry out its tasks. There is a close connection to the Ministry of Foreign Affairs which provides information on the political situation in various would-be recipient states. Special technical advice is, however, provided by two sources. For nuclear products[12] or products on the NSG list (or "NPT list" as it is called in most documents), the Ministry draws on the special competence of the nuclear division of Risø National Laboratory. For dual-use exports a business organization, the Confederation of Danish Industries (CDI), provides technical evaluation and advice.[13] However, there is nothing incriminating in the fact that the government goes outside its own agencies for this expertise. First of all, the CDI recognizes the necessity for an efficient export regulation, as it is not in its interest that a Danish business company should make dubious deals and run the risk of being blacklisted in other countries. Secondly, the CDI and business in general perceive exports to weapons programmes in turbulent regions as unnecessary contributions to tension, and this would by no means serve Danish export interests in the long run. Thirdly, it should not be forgotten that the close relationship between the individual companies and the CDI, can lend a credibility to the advice provided to the Ministry on whether a licence should be granted or not. On the whole, it can be said that the companies are very careful not to cross the border line between legal and illegal exports. Quite often, the Ministry and CDI receive preliminary inquiries as to whether a proposed export could in any way have undesirable consequences. Here, the standard answer tells companies to refrain from exports if there is any risk or suspicion involved.

---

[12] It should not be forgotten that there is also a nuclear COCOM list.

[13] It is necessary to add that the technical advice for dual-use had for a few years, until July 1993, been in the hands of the Agency of Trade and Industry. This is a Directorate of the Ministry of Industry. As all the export control competences have now been removed to the Ministry itself, this body is not included in the model shown on Figure 1.

When licences are granted and other products are in transit, the Customs Services have to establish that the product is in fact the licensed product. This is difficult as the Customs do not possess the technical expertise and because a detailed clearance is expensive and time-consuming. Therefore, detailed control mostly takes place when there is a reasonable suspicion. In these cases, the Customs Services can draw on technical assistance from CDI, Risø National Laboratory and other relevant institutions, such as the Army's special unit for nuclear, biological and chemical weapons.

4.2.2. Information or enforcement

From what has been said above, it is clear that the implementation of nuclear export controls owes less to a strict enforcement of the regulation than to close cooperation among the companies and institutions. A key word in this connection is information. This is not a one way traffic from the Ministries to the companies. If the companies were to see economic gains as their only task, the political institutions and administration of democratic societies would clearly have to counterbalance this in order to make it compatible with other requirements, such as international disarmament obligations. For export controls, this would mean that public authorities would have to place shackles on industry in order to be able to pursue political non-proliferation objectives as well.

It is hard to tell what lies behind the fact that such strong regulation has not been instituted in Denmark. But it is at least partially possible to explain why companies apparently also understand and accept these political considerations. It is a well-established fact that information on the importance of export controls is necessary for the creation of a common understanding on non-proliferation and its practical pursuit, and here Danish efforts are quite impressive.

The Ministry of Industry produces an updated directory at regular intervals when new amendments are made to the lists.[14] The directory contains : (a) an overview of the international obligations

---

[14] For instance, *Industri- og Handelsstyrelsen*, in : **Industriministeriet, International Handel : Orientering om im-og eksportforhold mv.**, nr.5, 15 July 1992.

that Denmark has to observe in relation to the various export control regimes, (b) an explanation of the legal provisions for the area, and (c) a more detailed description of licence and export procedures. The CDI also provides companies with a guide to this rather complicated issue.[15] The export control regimes are described in considerable detail, and there is also a list of recommendations on how the companies can take their own export precautions ; select responsible persons, establish procedures and gather information on the destination and end-use of the would-be export, etc. The handbook also includes an unofficial negative country list containing particularly sensitive recipient countries.

There may seem to be some duplication of efforts involved here. Although both publications address the same issue, they stress different aspects, and it is therefore more appropriate to see these efforts as complementary.[16] On the whole, there is close cooperation between these two institutions, and the hypothesis that their efforts are more complementary than duplicated is perhaps confirmed by the fact that the author received both agencies' guides or handbooks from the Ministry of Industry.

5. International Negotiations on Nuclear Export Controls

It has already been observed that the information processes concerning the implementation of nuclear export controls do not follow one path. Just as the business world is able and willing to make overall political judgements, so Denmark's participation in international negotiations reflects an acknowledgement of business interests and economic aspects in general.

There is a general perception on the part of the persons involved, and the institutions they represent that Denmark, just like any other

---

[15] Dansk Industri, **Eksportkontrol : Råd og vejledning**, maj. 1992, latest update : September 1994.

[16] A recent development has been to pool the efforts of the Ministry of Industry and CDI. The latter now issues a common and official handbook on behalf of both agencies.

adherent, has an influence in the NSG and Zangger Committee and on the lengthy negotiations on the EU dual-use export control regulation.[17] Negotiations take place among members that are formally more equal than their unequal nuclear status would lead one to believe. That this is the case is maybe most clearly seen in the attention that various interested parties pay to the formulation of Danish positions.

Proposals for changes in the product lists also allow the CDI to play a prominent role. The responsible Ministries, of Industry and Foreign Affairs, also inform and discuss these proposals with the CDI. The latter then consults the industries whose products will fall under the new restrictions and together they evaluate the proposals and formulate adjustments or protests. This procedure is well-established, and all institutions would consider it unthinkable that NSG proposals, for example, could be accepted by the government without having been discussed with the CDI.

There are two further dimensions to this procedure. First of all, the Danish delegations to EU and NSG meetings on nuclear and dual-use export controls do not exclusively consist of representatives from the ministries but also of CDI officials. Secondly, this shows how Denmark works to strengthen export controls while paying due attention to a range of considerations. From a Danish point of view, this cannot always be said of many of the other members ; they seem at times to pursue rigorous policies and only afterwards to discover the unnecessary problems that this leads to for their exporting firms and/or administrative procedures.

The adherents to the NSG usually have differing opinions on what should or should not be added to the list, but it can be said that Denmark sticks very close to the letter of agreements once they have been reached. These agreements have time limits attached to them,

---

[17] An official at the European Commission chose to say : «The Danes have an influence when they choose to show up». This is certainly one point on which it is possible to direct criticism against Danish priorities. Quite often there are no Danish delegates at the various NSG meetings and this makes it more difficult to build up the necessary expertise in this complex field.

within which they have to be adopted as national legislation. The Danish practice has without exception been to stay within these time limits but, on the other hand, not to implement the new standards much earlier than required, as this would give foreign firms competitive advantages.

Furthermore, the Danish authorities are convinced that all the products that have been agreed upon internationally are on the national list. This is not confirmed by studies made by the EU Commission, according to which eight items are missing.[18] Asked directly about this, official Danish sources have stated their knowledge of these studies and argue that the time gap between NSG decisions and national implementation is the cause of the discrepancies.

5.1. Denmark and the EU

Together with its partners in the EU, Denmark has worked for the establishment of common dual-use export regulations. The negotiations lasted for some years, and after the member states reached agreement on the overall regulation at the Corfu summit in June 1994, it is reasonable to expect an agreement on the last remaining details in the course of the German Presidency in the fall of 1994. Danish attitudes to the depth and width of the common regime are ambiguous . On the one hand, it is widely acknowledged that a catch-all clause and provisions on controlling intangible knowledge are necessary to strengthen the regime. On the other hand, there is considerable scepticism about the burdens that the catch-all clause may place on the transparency of export controls for exporting companies and for the administration. The process of cooperation between the various interests may change from being very informal and swift to being rigorous, formal and slow.

On the whole, Danish delegates regard their position as clearly in favour and pursuance of stricter export controls. This perception

---

[18] MÜLLER H., *"The Export Controls Debate In the 'New' European Community"*, in : **Arms Control Today**, March 1993, p.12.

is shared by officials from the European Commission. Although Denmark may be counted among the more reluctant EU members and sometimes considered a semi-enemy of the Commission, the particular issue of dual-use export controls is one where she pursues pragmatic policies, close to those of the Commission.

6. Conclusions

Returning to the questions posed at the beginning of this chapter, it can be stated that the prime consideration driving the pursuit of export controls is the goal of non-proliferation and the adherence to a club of like-minded countries has many more economic advantages in the long run than illegal exports in the short run. These attitudes are not confined to the separate political and economic strata in Denmark, but are present across all the relevant ministries, firms and organizations. Companies have considerable knowledge about and accept the overall non-proliferation objectives, and governmental agencies are willing to take the practical implications, as seen by the business world, into consideration.

Three findings stand out as most valuable in a wider perspective. First of all, it is advantageous for a state to be restrained by common export guidelines, as this facilitates a degree of economic interaction with valuable partners which could not be achieved by staying outside the NSG and exporting to dubious purposes. Secondly, the smaller countries can also influence and are important for the functioning of the NSG, and it is important that countries on the threshold of NSG membership should know this. Third, close cooperation between business and the authorities is attractive because it is cheap and relatively uncomplicated compared to strict regulatory measures. However, it is not clear how such a system of cooperation and consensus, if it is thought to be a desirable way forward, can be achieved elsewhere. As happened in Denmark, it is probably something that will have to evolve over the years. Nevertheless, the procedure of passing detailed information from the governmental and business organizations to companies is something that can be introduced relatively easy. If firms are made aware of the national importance that is attached to non-proliferation and of how this is compatible with overall economic interests, this may be a good starting-point for achieving a nuclear export control system that will not have to rely exclusively on detailed control and enforcement.

But the virtues of the nuclear and dual-use export control system as it stands also have their limits. There is no catch-all clause and no provision against the transfer of intangible knowledge or against extraterritorial trade, to mention the most salient issues. To the extent that the common EU regulation will encompass these issues, improvements will be introduced through the back door. But if the issues are not dealt with, the new national legislation that together with the EU export control regulation will soon replace the existing Ordinance will not greatly improve the situation. The member states are free to apply stricter requirements at the national level, but for Denmark this only seems to imply that the penalties are made stricter (profits from unlicensed trade may be confiscated) and can be treated under the general penalty code.

For obvious reasons, Danish export controls are not going to be exposed to the same kind of stress as was the case with the German system during Saddam Hussein's procurement raid. But even minor procurement attempts by proliferators may reveal that control is insufficient, as proliferators seem to discover the holes before national authorities do. This is one reason why it is desirable that the issue should at long last receive the political attention it merits. This is all the more important since the layman may ask why export controls are relevant in the first place.[19] And if this is how a debate is started, it will be difficult and time-consuming to re-set the right course after loop-holes have been exposed.

---

[19] If one believes that this fear is exaggerated, it can be said that many politicians are more likely to address the immediate aspects (e.g. perceived North-South discrimination) than the prospect of a distant country wanting a seemingly innocent product which could be put to far from innocent uses.

SWEDEN

Lars van Dassen

1. Introduction : Nuclear Turbulence and Stability

A general survey of Sweden's past and present nuclear activities in the civilian and military sector may not portray developments as smooth and incremental. However, the special area of nuclear export controls is an exception as changes have, on the whole, evolved slowly and gradually, responding to needs and requirements as they arose - both nationally and internationally.[1]

In recent times, the fact that Iraq was able to establish a clandestine nuclear weapons infrastructure was one reason for the decision

[1] This study has drawn on the expertise and kindness of a number of people. Dr. Jan PRAWITZ from the Swedish Institute of International Affairs (SIIA) arranged for me to stay at the Institute for a period of five weeks in April-May and again for two weeks in September 1994. Jan PRAWITZ's active interest in the present study and his numerous contacts to key persons opened many doors and have proven to be indispensable to the writing of this chapter. The author wishes to thank all the interviewed persons: one member of the Swedish Parliament, the officials from the Ministry for Foreign Affairs, the Ministry for Environment and Natural Resources, the Swedish Nuclear Power Inspectorate, the National Defence Research Establishment, the Board of Customs and ABB Atom in Västerås. The persons interviewed have had the opportunity to comment on a first draft of this text, and the preliminary findings were presented and discussed at a seminar, on May 17th 199, at SIIA. All responsibility for the content and opinions expressed remain exclusively with the author. Last but not least, I am most indebted to Gustav WILSON, Kirsten, Sara Maria, Emil and all other Navis-people for their hospitality and kindness.

to alter the Swedish export control system.[2] As will be described in this chapter, these changes should, however, to a larger extent be regarded as the result of Sweden's recognition of the need for a new international decisiveness on export controls rather than a consequence of leaks and an absence of export controls at the national level.

The widespread nuclear euphoria of the 1950s also affected Sweden, and in this period the nuclear energy sector was founded. It prospered and was expanded until the early 1980s, when people began to have second thoughts. Popular opinion in favour of the use of a cheap, reliable and non-polluting source of energy shifted, and the inherent problems related to nuclear safety, storage and the like caught people's attention. In 1981, the outcome of a referendum advised the government to abolish the nuclear power industry. But the advisory character of the referendum had to be interpreted, in the sense that it was uncertain whether, and if so when, the decision would have to be implemented. A few years later, during a debate in Parliament, the standard life-span of a reactor was used as the criterion, and therefore the general but also widely contested perception is that 2010 will be the last year of nuclear energy in Sweden.[3] The nuclear sector as it currently exists, consists of four sites comprising twelve light water reactors (three Westinghouse and nine ABB) with a total yearly consumption of 200-250 tonnes LEU fuel (3-4 % enrichment).

In the 1960s, there were investigations into the possibility of building a reprocessing facility, but the idea was abandoned in 1970 because the economic viability of the project turned out question-

---

[2] Later, a more detailed account will be given of the reasons behind the ongoing changes of the Swedish export controls. For now, it can be said that there are at least two additional reasons to the one mentioned above. First of all, the rising number of export control regimes has created a situation at the national level where it is increasingly difficult for the users, the business world, to find a way through the maze. A more transparent system is needed. Secondly, Sweden's recent membership of the EU necessitates the adaptation to EU export control regulations.

[3] The dispute mainly concerns what can substitute for nuclear energy in an economically and environmentally responsible manner. Those who doubt that anything can fill the gap have produced the joke that Sweden may well have to go from 220 to 110 volts to compensate for the missing 50 % of energy supplies!

able. Two companies, *Sandvik* and *ABB Atom*, are important importers of nuclear materials as well as manufacturers and exporters of
fuel elements, cladding and services.[4] All uranium for the industry
and fuel fabrication is imported, in spite of the fact that the largest
European uranium deposits are to be found in the region of Väster-
götland. The modest uranium concentrations as well as the low
prices on the world market stand in the way of profitable indigenous
production.[5]

Whereas the fate of nuclear power in Sweden is uncertain, the
question of nuclear weapons acquisition is certain in the sense that
it has been dead and buried for more than 25 years. Prior to that,
much effort had been put into research on a Swedish nuclear option. These efforts are of less concern in the present context[6] but a
brief mention of policies in both the civil and military sector makes
it possible to draw attention to major shifts and alterations. The
evolution of the nuclear export control system has not, however,
been subject to such shifting tides.

The changes regarding policies on the military application of
nuclear technology have been for the better, and accordingly, Sweden's nuclear non-proliferation policies have enjoyed high esteem

---

[4] The decision to abolish the nuclear power industry would not impede on the activities of ABB Atom and Sandvik that are mainly related to fuel production and
services. Without a Swedish nuclear power industry, these companies would, of
course, lose some most important costumers.

[5] According to *Uranium*, A joint report by NEA and IAEA, 1989 and 1991 eds.,
10,000 tonnes of uranium could be recovered at the cost of less than $ 130 pr. kg
75,000 tonnes could be extracted at a cost between $ 130 and $ 260 pr. kg. The total
deposits amount to 300,000 tonnes.

[6] This issue has received intensive attention in academic literature, for instance :
AGRELL W., *"The Bomb That Never Was : The Rise and Fall of the Swedish
Nuclear Weapons Programme"*, in : GLEDITSCH N.P. & NJØLSTAD O (eds),
Arms Races : Technological and Political Dynamics, PRIO/SAGE Publications,
London, 1990; AGRELL W., **Alliansfrihet och atombomber : Kontinuitet och
förandring i den svenska försvarsdoktrinen från 1945 till 1982**, Liber Förlag,
Stockholm, 1985, espec. pp.192-271; PRAWITZ J., **Non-Nuclear is Beautiful :
Or, Why and How Sweden Went Non-Nuclear**, Kungl. Krigsvetenskaps-
akademiens Handlingar och Tidskrift 6/94, Abrahamsons Tryckeri AB, Karlskrona,
1994; COLE P.M., **Sweden Without the Bomb : The Conduct of a Nuclear-
Capable Nation Without Nuclear Weapons**, RAND, 1994; FEHRM M.,
"Sweden", in : GOLDBLAT J. (ed.) **Non-proliferation : The why and wherefore ?**,
SIPRI/Taylor & Francis, 1985, pp.213-220.

internationally since the birth of the NPT. From the beginning, Sweden belonged to the "White Angels" or the "Group of Ten", a group of countries that since the second NPT Review Conference in 1980 has developed increasingly more stringent non-proliferation policies, above all with respect to the requirements for nuclear exports and cooperation but also where influencing other states to join the regime is concerned.

Sweden may with time have become a White Angel, though her prior military activities make clear that this was not always the case. When it comes to the efficiency and stable evolution of export controls, however, it is possible to view Sweden as a *'Musterknabe'* - also for the period before the birth of the NPT.[7]

2. The Birth of Nuclear Export Controls, 1944-1956

For specific reasons, nuclear export controls preceded any other substantial nuclear activity in Sweden. During World War II, the USA and UK had founded a uranium trust with the objective of buying up all available uranium in the Western world and hereby restraining the civilian and military application of nuclear technology elsewhere. British representatives of the trust visited Sweden as early as 1944 and with the secret assistance of a Swedish mining company were able to conduct investigations of the size and loca-

---

[7] Musterknabe is the German word for paragon or model boy. It is perhaps not the most common of the German words that have found their way into English, but it has been used before to portray aspects of Swedish policies and politics, for instance; MOURITZEN H., *"The Two Musterknaben and the Naughty Boy: Sweden, Finland and Denmark in the Process of European Integration"*, in : **Cooperation and Conflict**, vol.28, no.4, 1993, pp.373-402.

There are some good reasons why it is possible for nuclear export controls to remain stable despite fluctuations in other related fields. In a general perspective, a proliferating state would not want to contribute to others' nuclear weapons acquisition, as it would then lose a strategic advantage (in the real world, there are of course exceptions to this, for instance the French contribution to the Israeli nuclear weapons programme). In the other case, where a state does not want to become a nuclear weapons State, it does not want to see others undermine its security by means of qualitatively superior weapon systems. As was indicated above, for many years Sweden was unsure which track, she wanted to follow. But this did not change her attitude towards nuclear export controls.

tion of the uranium deposits.[8] In July 1945, the Swedish government received a British-American proposal suggesting that the trust should have exclusive access to the uranium ore for a thirty-year period with the option to extend this for another 30 years. Before the Swedish government could answer, the atomic bombs were dropped on Hiroshima and Nagasaki and this led to a new awareness of the combustible nature of the uranium resources. The Anglo-American proposal was rejected in September 1945, on the grounds that the fate of the nuclear weapon ought to be decided within the United Nations.

Sweden worked actively but fruitlessly for many year for such a settlement, initially within the United Nations Atomic Energy Commission when it was founded in January 1946. But the foreign interest in the Swedish uranium resources had further consequences at the national level. The Swedish Parliament added a new chapter to the law that had hitherto regulated access to coal mining. According to this revision, both uranium mining and the subsequent handling and processing would have to be authorized by the government (§§ 63, 67).[9] Moreover, it was stated that no uranium or products containing uranium could be exported. An exception was made for cases where the uranium content was insignificant, but such exports would, nevertheless, require permission from the government (§ 67). This early regulation, in fact, established a principle that has not been changed since - the need for a governmental authorization of exports containing significant quantities of fissile material.

3. Export Controls and Nuclear Energy, 1956-1984

The nuclear arms race between the USA and USSR made the prospect of international sharing through the UN or abolition of the

---

[8] HELMREICH J.E., **Gathering Rare Ores : The Diplomacy of Uranium Aquisition, 1943-1954**, Princeton University Press, Princeton, 1986, pp.60-71, 172-177; ÅSTRÖM S., **Ögonblick**, Bonus, Stockholm, 1992, pp.60-66.

[9] **Lag om tillägg till lagen den 28. maj 1886 (nr.46) angående stenkols-fyndigheter m. m.**; 21 December 1945.

weapons more and more remote. The peaceful uses of the atom were seen in the "Atoms for Peace" programme to be at least a partial compensation for the unequal distribution of nuclear knowledge and technology, and at the international level, peaceful nuclear use organizations and conferences mushroomed. In Sweden, a new law that would facilitate the uses of nuclear energy for peaceful purposes was passed in June 1956.

The revised law from 1945 that had previously regulated access to mining concessions was altered to encompass beryllium and thorium.[10] Beyond the expansion of this basic provision, the Atomic Energy Act[11] became the framework for all nuclear activities. In general, any handling of nuclear material needed government approval and so did the construction and operation of nuclear facilities. Further, § 3 stipulated that no nuclear materials *per se* or as compounds of other materials or minerals could be exported without governmental authorization. In another paragraph the establishment of an agency with the authority to supervise nuclear activities and to administer export controls was foreseen.

The competences of this body were stipulated in one of two ordinances that accompanied the Act.[12] The Atomic Energy Commission (*Delegationen för atomenergifrågor*) consisted of five members appointed by the government. It would regulate the implementation of the Act, administer all questions regarding nuclear energy and international nuclear cooperation, and cooperate with the various national agencies that would be concerned with the issue. In another ordinance, a few exceptions from the general requirements for governmental authorization were granted.[13] Uranium and thorium in small quantities could be handled, processed and experimented by industries for the production of secondary goods, and furthermore,

---

[10] **Lag om ändrad lydelse av 9 kap. lagen d. 28. maj 1886 (nr. 46) angående sten-kolsfyndigheter m. m**; 1 July 1956.

[11] **Lag om rätt at uttvinna atomenergi m. m.** (atomenergilag) 1 Juni 1956.

[12] **Kungl. Maj:ts Instruktion för delegationen för atomenergifrågor**, 1 Juni 1956.

[13] **Kungl. Maj:ts kungörelse med vissa tillstånd enligt atomenergilagen** d. 1 Juni 1956 (nr.306).

compounds where thorium or uranium did not exceed 50 gr pr. tonne could be exported. In the latter case, the content of the compound would still have to be verified by the authorities and further conditions could then be placed on the transfer.

In 1959 a new ordinance specified the industrial and scientific uses for which small quantities of uranium and thorium could be acquired at the national level. Exceptions from the general requirement for government permission for nuclear exports were allowed - as before, provided that the uranium and thorium did not exceed 50 gr pr. tonne. All such acquisitions and exports would, however, have to be reported to the Atomic Energy Commission and all transfers with national or external destinations would have to conform to the provisions for radiation protection that were implemented by law in 1958.[14]

Changes introduced in 1970 specified some definitions and added some products where exports would no longer be subject to governmental approval (e.g. depleted or natural uranium for counterweights in aeroplanes).[15] The origin of these changes is most probably that Sweden had a few years earlier, in 1967, joined a then secret club, and predecessor of the London Club, which tried to align the criteria for exports among the major exporters.[16]

There were also organizational changes at this stage. Over the years, the tasks assigned to the Atomic Energy Commission continued to grow. International safeguards agreements had to be imple-

---

[14] **Kungl. Maj:ts kungörelse med vissa tilstånd enligt atomenergilagen** d. 1 Juni 1956 (nr.306); 18 Dec.1959. Radiation protection is as old as the Atomic Energy Act and the Atomic Energy Commission (1956), in spite of the fact that a specific law on radiation protection was not implemented until 1958. Before the establishment of a radiation protection regulation, the issue resided with a sub-agency (Reaktor-förläggningskommittén) of the Atomic Energy Commission. It advised the Commission on the issue, and when the Commission followed these recommendations they were legally binding according to the Ordinance of 1956.

[15] **Kungl. Maj:ts kungörelse med vissa tillstånd enligt atomenergilagen** (1956: 306); 11 Dec.1970.

[16] PRAWITZ J., **Non-Nuclear is Beautiful**, *Op.cit.*, p.77; SIMPSON J., **The Independent Nuclear State : The United States, Britain and the Military Atom**, The Macmillan Press Ltd., London, 1983, p.152.

mented, and the staff had grown accordingly. In 1974 the institution was restructured and given its present name, the Swedish Nuclear Power Inspectorate (*Statens Kärnkraft-inspektion*, SKI).[17] Export controls was among its most important tasks, and when the Trigger List as established by the Zangger Committee was implemented nationally through an ordinance in 1975, it stated that applications for export licences would have to be forwarded to SKI, and as always that the permit would, in the event, be granted by the government.[18] With the Trigger List and Nuclear Suppliers Guidelines (NSG) implemented, export controls had been specified on the basis of an international agreement. The SKI was established as the appropriate forum for dealing with this expansion of technological and scientific evaluation of materials and applications.

In an overview, only minimal exemptions were allowed from the general provision of the Atomic Energy Act (§ 3) whereby nuclear exports would be subject to governmental approval. The Trigger List and the NSG were internationally agreed specifications of where Sweden would have to adapt her export controls. Another requirement for granting nuclear exports was of national origin and was introduced on March 30th 1977, when the Minister for Foreign Affairs, Karin Söder, declared during a parliamentary session that Sweden «would grant permission for export only to such states which are parties to the NPT or have committed themselves to apply IAEA safeguards to all their nuclear energy activities».[19]

---

[17] SKI, **Milstolpar i SKI's historia, Ett informationsblad från Statens Kärnkraft-inspektion**, 1994.

[18] **Förordning om förbud mot utförsel av utrustning eller material för utvinning av atomenergi**, m. m., 27 Feb.1975.

[19] Quoted from Jan PRAWITZ, *Op.cit.*, p.77. The formulation as quoted above is normally referred to as a full-scope safeguards (FSS) requirement and regarded as identical with NPT safeguards. However, it is possible to have FSS in other ways, for instance if old INFCIRC/66 safeguards apply to all nuclear activities (*de facto* FSS, something that once covered Albania and Spain). In Sweden as in the Guidelines, FSS means : «NPT, Treaty of Tlatelolco or a similar legally-binding agreement and an IAEA safeguards agreement in force».

4. Export Controls After the Referendum, 1984-1993

The Atomic Energy Act as presented above served the purpose of establishing the nuclear energy sector, and according to most observers it was a very effective framework with few loopholes and problem areas. But due to the perceptions of the time and the outcome of the referendum on nuclear energy, this sector suddenly found itself under pressure : even if it was not abolished in the short run, measures would have to be taken to prevent its expansion and to improve on safety and physical protection.

The Act on Nuclear Activities of 1984[20] and its later revisions of 1987, 1988, 1989 and 1992 reflected this shifting emphasis as the operators became subject to tighter requirements regarding control, research into safety, storage and the taxes they have to pay.[21] In 1987 an amendment to § 5 was passed whereby the construction of new reactors was forbidden.

However, the Act also contains some new elements concerning nuclear export controls. In the introductory paragraph, there is a definition of nuclear activities that goes far beyond what was found in the Atomic Energy Act of 1956. For nuclear exports, this means that the provisions (§ 1, Sections 3 and 4) in general terms reflect the Guidelines. Furthermore, there are general requirements that all nuclear activities (and therefore also export controls) must be conducted according to Sweden's international non-proliferation commitments. Since 1992 there have also been two sections that allow the government, or the agency it chooses, to revise the national instructions according to international agreements (§ 3), and require the operators to submit to the authorities all information relevant to the pursuit of Sweden's non-proliferation commitments (§ 17). The Act was accompanied by the Ordinance on Nuclear Activities[22] which included the NSG list of products that could not be exported

---

[20] **Lag om kärnteknisk verksamhet**, 1984:3, 12 January 1984.

[21] **Regeringens proposition 1992/93 om ändring i lagen om kärnteknisk verksamhet, m. m.** Riksdagen 1992/93. 1 samling nr.98, espec. pp.18-41.

[22] **Förordning om kärnteknisk verksamhet**, 1984:14, 12 January 1984.

without permission from the government. Whereas the Act itself defined nuclear activities very broadly and stated that all such activities would have to be permitted, the Ordinance specifies a substantial number of exceptions where "anyone" or specific legal persons (like universities and research institutions) may handle, process or import various products. Neither of these paragraphs, however, refers to exports, § 17 being the only exception. In these cases, SKI has the competence to decide on exports of smaller quantities (grammes) of uranium, plutonium, tritium and thorium.

In 1984, eight years before the adherents to the NSG decided to add a dual-use list, Sweden had already taken similar steps unilaterally and made hot isostatic presses and flash x-ray systems subject to export controls.[23] This manner of unilaterally pursuing stricter export controls than international obligations required was not unprecedented as it is also found with respect to the export control regimes which Sweden did not participate in. She never adhered to COCOM, and did not join the MTCR and the Australian Group till 1991. These regimes were dominated by the Western world, and therefore Swedish adherence was thought to encroach upon the country's neutrality. Throughout the Cold War business maintained self-restraint with respect to exporting goods listed in other countries. This protected Swedish companies against being blacklisted, and may be one reason why major exporting companies today are familiar with and accept export controls.[24] In another respect Sweden created an export control regulation on its own. In 1986, the Ordinance on High Technology[25] was passed with a twofold purpose. First of all, Sweden did not want to run the risk of becoming a transit route for exports from countries within export control re-

---

[23] The NSG clearly gives an adherent this right as paragraph 7 states that «the supplier reserves to itself discretion as to the application of the Guidelines to other items of significance in addition to those identified in the Annex...».

[24] The author has been given access to the internal export control system of Sweden's most important nuclear exporter, ABB Atom. ABB's knowledge of and seriousness about export controls is profound, comprising e.g. internally produced manuals and networks of export control officers and a system for updating legal changes and alterations of the lists. Furthermore, there is a recognition of the priority of certain political considerations over economic gains.

[25] **Förordningen om förbud mot viss utförsel** (1986: 89).

gimes in which Sweden did not participate to countries outside them. Secondly, the government wanted to ensure that industries could import without any restrictions that might arise from external fears of re-exports. The basic principle of the Ordinance was, therefore, that all imports to Sweden that had required a licence in the country of origin (adherents to COCOM, MTCR and Australian Group), would also need a Swedish licence, and depending on the requirements, prior consent from the country of origin, if the goods were to be re-exported.[26]

4.1. Procedures and the Implementation of Nuclear Export Controls

Nuclear export control is not merely a question of formal laws and paragraphs. Its effectiveness also rests upon on the competence and seriousness of the agencies involved , as well as cooperation between them. The following description of the procedures will not provide details of all alterations of routines, organizations and paragraphs, but will be limited to the main characteristics of nuclear export control since 1984.

It may be helpful to explain a few essentials about the administrative system in Sweden. First of all, the core ministries or political departments are small (normally not more than hundred persons, including clerical staff). There is a high degree of decentralization to relatively independent governmental agencies. These agencies have to observe the general and particular laws, ordinances and instructions, while the responsible minister cannot himself change the outcome of a specific decision.[27] If the minister disagrees with a

---

[26] Statens offentliga utredningar, **Kontrollen över export av strategiskt känsliga varor, 1993:56**, Utrikesdepartementet, Stockholm, pp.36-39.

[27] The head of an agency is, therefore, not the minister alone. The minister holds authority through his influence on budgets and legislation. But other than this, every agency has a director general, and a board appointed by the government which supervises the planning of activities and compliance with regulations and budgets. The number of board members vary from agency to agency, as does the board's composition. The members are normally politicians and representatives from organizations with special interests in the matters dealt with by the agency. Svenska Institutet, **Fact Sheets on Sweden : Swedish Government**, Graphic Systems, Stockholm, 1992.

particular decision, he will have to seek general alterations of the legal framework under which the agency operates. This would apply in the case of nuclear export controls if the minister was informed of and disagreed with a decision made by SKI in relation to § 17 of the Ordinance on Nuclear Activities which gives SKI the authority to decide over certain exports. But as shall be explained, for all other exports it is different, as a government authorization is required and this is based on the recommendation made by the appropriate agency and ministry.

The nuclear sector as a whole and the matters related to energy consumption, structure, planning etc. are the responsibility of the Ministry of Industry, but the latter has no influence over export controls, nuclear safety or physical security. The ministry responsible for these matters is the Ministry for Environment and Natural Resources, and SKI functions on its behalf as the competent agency in charge of safeguards and contacts with the IAEA. Another important agency is FOA (*Försvarets Forskningsanstalt*, the National Defence Research Establishment). One of its activities is to keep track of international defence and security developments, and by virtue of this function, it serves as a consultative body on proliferation risks for SKI. Furthermore, both the Political and the Foreign Trade Department of the Ministry for Foreign Affairs play important roles. Last but not least, the minister(s) responsible and the cabinet have the final word on nuclear exports.[28]

4.1.1. List 1 procedure : Nuclear materials and equipment

For the export of nuclear goods and equipment that are listed in the NSG list 1 (INFCIRC/254) and in the Ordinance, an application has to be forwarded by the exporting company to SKI.[29] The first

---

[28] It is necessary to explain that though the Foreign Trade Department is part of the Ministry for Foreign Affairs, the former has its own minister, the Minister for Foreign Trade.

[29] As already indicated, the Swedish nuclear export control system is in a transitional phase. Therefore, the description of the system in 4.1.1. and 4.1.2. should be read with this in mind. However, this is what the export controls looked like when the author conducted the research, while the changes that are portrayed as belonging to the near future in 5., 5.1. and 5.2. are being implemented at the time of completion of this study (February 1995)

basic step is to consider the safeguards situation of the recipient state. If the full-scope safeguards requirements is met, the further requirements of the NSG are also evaluated. According to these, the recipient state must have an adequate system for physical security. Further, it must be ascertained that the proposed export is «appropriate for the stated end-use and that the stated end-use is appropriate for the end-user» (quoted from the Guidelines).

Next, the credentials of the recipient company are evaluated. If these cannot immediately be established, for example, because the company is new or unknown, the Ministry for Foreign Affairs is asked to seek further information from the recipient state. The vast majority of applications are matters of routine as the exporters and customers are well-known to SKI, and therefore the initial steps at SKI can be completed fairly quickly. But when there is any uncertainty, FOA is asked to provide advice on the political situation in the recipient country, as well as a technical evaluation of the potential military implications of the planned export.[30] As the next step, SKI sends the application with its recommendation to the Ministry for Environment and Natural Resources. If there are no further objections here, the Ministry for Foreign Affairs is contacted and requested to inform the recipient country that when a peaceful uses guarantee has been obtained, the case will be submitted to the cabinet for final decision.

As soon as the peaceful uses guarantee is received (in most cases from the recipient country's diplomatic representation in Sweden), it is passed on by the Ministry for Foreign Affairs to the Ministry for Environment and Natural Resources. Hereafter the final approval is prepared and signed by the competent minister. The minister responsible then has to present the case to the cabinet and if there are no objections, the export can go ahead.

---

[30] In particularly tricky but also very rare cases where the situation in a would-be recipient state is unclear or disputed, it is possible to decide on the matter within a collective body, consisting of representatives from the Ministry for Foreign Affairs, the Ministry for Environment and Natural Resources, SKI, the National Institute of Radiation Protection and FOA.

List 1 Procedure

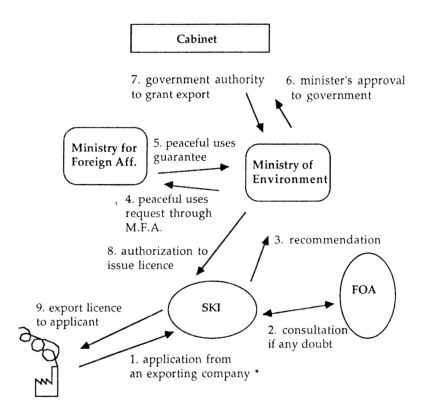

* As stated above, SKI decides according to § 17 of the Ordinance on Nuclear Activities on exports of certain small quantities of fissile material

The authorization to export is communicated to SKI which issues a licence and forwards it to the exporter. The exporting company then has to inform SKI about the exact date and circumstances of the export at least three weeks before it takes place. With this specification of the export, SKI can inform the IAEA early enough to allow the latter to make an inspection.[31] The Customs are informed of the export at least one week before it is scheduled to take place, which makes it possible to check the product and make sure it corresponds to the licence. This control takes place when the good is packed and shipped from the exporting company. The Customs do not have especially equipped units for handling and controlling single-use products, but in case of doubt they draw on expertise from SKI and FOA.

There are variations to the procedure presented above, and they arise with respect to the countries with which Sweden has a bilateral agreement.[32] In these cases, the exchange of notes regarding the peaceful use guarantees does not take place through the Ministry for Foreign Affairs. Instead, the bilateral agreement contains the same assurances, and therefore, the communication on guarantees for the specific export as well as inventory changes takes place between SKI and its counterpart abroad. Where export controls are concerned, the existence of bilateral agreements also has an additional significance with respect to prior consents. If nuclear materials and equipment are re-exported from Sweden, prior consent from the country of origin must in most cases be obtained. This is not necessary if a bilateral agreement between the country of origin and Sweden provides for this.

---

[31] As stated earlier, most of these cases are routine, both for companies and agencies. There is a possibility that a company may want to speed up or jump the procedure, deliberately or by accident. This could, for instance, be done by forwarding a notification on one particular export and the inventory change documentation **before** the licence has actually been obtained. The probability of detecting such an attempt is high, but to reduce the risk of such errors, the computers at ABB Atom are programmed in such a manner that they cannot issue an export notification before the licence has actually been received and registered.

[32] These countries are: Australia, Canada, Finland, the USA, Switzerland and Great Britain.

4.1.2. List 2 procedure : Dual-use goods

It has already been mentioned that Sweden introduced export controls on a few nuclear related dual-use products in 1984. For a number of years, these products were on the nuclear list of the Ordinance on Nuclear Activities and submitted to the procedure explained above. In 1991 a Law on Weapons of Mass Destruction[33] was introduced to implement the Swedish non-proliferation efforts with respect to missile technology and chemical and biological weapons. This regulation also covers the dual-use lists of the regimes mentioned above, and it was therefore thought the suitable place for the NSG list 2 when it was established in April 1992. Nuclear dual-use products have been covered by this new framework since April 1993, and therefore the procedure has come to deviate from the one described above. As will be explained later, this is one of many steps that have been taken to centralize and harmonize the export control provisions of all these regimes.

The most important agency with respect to nuclear dual-use export controls is the Foreign Trade Department.[34] This department receives the application from an exporter and evaluates it according to three criteria. First of all, the relationship to the NPT and non-proliferation commitments is considered. Secondly, there is an evaluation of the risk that the recipient country and/or company may re-export the item. Thirdly, the political and strategic situation of the recipient country is an important parameter. In addition, the recipient's stated use of the product is evaluated.[35] If it is estimated that the criteria are on the whole fulfilled and do not imply any proliferation risks, an export licence can be granted. The recipient

---

[33] **Lagen om förbud mot utförsel av vissa varor som kan användas i massförstörelsesyfte vilken omfattar missilprodukter, kemiska och biologiska produkter och relaterad tillverkningsutrustning, samt produkter av dual-use karaktär;** 1 July, 1991, (1991: 341)

[34] Within the Foreign Trade Department the export controls of dual-use products were initially carried out by the Inspectorate General of Military Equipment. As will be explained later in more detail, a new unit, the Strategic Export Control Division has been established (1 July 1994) to handle the non-military export control.

[35] **Krigsmaterielinspektionens handledning för utförsel av produkter som kan användes i massförstörelsesyfte**, Utrikesdepartementet, KMI, 1993, p.7.

state is subsequently informed that it may import the desired item on the condition that it issues a peaceful uses guarantee. The responsibility for obtaining the peaceful uses guarantees has until recently, resided with the Political Department of the Ministry for Foreign Affairs, but it is now being taken over by the Foreign Trade Department.

If a recipient state is also an adherent to the particular export control regime, it is possible to issue general licences for a certain product, destination and period of time. For non-adherents, on the other hand, the recipient company must guarantee peaceful uses and that the product will not be re-exported or moved to another location. These demands can be extended to include the requirement that the exporting company must verify and certify that the product has been received and installed by the importer. Moreover, the exporter can be required to include a clause in the contract whereby the exporting company may carry out inspections to ensure that these requirements are respected.[36]

Once the guarantees have been received, the case is presented to the Minister for Foreign Trade. Upon signature, the permission to export is submitted to the cabinet, and if no further objections arise, the licence is forwarded to the exporter. Concerning the actual export of the item, the Customs must be notified one week in advance. This allows for an inspection when the item is loaded and shipped, and if technical assistance is needed it is provided by the Foreign Trade Department.

5. Changing the Export Control System

It has been stated already that the Swedish export control system and its procedures have undergone changes over the last couple of years. This is a process that has not yet finished, but it is possible to

---

[36] *Ibid.* pp.7, 10. A typical case where such additional conditions would apply would be in cases where an export to a non-NPT country is allowed. The statement on full-scope safeguards from the NSG meeting in Warsaw, April 1993, identifies considerations of the safe operation of existing nuclear facilities and provisions in existing contracts as exceptions to the FSS requirement.

sketch the reasons for the changes and the contours of the future system. There are three main reasons why these changes have been introduced.[37]

First of all, Iraq's clandestine nuclear weapons programme and the accompanying acquisition of the necessary technology and materials proved that it was necessary to strengthen international and national efforts. Two products of Swedish origin were found by the IAEA and UNSCOM, but this did not in itself cause the changes. The one export was a hot isostatic press, which was on Sweden's then unilateral dual-use list. It had been exported under the conditions applying to dual-use products, by which they could not be moved and were to be for peaceful uses only. These conditions had not been breached, as the product was found at the intended location, outside the nuclear weapons facilities. The other export of Swedish origin was a cold isostatic press, but this had been on neither the national nor the NSG list at that time. The Iraqi nuclear programme, nevertheless, increased awareness of export controls and of the importance of adherence to an expanding number of export control regimes. Earlier, membership of MTCR and the Australian Group had been thought to conflict with Swedish neutrality but as East-West tensions vanished and more and more countries from both sides joined various regimes, Sweden decided to do the same.

Secondly, the rising number of export control regimes has led to a steady increase in the number of lists and goods. This has created a situation where the users, the companies, find it more and more difficult to maintain an overview of the products that need a licence and from which agency or ministry this licence will have to be obtained. Therefore, the changes have the clear objective of providing as few impediments to free trade as possible, and simultaneously of ensuring the system's efficiency.

A third reason for the alterations to the national legislation was the Swedish application for membership of the EU. Even if Swe-

---

[37] All three are referred to in: Statens offentliga utredningar, **Kontrollen över export av strategiskt känsliga varor, 1993: 56**, *Op.cit.*, pp.6-12.

den had not joined the EU after the referendum in November 1994 (Sweden became a member of the European Union on 1 January 1995), there was a recognition among many export control officials that changes in the national legislation would serve a purpose as they would facilitate free trade by ensuring a high degree of compatibility between the EU's and Sweden's export control systems.[38]

The new national legislation was approved by Parliament in June 1994. The Government decided that it would enter into force on 1 January 1995 and be implemented in the following months, as the new regulation will also be accompanied by the conclusion of a major reorganization of the export controls administration and procedures. Regarding the legal changes, the Law on Weapons of Mass Destruction will encompass all other export control regulations. This means that the Ordinance on High Technology and the provisions on nuclear export controls within the Act and Ordinance on Nuclear Activities will be incorporated within this law. As the regulation has with time come to encompass so many different products, not all of which are related to weapons of mass destruction, the name of the regulation has been changed into the Act on Strategic Products.[39]

Concerning the organization of the system, it has already been mentioned that a new unit, the Strategic Export Control Division, has been established within the Foreign Trade Department. There will therefore be two bodies dealing with export controls : the Inspectorate General of Military Equipment is charged with controlling military exports only, while the Strategic Export Control Division covers all other exports intended for civil purposes.

There is one exception. While all applications regarding non-nuclear exports go directly to the Strategic Export Control Division, applications related to nuclear material and equipment are forwarded to SKI to receive a technical evaluation and recommendation.

---

[38] **Regeringens proposition, 1993/94 : 176, Ändringar i lagen (1991: 341) om förbud mot utförsel av vissa produkter som kan användas i massförstörelsessyfte**, m. m., pp.12-14, 21.

[39] **Lag om strategiska produkter**, 1994: 341.

Moreover, the competence to decide over exports of small quantities of nuclear materials, according to § 17 of the Ordinance on Nuclear Activities, is retained by SKI. In addition, it is foreseen that SKI will have at least two new competences added. First, SKI will have the power to decide over exports to states with which Sweden has a bilateral agreement. Second, it is foreseen that SKI, in cooperation with the Ministry for Environment and Natural Resources, will take the final decision in cases where nuclear material is not only exported but also changes ownership.[40]

The procedure will be the following. An application regarding the export of nuclear goods is sent to SKI. Except for the cases mentioned above, where the latter has authority to grant the licence, a recommendation is added to the application and then both are forwarded to the Strategic Export Control Division. After an individual examination of each case on the basis of the criteria mentioned earlier and the reception of peaceful uses guarantees from the recipient state (and in some cases additional assurances from the exporting and importing company), the case is presented to the Minister for Foreign Trade. If the Cabinet has no further objections, the Strategic Export Control Division issues the licence. The company is then obliged to notify the Customs of the time and circumstances of the export one week in advance.

5.1. Other Characteristics and Changes

The account so far does not cover the full spectrum of Swedish legislation on nuclear export controls in its past, present and future forms. Therefore, it is important to dwell on certain specific elements of the system, as this helps us to identify the improvements and possible remaining weaknesses.

Regarding **breaches of the export control regulation**, attention may be drawn to the penalties, the scope of active participation leading to different penalties and the possibility of confiscating the value

---

[40] **Regeringens proposition, 1993/94: 176,** *Op.cit.*, pp.25, 31. It is necessary to stress that in most cases when nuclear material is exported, or for that matter imported, the material is leased and does not change ownership.

of or profit from illegal sales. If an export of nuclear material or equipment takes place without the necessary authorization and licence, or there is a breach of the conditions laid down by the governmental agencies, the Act on Nuclear Activities (§§ 5, 25 and 27) provides for penalties ranging from fines to a maximum of two years imprisonment.

While this regulation makes no mention of confiscation or of the exporter's active involvement, these are mentioned in the Law on Weapons of Mass Destruction as well as in the Act on Strategic Products that began to be implemented on 1. January 1995. In both cases, the transfer of listed goods without an appropriate licence can be punished by fines or sentences of between six months and two years. Intentional acts receive harsher punishments while neglect or other unintentional breaches are dealt with more leniently (§ 10). In special cases where an intentional act considered to be particularly harmful is involved, sentences of up to four years may be imposed. The regulations also contain a provision by which profits from illegal sales can be confiscated (§ 14).

Additionally, all three regulations refer to similar paragraphs in the customs regulations as covering the cases where an attempt is made to smuggle listed goods as a way of circumventing export controls.

A further important aspect is the range of the **technology definition**, i.e. the question of whether intangible technology is also covered. Neither the Act nor the Ordinance on Nuclear Activities contains provisions on intangible knowledge beyond the statement that permission to conduct nuclear activities cannot without an additional authorization be considered to cover similar activities abroad (in §§ 1 and 2). In the Law on Weapons of Mass Destruction and the Act on Strategic Products, new clauses have been added whereby the necessary computer soft- and hardware accompanying any product needs a licence. If this is exported with the product, the application has to state this. An isolated export of technological knowledge, without the primary good, requires an independent licence, as does transmission by means of computer networks, fax, telephone etc. (§ 3). Most important are the restrictions on the right of companies, public agencies or any person living in Sweden to produce the components, material and equipment related to the listed goods outside the country without a licence (§ 5). As stated earlier, nuclear material and equipment are from 1 January 1995 also covered by the provisions of the Act on Strategic Products.

The new regulations will also bring improvements in the field of **extraterritorial transfers**. Under the Act on Nuclear Activities, there are no provisions that can prevent a company from trading listed goods outside Swedish territory. According to the Law on Weapons of Mass Destruction and the Act on Strategic Products, such activities will need a licence (§ 6).

None of the three regulations that have significance for export controls have any positive **country lists** attached, listing the destinations to which exports are possible with fewer restrictions and conditions. There are two reasons for this. First of all, it is thought that this will create a fixed order or discrimination and possibly diplomatic difficulties if revealed. Secondly, the procedure has traditionally been one where every application is treated individually in relation to the criteria mentioned earlier. Therefore, checklists are not regarded as significant additions to the procedure.

In the Swedish export control system, there is **no catch-all clause** to cover the cases where there is any reasonable risk that an export of an unlisted item is intended for the production of missiles or weapons of mass destruction. However, this issue has been thoroughly discussed after it became clear that the EU intended to make a catch-all clause a component of the Union's common export controls. Two agencies have advocated a catch-all clause as it is hard, if not impossible, to agree internationally on new products for the list at the same speed as these products become relevant for military purposes.[41] The proposal to introduce a catch-all clause is also

---

[41] *Ibid.*, p.28. One option that has been under consideration is to use the government's authority to change lists and swiftly to add new products as soon as a suspicion of non-civil use arises. However, this proposal ignores earlier experiences when non-listed goods that were being exported for sensitive purposes could not legally be stopped by adding the product to the list after the application had been forwarded to SKI. In these particular cases, SKI was able to convince the companies to refrain from the exports.

based on the fear that Sweden may become a transit route for goods that are controlled by means of a catch-all procedure elsewhere.[42] Although there is as yet no catch-all clause in the national regulations, this is an issue on which the ongoing debate does not become void as long as the EU dual-use export regulation allows member states to decide on the full extent of the catch-all clause.

In the Swedish export controls system the close, and often informal, **communication between officials and agencies** is an invaluable element whereby problems are easily communicated and resolved, and it also ensures a fairly swift procedure, in view of the complicated and thorough procedures involved. The informality has other advantages, as it is also easy for companies to get advice and instructions from the relevant authorities. Various business organizations also provide this, but the study that preceded the new legislation noted that the many export control regimes and new procedures make it advisable to issue an official handbook. All agencies involved have supported this proposal.[43]

5.2. Sweden and the European Union

The possible consequences for the nuclear sector of Sweden joining the EU received much attention during the membership negotiations between Sweden and the Union. However, the official assessment is that there will be no radical changes in the present situation.[44] Euratom safeguards agreements will have to be implemented, the existing bilateral agreement between Sweden and the Joint Research Centre will become void and some adaptations to the practice of the Euratom Supply Agency will have to be implemented.

---

[42] **Regeringens proposition, 1993/94: 176**, *Op. cit.*, p.27-28, 56. According to this source the catch-all clause has been suggested by the Inspectorate General of Military Equipment and the Board of Customs.

[43] *Ibid.*, p.44.

[44] This evaluation is found in the official study on the consequences of Swedish EU membership, **Sveriges medlemskap i Europäiska Unionen, Regeringens proposition 1994/95: 19, del. 1.**, pp.275-287.

The provisions of the Euratom Treaty state that Euratom nominally owns all the fissile material within the Community and that the Supply Agency negotiates contracts for supplies on behalf of the operators. The reality is different as the unimpeded use of the fissile material by the operators means more than *de jure* common ownership, and when contracts on exports and imports are drawn up, the role of the Supply Agency is to authorize contracts, register transfers and establish criteria for the conclusion of contracts.[45]

For dual-use goods, measures to ensure free and unrestricted trade within the EU and uniform standards for licensing exports out of the Union have been negotiated since 1991.[46] The most important elements of the new regulation are the following. First of all, a catch-all clause will oblige an exporter to submit non-listed goods if he is informed by the authorities or has knowledge by other means of a possible proliferation risk. Secondly, the member state through which an export takes place may veto a licence issued in another member state. Moreover, the regulation establishes new criteria beyond the NSG provisions (for instance, the human rights situation of the recipient state). Fourth, the member states are obliged to keep registers and to exchange of information, in order to eliminate the risk of disparities of procedure. Fifth, the members are required to apply their own enforcement measures, determine penalties and inform the Commission and member states of their national regulations and administrative practices. Finally, the procedure and requirements for goods in transit remain under the member state's authority and each state has the right to demand statements of end-use and re-export.

Membership of the EU necessitates some additional changes to the Swedish export controls system, but they do not seem to be revolutionary. A catch-all clause will have to be introduced, although this proposal was disputed by some agencies and politicians. The additional criteria for exports are immediately acceptable, as Swe-

---

[45] *Ibid.*, pp.282-283.

[46] WENZEL J., *"The European Commnunity's Approach to Export Controls"*, in : BAILEY K. & RUDNEY R. (eds), **Proliferation and Export Controls**, University Press of America, Lanham, 1993, p.96.

den has in many respects been in the forefront of developments which fosters peace and stability. Similarly, the exchange of information and the national enforcement of penalties are unproblematic.

To the extent that there are fears that a common EU regulation waters down the effectiveness of the national system, and such fears do exist, the right to veto other member states' decisions can only serve to ease these concerns. Also, the right to apply conditions on end-use and re-export ensures that the most valuable established practices in this field may continue.

However, there is still a risk that on the issues where Swedish regulations are stricter than the common EU regulation (intangible knowledge, conditions on end-use and re-export), companies may be tempted to export to the Union members where these restrictions do not exist. From here, they can be re-exported to a third country outside the EU and give rise to proliferation risks.

6. Conclusions

In a broad overview, it is possible to see the Swedish export control system as consisting of three pillars that with time have increasingly complemented one another.

The **first** is the national preoccupation with nuclear export controls with its roots in the 1940s. The Swedish system has continuously integrated the scientific competences of various agencies with a procedure involving even the Cabinet. Export control has become a salient issue about which all relevant political and administrative levels are remarkably well informed. This is also true of the business world.

The **second** pillar relates to international efforts to curb the arms race, particularly nuclear proliferation. From an early date in the late sixties, Sweden participated in this endeavour and has implemented all agreements on nuclear trade with great care at the national level.

These efforts are ongoing and received a new impetus after the Gulf War, more or less simultaneously with the rise of the **third** (European) pillar. While national and international efforts have continued and have already resulted in new national legislation, adaptation to a common EU regulation is now taking place. There is still more to be done here, and as stated earlier some of the European aspects may not immediately be characterized as improvements compared to the national export controls. But this is where a *"Musterknabe"* meets his test. Sweden has a long and interesting export controls history and it contains a valuable legacy for all who want to learn. The EU, as a body where arguments count more than muscle, constitutes the ideal forum for convincing others that stricter policies and criteria serve everybody better than weak ones.

In the official study on the consequences of membership of the EU, the government stresses the positive influences that Sweden can have on issues related to the common non-proliferation and foreign policy.[47] Sweden's implementation of nuclear export controls shows that the foundations for such aspirations really do exist.

---

[47] **Sveriges medlemskap i Europäiska Unionen,** *Op.cit.,* pp.40-41, 275-287, 387-393.

GREECE

Thanos Dokos

1. Introduction

Like most states, Greece has an interest in preventing the nuclear chaos that could result from a weakening or collapse of the international non-proliferation regime. Such a collapse could be followed, sooner or later, by the widespread and unchecked proliferation of nuclear and other weapons of mass destruction. In an era of tremendous upheaval and fluidity in international relations, when alliances are being reshaped and even eliminated and other international security arrangements restructured, the proliferation of weapons of mass destruction could complicate the security equation, destabilizing the situation and seriously aggravating various regional conflicts.

Greece is situated within a vast "arc of nuclear crisis", extending from Russia in the north to Japan in the far east, India in the south and the Maghreb in the south-west. This region contains an explosive mix of nuclear weapon states (NWS), inheritors of the former Soviet nuclear arsenal, covert NWS, nuclear aspirants, and states which would feel threatened by the nuclearization of their neighbours and have the technological capability to develop their own nuclear weapons. In this region nuclear weapons play (or have the potential to play) a significant role.

In addition, there is some concern in Athens about Turkey. Although Turkey does not possess the technological capability to develop nuclear weapons in the near future, Greece is worried of the alleged nuclear cooperation between Ankara and Islamabad, the rise of Islamic fundamentalism and (unconfirmed) reports that Turkey might try to acquire nuclear weapons material and technology and recruit nuclear scientists from the Muslim republics of the former Soviet Union. Also, the proliferation of advanced military technology and weapons of mass destruction in the region may eventually force Turkey, already worried about the acquisition of such weapons by regional adversaries like Syria, Iran and Iraq, to try to acquire such weapons itself. Greece, therefore, has a strong interest in preventing the nuclearization of the region, so that Turkey does not feel threatened and decide to follow the same path.

2. Greece and the Non-Proliferation Regime

During the Cold War, the non-proliferation of nuclear and other weapons of mass destruction was never an issue of high priority for Greece. The low priority accorded to nuclear non-proliferation can be partly explained by the absence of major nuclear proliferation problems in Greece's immediate vicinity, by the country's other pressing security problems and by the fact that Greece's own nuclear activities are very limited and for peaceful purposes only.[1] Indeed, the only nuclear installations in the country are a 5 MW pool-type research reactor which uses 20 % enriched uranium, situated at the Demokritos National Research Centre, and a sub-critical installation at the Polytechnic School of Athens. The Demokritos reactor is mainly used for the training of scientists and for the production of radioisotopes for medical uses. Both facilities are under IAEA/EURATOM safeguards. The country is not engaged in any kind of nuclear trade.

---

[1] The official position is that there are no plans for the introduction of nuclear energy in Greece. The country's energy needs will continue to be covered by coal, imported oil and hydroelectricity. Although it is generally believed that the issue of nuclear energy will surface again internationally because of worldwide concerns about the environment, it is not expected that a re-examination of the nuclear energy option will take place in Greece, mainly because public opinion is firmly anti-nuclear.

Despite its low level of activity in the field of non-proliferation, Greece has participated enthusiastically in international efforts to stem the proliferation of nuclear weapons. It ratified the NPT in 1970. When the country became a member of the EC in 1981, it acceded to the agreement between the Non-Nuclear Weapon States of EURATOM and the IAEA. Although it exports virtually no nuclear or nuclear-usable items, Athens complies fully with the Zangger Committee's "trigger" lists and applies safeguards in the rare case of transhipments of nuclear technology through its territory. In 1991, Greece declared its intention to observe the Nuclear Exports Guidelines and became a member of the London Club.

It should also be noted that Greece has signed the Biological Weapons Convention and the Chemical Weapons Convention and is also a member of the Australia Group for the Control of Chemical Exports and of the Missile Technology Control Regime (MTCR).

3. The Non-proliferation Issue After the Gulf War

The end of the Cold War has had little effect on Greece's non-proliferation policy. As for the Gulf War, although it threw into sharp relief the problem of the proliferation of weapons of mass destruction in regions fairly close to Greece (the Middle East and the eastern Mediterranean), it did not cause the Athens government to attach a significantly higher priority to the non-proliferation issue. The main effect of the Gulf War was to prompt Athens to draw some vague conclusions to the effect that the issue was a potentially serious threat to regional and international security. It must be noted, however, that the potential proliferation consequences of the breakup of the Soviet Union are of great concern to the Greek government. Greek officials and diplomats have on numerous occasions expressed their concern about the control of the former Soviet nuclear arsenal and about the possible diffusion of nuclear weapons, material, technology or know-how from the CIS states.

At the same time, experts and officials in various European Union countries and the European Commission have expressed the concern that with the advent of the European Union's single market in 1993 and the elimination of internal barriers in the movement of goods and technology Greece may be used as a transit point for clandestine exports of nuclear materials and technology, mainly because the country lacks the infrastructure and experience necessary to handle and inspect such materials.

This concern cannot be dismissed out of hand, in view of the export control problems faced by other European states with significantly greater experience and expertise than Greece and the weaknesses of Greece's own export control system, which will be explained below.

In the framework of the European Union, Greece has been somewhat more active in the field of non-proliferation. In a statement of December 23, 1993 Greece's Minister for European Affairs, Mr. Theodore Pangalos, envisaged non-proliferation as a priority area for the Greek EU presidency. The Greek Presidency did, against considerable odds, succeed in getting agreement on the dual use regulation as resolved by the Corfu summit (even if other member states were the driving forces behind this move, it should be seen as an achievement for Greece).

In the conclusions of the Presidency, there were references to the nuclear situation in Ukraine («support for the full implementation of nuclear and conventional disarmament agreements»), North Korea («[...] The European Council considers nuclear proliferation a major threat to international peace and security and recalls its long-standing commitment to the aims of the NPT. The European Council calls again on the DPRK to recognise and respect its international responsibilities and confirms that prospects for a better relationship with North Korea would be greatly enhanced if concerns about its nuclear activities could be alleviated.») and the 1995 NPT Conference («[...] in order to enhance the prospects for a successful outcome of the 1995 NPT Conference, démarches have to be made with a view to : (a) promoting participation in the remaining two PREPCOM sessions in Geneva and New York respectively and the 1995 Conference itself ; and (b) widening consensus on the aim of indefinite and unconditional extension of the NPT.»)

One should also mention a meeting in March 1994 between members of the Committee on Foreign Affairs and Defence of the Greek parliament and members of Bundestag's Foreign Affairs Committee, at which arms control and non-proliferation issues were discussed.

In the meeting of NATO's defence ministers in Seville in late September 1994, Greek Defence Minister Gerasimos Arsenis proposed the creation of zones free from nuclear, chemical and biological weapons in the Balkans, the Mediterranean and the Middle East.

In the two Prepcoms and the 1995 NPT Review and Extension conference, Greece will fully support the common position of the Twelve as expressed by the Council of the European Union (Council Decision 94/509/CSFP of 25 July 1994). According to this decision, the member states of the European Union will «strengthen the international non-proliferation system by promoting the universality of the Treaty on the Non-Proliferation of Nuclear Weapons and by extending it indefinitely and unconditionally».

4. The Greek Nuclear (Import-)Export Control System

4.1. Law and Organization

The main laws regulating Greek export controls are : Law 936/30.6.1979 on "Amendments and supplements to external trade legislation" ; Regulation 260/69 "Establishing common rules for exports" ; and Regulation 91/477/EEC on "Arms shipments between European Union member states". There are also a number of Ministerial Decisions, such as Ministerial Decision No.5408/E3/2362/31.08.93, followed by Appendix INFCIRC/254/REV.1/PART1, covering nuclear goods and technologies, No.3286/E3/2757/24.05.93 relating to missile technology and No.3285/E3/4136/05.93 on export controls for chemical and biological substances.

The goods restricted by Greek export control legislation are those included in the (former) COCOM, Zangger, London Suppliers and Dual-Use lists.

In the past, one of the main characteristics of Greek non-proliferation policy was the low level of inter-ministerial cooperation. This was mainly due to the low priority accorded to the issue, the lack of nuclear activities and, to some extent, the weaknesses of Greek public administration. In order to understand the precise dimensions of the problem, it is essential to have a clear picture of the Greek non-proliferation mechanism.

Because of the multifaceted nature of the issue, there are a number of agencies involved in the export control system. These agencies include the ministries of National Economy, Foreign Affairs, Defence, Finance, Industry & Technology, the Greek Atomic Energy and the National Intelligence Agency.

The Ministry of National Economy (and more specifically the Directorate for External Trade Procedures) has the principal responsibility for granting licences. There are three types of licence : the Individual Licence, valid for one end-user in one country for up to one year ; the General Licence, valid for one or several countries where the consignee is a regular customer and with the condition that exporters are required to provide the Ministry of National Economy with a list of goods exported under such a licence ; and the Intra COCOM General Licence, which can be used for goods which would usually require a licence. This last can also be used for shipments to more than one destination, as long as the countries are members of COCOM.

The general philosophy of the Ministry is the strict application of the regulations. So far, however, there **hasn't been a single application for an import or export licence for any items appearing on any of the nuclear or nuclear-related lists**.

The Ministry of Finance, and more specifically the Customs Directorate, is the "executive arm" of the Ministry of National Economy. However, due to changes of personnel and other organisational problems, the Ministry has had very little involvement in nuclear export control issues in the past year or so. In 1992, a group of approximately 25 customs controllers took the initiative and asked for training in order to become the nucleus of a force of inspectors, but so far nothing has happened.

In the Foreign Ministry, the Directorate for International Organisations and Disarmament (B1) has a dual function : (a) to represent Greece in international fora and meetings, to monitor all developments in the field of nuclear proliferation (as well as a number of multilateral arms-control negotiations), and to draft policy papers on those issues ; and (b) inside the country, to brief other agencies about developments in the field of non-proliferation and export control and to co-ordinate their activities. It should be noted, however, that, despite its key role, the B1 Directorate is understaffed and export controls is not among its high-priority concerns.

In the Foreign Ministry, the Directorate for International Economic Relations (B3) - dealing with the former COCOM issues - is also involved in export control issues. Mainly because of the problem of understaffing, there have been some complaints from other agencies about the lack of regular briefings from the Foreign Ministry on international developments in export controls.

The body solely responsible for providing technical advice on whether an import/export licence should be granted is the Greek Atomic Energy Committee (GAEC). The GAEC has a staff of approximately 25 people (of whom 13 are scientists). According to Law 181/1974, no nuclear material can enter or leave the country without permission from the GAEC. However, the Committee is not involved in cases of dual-use materials. By any standards, the GAEC is a highly professional and competent scientific body which can be relied on for technical advice on nuclear import/export issues.

The National Intelligence Agency has an advisory role in export controls. The Agency has a veto power over the granting of a licence, in order to ensure that national security interests are not threatened. Because of developments in the CIS states there has recently been a slight increase of interest in and monitoring of nuclear issues.

In the Ministry of Defence, the agency dealing with nuclear issues is the Defence Industry Directorate (YPOVI). The interest and involvement of YPOVI in matters affecting weapons of mass destruction is rather limited. It is mostly interested in exports and control of conventional weapons exports. The Directorate of Defence Policy and the Military Intelligence Agency occasionally take an interest in nuclear non-proliferation issues and monitor developments in this field, particularly where Turkey is involved. But the Defence Ministry has no policy-making functions or direct involvement in non-proliferation matters, only an advisory role.

4.2. Greece's Approach on Specific Export Control Issues

The law regulating issues of external commerce is a general law (936 of 30/6/1979), and does not include any special clauses on nuclear export control issues. As a consequence, issues such as the definition of technology (tangible/intangible), as well as the scope of participation (direct breaches law, instigation, support, negligence) and the approach to extraterritorial actions (services on the spot/brokerage/transit trade transactions) are not explicitly dealt with.

As far as penalties are concerned, the maximum prison term is two years and the maximum fine is equal to the value of the goods. In some cases a heavier penalty may be imposed if other laws are violated. A prison term cannot be converted into a fine, even if such a possibility would exist in normal circumstances. Finally, the law gives the ministries involved the right to confiscate the profits or sale value of illegally transferred goods and to suspend the company's operation licence.

On the issue of end-use controls, it is obligatory to possess and submit an end-user certificate (IC/DV system).

The issue of catch-all clauses is not clear at all, but it seems that there is no such provision.

Where possible changes in the attitude of the business community are concerned, the lack of commercial activities renders meaningless or irrelevant questions as to whether companies and business associations have installed a company policy on export controls, an internal export control system, organisational interfaces, special incentives for business to behave, information programs for companies, etc.

4.3. Weaknesses in the Greek Export Control System

The only nuclear material that is legally imported and re-exported from the country comes from the Democritos reactor and is, therefore, easily controlled. The situation may be different regarding dual-use items, as their control is a much more demanding task.

There have reportedly been a few cases of smuggling of nuclear materials or sensitive technologies. *Nucleonics Week* published a report that «according to investigative sources in Germany, [...] a large quantity of plutonium-containing material, said to be 100-150 kilograms, was shipped by sea from the Bulgarian port of Varna to Athens. Sources said that, in the Greek capital, investigators were given leads suggesting that the large consignment of plutonium had been sent to Switzerland».[2] There was virtually no publicity in Greece related to this event. Of course, even if the report is accurate, this is not a case of import/export, but of illegal smuggling of nuclear material.

A brief reference should be made to past cases of illegal transfer of sensitive technologies through Greek territory or involving Greek companies.

One Greek company was among the large number that exported to Iraq substances and technology with possible applications in the manufacture of chemical weapons. Of course, it could be argued that the fact that a single Greek company was involved (as against the tens or hundreds of companies from countries with allegedly stricter export control systems) should be a reason for optimism rather than for concern. The situation is quite satisfactory today as far as chemical substances are concerned, since every substance that goes through customs is inspected (even non dual-use items) and there is no indigenous production of chemical substances.

Another example is the Iraqi "supergun", parts of which were seized in Greece, Turkey, Italy and Britain. It seems that Greek

---

[2] **Nucleonics Week**, July 21, 1994.

customs acted only after being tipped off by the security agency of another state (Israel), and it seems that the same thing happened in Italy. It should not be forgotten, however, that the British authorities were responsible for allowing the weapon parts to be exported in the first place.

In December 1991/January 1992, Greek intelligence was reported to be keeping close tabs on a ring of Hungarian nationals (including at least one diplomat) who were apparently trying to sell nuclear materials and technology, involving "red mercury" (a "phony" material). A similar case involving "East Europeans" trying to sell "red mercury" was reported in October 1993.[3] It seems that in none of the above cases were there any convictions.

There is a sense of general optimism among officials in the agencies involved. Unfortunately, this optimism appears to be based more on goodwill and ignorance than on the efficiency of the Greek export control system. Practically nobody shares the fear that Greece may become a conduit for the smuggling of technology that can be used by Third World countries to develop nuclear and other weapons of mass destruction. The issue is of low priority, and this will continue to be the case for the foreseeable future unless some dramatic event takes place. Theoretically, the export control system should work in a fairly satisfactory way. In practice, however, it is impossible to tell. To the best of this author's knowledge, it has never been tested in the form of applications from companies for export licences.

What can one expect from Greece in the future ? The country will sign all relevant international agreements and try in good faith to implement them, but lack of expertise and of full awareness of the problem may cause significant difficulties. Greece's ability to intercept the illegal transfer of nuclear materials would be very ques-

---

[3] One should also mention the case of the so-called Athens Uranium smugglers. In October 1989, a foreigner contacted an official from the Democritos National Research Centre and offered to sell uranium (illegally) imported from South Africa. The price was exorbitant ($80 million for a few pounds). The Greek police arrested the smuggler, and analysis of the smuggled uranium showed that it was barely processed natural uranium.

tionable, especially when faced with intelligent and experienced smugglers who (after breaking through the German and other Western European export control systems) could easily find loopholes in the Greek export control system and inspection mechanism.

5. Conclusion : What should be done ?

What should be done to strengthen the Greek nuclear export control system ? Economic and training assistance from the European Commission can play a significant role. Such assistance has not so far been provided. If necessary, the creation of multinational customs inspection teams is a possibility that could be examined, probably on a temporary basis until Greek officials can receive the necessary training. The appointment of Christos Papoutsis as European Union Commissioner responsible for Energy and EURATOM is expected to improve the prospects for the strengthening of the Greek export control system. Finally, while tribute should be paid to the efforts of the permanently understaffed agencies involved in non-proliferation efforts, the various ministries should take measures to address the problem of understaffing.

Furthermore, there is a pressing need for improvements in the work of the Greek intelligence agencies. Here, training may not be enough. The establishment of an information exchange system and of closer co-operation between EU (and other) states would be necessary.

In Greece's view, police-type measures are not enough. The root cause of the alleged security threat which provides the motives for the acquisition of nuclear and other weapons of mass destruction must be addressed. A political solution to an emerging conflict constitutes the most effective arms control measure. In this context, the European Union (especially if it is more closely integrated politically) can play a very important stabilizing role in the Mediterranean and the post-Gulf War Middle East and Greece's traditionally good relations with the Arab world (and, lately, with Israel) might prove a significant factor in facilitating such a process.

HUNGARY

Erzsébet N. Rózsa

1. Hungary : A Nuclear Summary

Hungary is a small non-nuclear weapon state, party to the NPT since 1970 when the Treaty entered into force. During the Cold War it was a member of the Warsaw Treaty Organization and bordered on the Soviet Union, the WTO's and the region's only nuclear weapon state. At that time there was great public concern about the possibility of a nuclear war between the two superpowers, but there was no Hungarian perception of a direct nuclear threat from the Soviet Union. Since the collapse of the Soviet Union, Hungary has no border with the acknowledged nuclear weapon successor state, Russia, but the country borders on the Ukraine, which still has nuclear weapons on its soil. In spite of this fact, there is no public perception of a possible nuclear threat from Russia, Ukraine, or any other party.[1]

Nevertheless, it is in Hungary's best interests to support nuclear disarmament and to stop the nuclear arms race in order to contribute to international stability and security. Therefore, Hungary is an

---

[1] This conclusion is based on the findings of a 2-year project conducted by Brown University, Providence, Rhode Island on "Security in Europe". In the framework of this project some 10 focus group meetings were held in Hungary and the question of the nuclear threat from Russia was discussed.

active participant in all the relevant international fora, has joined all the international control regimes (the Zangger Committee, the Nuclear Suppliers Group, the Australia Group and the Missile Technology Control Regime), and also applies the COCOM control measures. This means that the lists of these regimes are introduced and observed in Hungary and a reliable export control system has been set up, for the most part since 1990, when the first democratically elected government entered office.

Hungary is, at the same time, a user of nuclear energy in several peaceful, civilian fields ; the utilization of nuclear energy for power generation is the most significant application, but it is also used in industry, agriculture, medical treatment and scientific research.

Hungary has one nuclear power station, at Paks, which provides approximately 50 % of Hungary's electricity. The dependence of the country on nuclear energy is challenged not only by the "green" movements, but also by some of the parliamentary parties, mostly due to environmental considerations. Recently, a new dimension has been added to the problem : the return of the spent fuel to Russia, which had been functioning more or less smoothly, has been stopped and the future is uncertain.

The safe operation of the Paks nuclear power plant and the other installations where radioactive materials are handled has always been a priority. The original safety system of the power plant has been revised and further developed by Hungarian scientists. Hungary has not only undergone regular safeguards inspections from the IAEA, but has asked for examinations of the safety of the nuclear power plant itself. Hungary has also offered its help and expertise on nuclear safety to Russia, Ukraine and the IAEA.

Hungary's stance on the nuclear issue can be best summed up as stated in the Law on Atomic Energy of 1980 :

- Hungary has to do its best to stop the nuclear arms race and to promote nuclear disarmament ; therefore, nuclear energy can only be used for peaceful purposes in Hungary.

-   Hungary is increasingly dependent on the peaceful use of nuclear energy, in industry, agriculture, health care and scientific research, as well as in the generation of electricity.

-   Unsafe uses of nuclear energy may harm mankind and development ; therefore, safety of operation is a priority and must be ensured by all possible means.

These main principles of Hungary's nuclear policy and the changed international environment (Hungary lost its former allies, which made a re-orientation and redefinition of its priorities inevitable) have brought Hungary closer to the Western world and Western values. It is against this background that Hungary has in the past four years (1990-1994) built up and completed an export control system comparable to those of the Western countries.[2]

2. Reform of the Export Control System

2.1. Laws and Regulations

Hungary's first commitment to control the trade in and movement of nuclear materials was undertaken when the country signed the NPT in 1968.[3] It was published by the Law-Decree No.1970 :12, which was followed, in 1972, by the conclusion of a safeguards agreement of the INFCIRC/153 type with the IAEA. Hungary became a member of the Zangger Committee in 1974.

---

[2] It should be noted that the beginnings of this export control system can be traced back to the years of the communist-socialist regime: membership in the NSG in 1985 and renewal of activities in the Zangger Committee together with the Decree of the Council of Ministers No.2/1986 resulted in a control system valid for the then centralized conditions.

[3] Article III paragraph 2 says : «Each State Party to the Treaty undertakes not to provide :

(a) source or special fissionable material, or

(b) equipment or material especially designed or prepared for the processing, use or production of special fissionable material, to any non-nuclear-weapon State for peaceful purposes, unless the source or special fissionable material shall be subject to the safeguards required by this Article.»

The Law on Atomic Energy[4] was passed in 1980 (No.I.). It states that «Hungary does its best to help stop the nuclear arms race and to take efficient measures towards nuclear disarmament». In paragraph 4 this law also adds that «any trade/commercial transaction with them [nuclear materials, equipment and machinery] is the monopoly of the state,[5] which is practised via the organizations appointed for this task».

Hungary joined the Nuclear Suppliers Group in 1985. The Decree of the Council of Ministers No.2/1986 on Nuclear Export combined in its annex the lists of both the Zangger Committee and the NSG. In all overlapping cases the stricter variant was preferred. The decree ruled that all nuclear exports to non-nuclear weapon states should be licensed by the National Atomic Energy Commission before the general export licence was issued. The decree also stated that the importing country should give a written undertaking :

- not to use the imported goods for the production of nuclear weapons or any other nuclear explosive devices ;
- to place the imported goods under IAEA safeguards ;
- to place the imported goods under physical protection ; and
- not to re-export them without previous written approval from the Hungarian party.

This decree on nuclear exports has subsequently been modified twice (by Governmental Decrees Nos.62/1992 and 54/1993). Nuclear imports were also drawn into the scope of the decree, to which the combined list of the Zangger Committee, the NSG[6] and the

---

[4] A new law on atomic energy is currently under elaboration by a working group of some 40 experts delegated by the relevant authorities and organizations. In the draft all the new developments in Hungary, the new administrative and financial systems, the dismantling principles, the prevention of accidents, the responsibility for damage, etc. will be considered. This draft will be judged by a committee of technical and legal experts. The new law will also allow the privatization of the Paks Nuclear Power Plant, provided the privatizing company is registered in Hungary.

[5] Although the monopoly of the State ceased to exist as a result of the liberation of all trade activities, transactions in nuclear and other internationally controlled materials, goods and technologies have to be licensed.

[6] These two had already been in force since the Decree of the Council of Ministers No.2/1986.

COCOM International Nuclear List was added. At the same time the decree ruled that the non-proliferation behaviour of the importing countries should also be taken into consideration when an export licence was requested. That meant that the country's political commitments and activities had to be examined, and also whether the country in question had a full-scope safeguards agreement with the IAEA.[7] In 1993 the NSG Nuclear Related Dual Use Items List was also attached to the decree, and from that time on the non-proliferation behaviour of nuclear weapon states that wished to import Hungarian goods appearing on these lists, could also be examined.

Parallel to these steps in the field of control over the export/import of nuclear goods and technologies, Governmental Decree No.61/1990 on the Licensing of Certain Internationally Controlled Goods and Technologies introduced important changes in the field of export control in general. It was this decree which settled the interpretation of the terms "export" and "import", and which, by attaching the COCOM Industrial List to the decree, determined the scope of the goods and technologies placed under control.

At the same time, the decree required the establishment of the Interagency Committee on Export Control and the Export Control Office within the Ministry of International Economic Relations.

After the lifting of restrictions on export and import in general, the conclusion of contracts did not need to be licensed. Therefore, another decree was issued in the same year (No.112/1990) which stated that **any activities** related to certain items were licence-bound in themselves. This decree acknowledges two types of licences : a licence for a certain activity,[8] e.g. export, import or inland trade, etc. of a licence-bound item, and a case-to-case licence, i.e. a licence for a single transaction involving one of the licence-bound items.[9] Although the scope of this decree is redefined every year,

---

[7] These modifications were preceded by Hungary's joining the G-10 in 1990.

[8] The activity licence is issued by the Licensing Division, to which the Export Control Office also belongs.

[9] This is issued by the Export Control Office.

all radioactive materials and relevant technologies are covered by it.

Decree 61/1990 has been modified five times. In 1991 the Australia Group Control List (Governmental Decree No.143/1991)[10] and the combined NSG and Zangger List from the Annex of the 2/1986 decree on nuclear export were attached to it. In 1992 it was further amended by the COCOM International Nuclear List (Governmental Decree No.62/1992), the COCOM International Munitions List (Governmental Decree No.66/1992) and the MTCR List (Governmental Decree No.166/1992).[11] The latter modification introduced the "catch-all" clause not only with regard to nuclear, but also for biological, chemical, missile technology and conventional equipment and technologies. In the nuclear field these amendments meant no modification, as - although they referred to the Decree of the Council of Ministers No.2/1986 and its modification by the Governmental Decree No.62/1992 - these two were not annexed to the decree.

Having introduced all the relevant lists of internationally controlled goods and technologies, Hungary had to face the same problem as the EU, namely the comparison and co-ordination of these lists. The outgoing government's last cabinet meeting approved the EU-list No.9.4, which was introduced at the beginning of June 1994 by Governmental Decree No.87/1994. This decree finalized the country list in force in Hungary, which is a positive list, i.e. if an item is exported to the countries on the list, it is not necessary to attach the International Import Certificate and the End-use Certificate (Statement by Ultimate Consignee and Purchaser for Import) to the application for an export licence. There are exceptions, however, namely the 0 category and those items in the categories 1-9, which are marked with N, T and CA (N = NSG Dual-Use Items, INFCIRC 254, 2nd part ; T = NSG Trigger List, INFCIRC 254, 1st part ; CA = EU Nuclear Control List). Countries on the country list are : Argentina, Australia, Austria, Belgium, Canada, Denmark, Fin-

---

[10] Hungary became a member of the Australia Group in December 1992.

[11] Hungary became a member of the MTCR in December 1993.

land, France, Germany, Great Britain, Greece, Iceland, Ireland, Italy, Japan, Luxembourg, the Netherlands, New Zealand, Norway, Portugal, Spain, Sweden, Switzerland, USA.

Nuclear weapons items are included in the military list, which is the first chapter of the decree, while civilian nuclear and other internationally controlled goods are included in the second chapter of the same decree.

With regard to such questions as the extraterritorial actions and the distinction between tangible and intangible technologies, no regulations have been passed up to now. With regard to the former, Hungary is a small country with limited possibilities. However, agent activities in connection with internationally controlled goods and technologies, e.g. in case of transfer, are covered by the regulations.[12]

In the Penal Code violations of the regulations are dealt with in two places. Radioactive materials are dealt with in § 264[13] : «The person who - without licence - prepares, obtains, trades with radioactive material dangerous to health, or gives such material over to another person, who is not authorized to hold it, commits a crime and is to be punished with up to 5 years imprisonment.» This paragraph was amended in March 1994[14] by the addition of Article (2) : «The person committing the crime defined in Article (1) in complicity can be punished with 2 to 8 years imprisonment.»

With regard to the trade in internationally controlled goods and technologies, the Penal Code was changed in 1993 by Law No.XVII. If the provisions concerning the turnover of internationally controlled goods and technologies have been violated or the end-use of the goods and technologies has been realized in another way than that stated in the Statement by Ultimate Consignee and Purchaser, the offender is guilty of a criminal offence and can be

---

[12] This has been the case since the Governmental Decree 61/1990 entered into force.

[13] Law No.IV/1978.

[14] Law No.IX/1994.

punished by up to five years imprisonment (Section 287). The criminal offence of foreign trade activity without a licence (in the case of licence-bound foreign trade activity) or the export or import of controlled goods can be punished by a maximum of three years imprisonment. In addition, suspension of activities under the authorization of the regulations can be ordered, e.g. the "activity licence" can be withdrawn.

2.2. The Administrative Setting

Decision-making on export control is basically dependent on the following bodies and organizations :

The **Interagency Committee on Export Control**, in which all the relevant ministries and other organizations are represented at head of division level, was established in 1990.[15] The Committee meets every 6-8 weeks. Its task is to co-ordinate export control policy and the interests and opinions of the different authorities on relevant export control issues ; it compiles the list of controlled goods and technologies and co-ordinates it with international lists and commitments ; and gives its judgment on export licence applications in case of export to sensitive regions (in case of military end use, it forwards the proposal to the Interagency Committee on Military Equipment and Services). This committee thus has an important role in decision-making (see Chart 1). Its members are :

- the Ministry of Industry and Trade, which is represented by an Advisor to the Minister, who is also the Chairman of the Committee ;[16]
- the Head of the Export Control Office and the Deputy Head of the Export Control Office, who acts as Secretary to the Committee ;
- the Ministry of Foreign Affairs ;

---

[15] Government Decree No.61/1990.

[16] As of July 1994 the Ministry of International Economic Relations ceased to exist and its functions were taken over by the Ministry of Industry and Trade. However, the Chairman of the Committee remained the same person.

- the Ministry of the Interior ;
- the Ministry of Defence ;
- the Ministry of Finance ;
- the Ministry of Transport, Communication and Water Management ;
- the Ministry for Environment and Regional Policy ;
- the National Committee for Technological Development ;
- the National Customs and Excise ;
- the Hungarian Atomic Energy Commission ;
- the Information Office, and
- the National Security Office.

(The Military Industry Office, which used to be an independent unit and as such a member of the Committee, has been placed under the auspices of the Ministry of Industry and Trade. The head of this Office is now an additional representative of the Ministry in the Committee.)

The Interagency Committee on Export Control is undergoing gradual reorganization at the moment, due partly to structural reorganization of the state administration following the change of the government, and partly to the increasing demand for participation by other, hitherto unrepresented ministries like the ministries of Justice, of Public Welfare and of Agriculture.

It should be noted, however, that in spite of the fact that Hungary introduced the Australia Group Control List in December 1991,[17] the Ministry of Health has not yet been invited to join the Committee.

In January 1993 two working groups were set up within the Committee. One deals with the non-proliferation aspect of export control, and is headed by the Ministry of Foreign Affairs. In November 1994 in the Ministry of Foreign Affairs appointed Commissioner for Non-Proliferation Issues. This post is new, and was created in the context of preparations for the 1995 NPT Extension

---

[17] Government Decree No.143/1991.

Conference. The other committee deals with the prevention of illegal transfers, and is headed by the National Security Office. Between meetings there is continuous co-ordination between the committee members.

The **Export Control Office** was established in 1990[18] and acts as the secretariat of the Interagency Committee on Export Control. The Office operated within the Ministry of International Economic Relations until July 1994, and since then it has been part of the Ministry of Industry and Trade. In addition to its role in the decision-making process, its task is to control and license the export/import of items on the lists introduced in Hungary, to track the routes of the licensed items and to co-ordinate and update these lists. In its licensing capacity this body is in continuous contact with the National Atomic Energy Commission, whose licence is a precondition for any other licence related to items on the nuclear lists.

The **Technical Independent Department**, also part of the Ministry of International Economic Relations before it ceased to exist and now operating within the Ministry of Industry and Trade, performed similar control functions in relation to military equipment and services, above all the observation of the COCOM Munitions List which was introduced in Hungary in 1992.[19] Although there was continuous co-ordination between the Department and the Export Control Office, the Minister of International Economic Relations decided to unite the two in April 1993. The head of the united division is a member of the Interagency Committee on Export Control, and is, at the same time, the Secretary of the Interagency Committee on Military Equipment and Services. (The Committee has as members the five ministers of the Interior, Defence, Foreign Affairs, Industry and Trade and the Minister without Portfolio responsible for National Security. Due to the importance of military matters, the only officials permitted to represent the ministers at meetings of this body are their secretaries of state. The Committee meets every two weeks and maintains strict control over military exports, imports, re-exports, transit transactions, etc. The two Interagency Commit-

---

[18] Government Decree No.61/1990.

[19] Government Decree No.66/1992.

tees are in continuous and direct contact through the united Division of Export Control and its head.)

The **National Security Office** also has a role in licensing ; it gives its opinion every week on the applications for licences submitted to the Export Control Office. This office acts in an advisory capacity, giving complementary information and checking the applicants to see if they really exist or not. Within the Office there is a group for non-proliferation matters, and it participates in all the relevant meetings.

On the political level export control related issues are dealt with in the Ministry of Foreign Affairs and at the Permanent Missions of Hungary to the United Nations Organizations in Vienna (the head of the Mission is also Hungary's official coordinator to the NSG, while the official Hungarian body to represent Hungary at the NSG meetings is the National Atomic Energy Commission), Geneva and New York. Within the Ministry of Foreign Affairs, the United Nations Division deals with matters that are related to any organization under the umbrella of the UN. The Security Division provides the political background to the operation in the different international regimes. As mentioned before, the new post of a Commissioner for Non-Proliferation Issues was created in November 1994.

The process of decision-making on export control issues in Hungary is shown in Chart 1 :

The Export Control Office draws up the proposal for a new decree, and co-ordinates it with the Department of Legal Affairs within the Ministry. After co-ordination, the Heads of Divisions within the Ministry meet to discuss the proposal, which is then handed to the Interagency Committee on Export Control. If it is approved, the Administrative Secretary of State of the Prime Ministerial Office will have to study it and he then submits it to a meeting of the administrative secretaries of state of the relevant ministries. Upon approval they forward the proposal to the Minister of Industry and Trade (formerly to the Minister of International Economic Relations), who introduces it to the government. If there is no problem with the proposal, the government approves it without putting the issue on its agenda. However, if there are any problems, the government puts the issue on its agenda, discusses it, makes a decision and only then forwards the proposal to the Minister of Justice, who will pass it back to the government after examining it from the legal point of view. When the government has approved the proposal, the decree is published in the *Hungarian Official Gazette*. The decree enters into force on the day of publication, if not otherwise stated.

Chart 1 :
Decision-Making Procedure on Export Control Issues

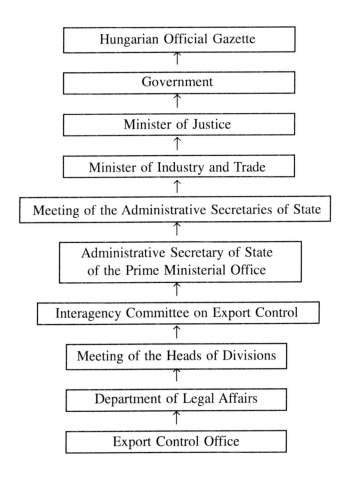

With regard to nuclear issues, however, it is the **National Atomic Energy Commission** which deals with conceptual questions. It was established as early as 1955 as an advisory and policy-making organ dealing with the peaceful uses of nuclear energy. In 1990 it was reorganized and became an independent body responsible for the regulation, licensing and inspection of all nuclear facilities in Hungary.[20] The Commission prepares proposals, reviews and studies to support government decision-making. In questions related to the peaceful utilization of nuclear energy, it acts as an advisory body to the government, co-ordinating and controlling the tasks of the authorities. It co-ordinates all activities related to the utilization of nuclear energy, its control, operation and dismantling, the manufacture and import of the relevant equipment ; the production, utilization, storage and transport of fissile and radioactive materials ; and any other activity related to radiation protection and nuclear safety. It issues licences for the construction, operation, reconstruction and dismantling of nuclear power plants. It informs the public of proposals and decisions on the utilization of nuclear energy, and co-ordinates research and technical development.

The Commission has a president and two vice-presidents appointed by the Prime Minister. Its members are delegated by the ministers of the Interior, Agriculture, Defence, Industry and Trade, Environment and Regional Policy, Transport, Communication and Water Management, Foreign Affairs, Culture and Education, Public Welfare, and Finance, and by the Chairman of the National Committee for Technological Development and the Secretary General of the Hungarian Academy of Sciences. These members are usually of the rank of an undersecretary of state. The President of the Commission also appoints leading experts to the Commission.

The Commission also has a Technical Scientific Board as a consulting body, the head of which is also appointed by the President of the Commission (see Chart 2).[21]

---

[20] Government Decree No.104/1990.

[21] All the relevant ministries and State organizations are represented in the Commission : the ministries of the Interior, Agriculture, Defence, Industry and Trade, Environment and Regional Policy, Transport, Communication and Water Management, Culture and Education, International Economic Relations, Public Welfare, Finance, the National Committee for Technological Development and the Hungarian Academy of Sciences.

Chart 2 :

The National Atomic Energy Commission

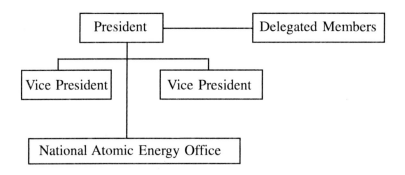

Chart 3 :

The Nuclear Decision-Making Procedure

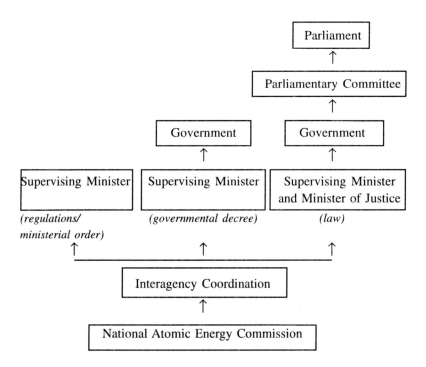

The process of decision-making on nuclear issues differs from general export control decision-making in that the National Atomic Energy Commission elaborates the drafts. If it is a new regulation, the President of the Commission publishes it after the inter-agency co-ordination in his capacity as minister supervising the Commission on behalf of the government (at the moment the Minister of Industry and Trade is responsible)[22] in the form of a ministerial order. If it is a new governmental decree, the supervising minister forwards the draft to the government. If it is a new law, the law is introduced to the government after the interagency co-ordination by the supervising minister and the Minister of Justice. After discussion in the relevant parliamentary committees, Parliament passes the law.

Export licences for nuclear materials, goods and technologies are approved or rejected by the **National Atomic Energy Office**,[23] which operates as the secretariat of the National Atomic Energy Commission under the control of its President.

Physical export control is performed at the regional customs centres, where there is one official on each shift who is trained in export control regulations and methods of detecting forbidden activities. (At the border only external inspection is performed.) This national export control network was established in 1990, following the introduction of the relevant regulations. Both in 1991 and in 1992 seminars were organized for the customs officers - altogether 120 customs officials have been trained - with the participation of foreign experts and officials. The first seminar was an introduction to the general, theoretical aspects of export control regulation, while the second one discussed practical questions and experiences.

Where the export of internationally controlled goods and technologies is concerned, reaction procedures have been greatly

---

[22] The Commission is an independent body under direct governmental control and it is outside the scope of the portfolio of the supervising minister.

[23] An average of 50 licences per year.

speeded up. Should an emergency arise, the customs officer can get directly in touch with the Export Control Group at the headquarters of the National Customs and Excise.

Customs officers-to-be are also currently being trained in export controls and the relevant regulations. Within the National Customs and Excise there are internal regulations concerning internationally controlled goods and technologies, which are also made known to the trading companies involved in such activities.

Nevertheless, customs officers have to face several problems. Besides such common ones as the unreliability of transporters, i.e. that they often lack information on the goods being transported, Hungarian customs officers are overburdened. Those responsible for internationally controlled goods and technologies have several other duties as well. Another problem is that the Hungarian customs system is based on the control of imports. Traditionally, imported items have been controlled and supervised at least once a year, if necessary several times, and the importers were obliged to account for such materials. If import control is abolished, as planned, the whole Hungarian customs system will have to be changed and new regulations introduced immediately. With regard to export activities, the National Customs and Excise has a full picture of the companies involved in licence-bound activities and of those trading in licence-bound goods and technologies. As regards transit, according to the Hungarian regulations it is the task of the customs officers to make sure that the items passing through the country are provided with the necessary licences issued by both the country of origin and the recipient country.

The Export Control Group in the National Customs and Excise has suggested that an internal export control group be set up within the army itself. This would make control easier, but the idea has not yet been put into practice.

3. The Political Actors

3.1. The Government

As early as 1968 Hungary decided to join the NPT, and successive Hungarian governments have followed - and later developed further - this "tradition" in handling nuclear issues. Hungary concluded an agreement with the IAEA in 1972, joined the Zangger Committee in 1974 and the NSG in 1985 and passed the 2/1986 Decree of the Council of Ministers.

During the last years of the former regime, however, it became clear that **access to the most modern technology and know-how** would only be possible if Hungary met international requirements and introduced a reliable and broad export control regime. The government that entered office in May 1990 gradually established an administrative and legal system of export control, passed decrees, established new administrative bodies, supported the setting-up of groups responsible for and involved in export control at already existing institutions and involved all the relevant authorities in the decision-making process on (nuclear) export control.

In recognition of these efforts, Hungary achieved "favourable consideration treatment" status in December 1990 and was taken off the COCOM list of proscribed destinations in February 1992. At the moment Hungary has "free world" status and is a member of all four regimes, the NSG, the Australia Group, the MTCR and COCOM. It is Hungary's intention to become a founding member of the new COCOM which is presently undergoing reorganization.

Hungary chaired the 1992 Review Conference of the Convention on the Physical Protection of Nuclear Materials and also the Second Preparatory Committee to the 1995 NPT Extension Conference.

In the field of the civilian use of nuclear energy, Hungary has made several commitments with regard to the safeguards system. In addition to promising full cooperation, Hungary gave up its right to refuse inspectors appointed by the IAEA. The work of such inspectors is supported by giving them a visa for the period of one year, which enables the inspectors to visit the country as many times within the given period as they wish.

Hungary has joined the universal reporting scheme of exports and imports of the IAEA and decided in 1972 to provide the IAEA with early design information, which meant that information on nuclear-related facilities is given to the IAEA 180 days before the nuclear material arrives on site. This undertaking has now been modified so that as soon as a decision is taken on a nuclear facility, Hungary informs the IAEA.[24] Hungary has also offered to participate in efforts to strengthen the IAEA's safeguards system, for example by strengthening the state system of nuclear material accountancy and control.[25]

Hungary offered to do all it could to help and move forward the 93+2 plan aimed at the unveiling of undeclared facilities. Environmental monitoring is one examination method to this end. Some water sampling and measurements have already been conducted on the Danube around the Paks nuclear power station.

The third factor is **political**, which was perhaps the most important for the Hungarian government. After the end of the Cold War and the dissolution of the Eastern bloc organizations, the Warsaw Treaty Pact and COMECON, Hungary found itself in a political and security vacuum which faced the country with the task of finding itself a new place in the international community and redefining its security needs and possibilities. Hungary's political re-orientation was also influenced by the fact that former (socialist) economic ties were suddenly cut, the bipolar balance came to an end and the Soviet Union as a whole ceased to exist. With the unpredictability on the eastern border and the former socialist countries' uncertainty and search for new contacts, it became one of the main priorities of

---

[24] In the case of the dry spent fuel storage for the Paks nuclear power plant, the information has already been sent to the IAEA even though construction work has not yet started.

[25] The Hungarian State system of nuclear material accountancy and control was first established in 1972.

Hungarian foreign policy to aim at integration into the Western world in the shape of membership of the European Union and of NATO. However, to achieve that aim, Hungary had to abide by all international regulations, had to make its policy conform as closely as possible to that of the Western countries, and had to show that their priorities were also priorities for Hungary.

It is in the framework of these three decisive factors (tradition, the Hungarian economy's need for technology and the political goals of the country) that Hungarian non-proliferation behaviour and (nuclear) export control policy can be understood and analysed. This explains the great efforts made by the Hungarian government to make sure that its non-proliferation behaviour is impeccable and that the Hungarian (nuclear) export control system operates without a flaw.

The unbroken continuity of Hungary's activity in the nuclear field in the past decades, the existence and operation of the export control system, the expert staff who have in the past four years helped form the new Hungarian export control, and the recent improvements in the organization of the system give us reason to hope that there will be no discontinuities in Hungarian non-proliferation and export control policy. Nevertheless, taking into consideration the structure and the status of the members of the interagency committees, especially the Interagency Committee on Military Equipment and Services, where all the members are of ministerial rank, the question arises of whether and to what extent a change of government could influence decision-making and the smooth operation of the established system. After half a year with the government in office that was elected in May 1994 continuity seems ensured and intense preparation for the 1995 NPT Extension Conference has begun.

3.2. Parliament

In 1989, under the government headed by Miklòs Németh, an operative committee was formed to make the necessary preparations for the 4th NPT Review Conference. The committee was led by the

Ministry of Foreign Affairs and all the relevant portfolios were represented in it. During the preparations for the conference, it was proposed that a hearing on nuclear non-proliferation should be organized for Parliament. However, as elections were already approaching, the hearing never took place and up to now the non-proliferation issue has not been raised in Parliament.

There has, however, been a development in the field of the peaceful use of nuclear energy. In April 1989 the National Atomic Energy Commission produced a report for the Environment and Regional Policy Committee of the Parliament on the application of the Law on Atomic Energy of 1980, with special attention paid to environmental protection. In autumn 1990, shortly after the new Parliament convened, a delegation of the parliamentary parties visited the IAEA Headquarters in Vienna to discuss energy policy issues and to examine the possibility of the construction of a new nuclear power plant. In 1991, in response to this visit, a group of IAEA experts was invited by the Hungarian Parliament (the visit was organized by the Economic Committee of the Parliament) to discuss the main concepts of Hungarian energy policy.

In the spring of 1994 the Interparliamentary Union put the non-proliferation issue on its agenda, which might have provided a fresh input for the Hungarian Parliament had it not happened just before the general election.

These were the only occasions on which the Hungarian Parliament held a hearing or was given information on nuclear issues. It should be noted, however, that the outgoing Parliament was elected as a result of the change of regime. Its main task was to complete this change and provide the necessary legislative background. Consequently, it was severely overburdened. However, as contacts with the West are becoming closer and integration of Hungary is gradually proceeding, Parliament will reach a stage when it has to discuss and deal with issues with which it has not hitherto been confronted, and non-proliferation - especially in view of the forthcoming 1995 NPT Extension Conference - is one of these issues.[26]

3.3. The Parties

The same ignorance - and in the last months of the 1994 election campaign the same lack of interest - can be observed on the part of the six parliamentary parties. Perhaps it was justifiable before the elections, when even foreign policy was of secondary interest only, that the parties did not deal with this issue specifically. During the research for this paper, 4 of the six parliamentary parties[27] were examined and interviewed in respect of their perceptions of non-proliferation and export control. At first their foreign policy programmes were examined : none of these mentioned the issue at all. There were some vague statements which could be interpreted as references to the nuclear non-proliferation issue, but it seemed that non-proliferation and the international commitments undertaken by Hungary only had relevance for the parties to the extent that they help and are a precondition for Hungary's integration into Western structures.[28] It should be noted, however, that most parties expressed a definite interest in the topic at a later stage, after the elections.

The parties - and for that matter the public as well - have much more knowledge about the Chernobyl catastrophe and its aftermath, the Paks nuclear power station and environmental threats, especially now that the media have covered the controversy over the return of spent fuel to Russia. There is also a debate going on on the issue of the interim storage facilities to be built. But very few people are aware of the strict regulations and preparations necessary for the

---

[26] The text of the NPT and Hungary's documents of accession were published in Law-Decree No.12 of 1970, and in 1995 this will have to be modified, depending on the outcome of the NPT Extension Conference. The new Law on Atomic Energy is under elaboration. Both of these factors should prompt Parliament to deal with nuclear issues.

[27] MDF (Hungarian Democratic Forum), SZDSZ (Alliance of Free Democrats), FIDESZ (Alliance of Young Democrats) and MSZP (Hungarian Socialist Party); the other two parties in Parliament had no foreign policy programmes worth mentioning.

[28] It should not be forgotten that these interviews were conducted shortly **before** the elections.

transport of nuclear goods, or the safety measures at the power plant, not to mention international regulations and the NPT.

At the moment all we can say is that there is a consensus among the parties, Parliament, the government and even the public that «we are against the proliferation of nuclear weapons and we abide by all the international commitments undertaken by Hungary». Some of the representatives of the parties were very frank saying that they «would be very much surprised, if the others [parties] had had any thoughts on the issue [non-proliferation] ... and [we] will deal with the issue when it comes before Parliament [in 1995]».

4. Continuity and Change in the Behaviour of Industry

Hungary is also a nuclear supplier. Most of its nuclear activity, especially nuclear export, is related to the Paks nuclear power station. There are also other goods and technologies related to nuclear activities which originate in Hungary and are regulated by international controls :

- Within the former COMECON, Hungary specialized in the manufacture of refuelling machines, which means that if there is a reconstruction going on anywhere in the nuclear power plants of the former socialist countries, they have to turn to the Hungarian suppliers.

- Hungary mines uranium ore concentrate and also manufactures radiation detectors and simulators.

- Another specific field of interest is safety software. Hungarian experts developed a new safety system for the Paks plant, which is internationally considered very efficient.[29]

---

[29] In recent years in the framework of different programmes several safety inspections have been carried out at Paks : IAEA OSART (1988, 1991); WANO (1992); IAEA ASSET (1992), AGNES (1991-1994). The last one is a Hungarian programme (Advanced General and New Evaluation of Safety), financed by the Paks Plant and the National Atomic Energy Commission and performed by relevant Hungarian institutes.

- In the area of dual-use goods and technologies, Hungary manufactures machine tools which are on the lists and should therefore be controlled.

4.1. The Paks Nuclear Power Station

Hungary's only nuclear power plant is situated at Paks, some 100 km to the south of Budapest. The power plant (V-213 design of the reactor series WWER-440) was supplied by the Soviet Union and its four units came into operation between 1983 and 1987. As mentioned before, it generates approximately 50 % of Hungary's energy.

The fuel used at Paks originates in Hungary. "Yellow cake" mined in the Mecsek Mountains in the south of Hungary is processed into fuel elements in Russia and is then returned to Paks. The same fuel elements, when spent, are returned to Russia for reprocessing after 5 years of cooling in the spent fuel pond. In the past this meant an average of 466 high activity spent fuel elements per year. At the moment there are approximately 2,800 spent fuel elements in the pools at Paks.

In the near future, however, this major contribution to Hungarian nuclear exports might be severely cut back, depending on the outcome of two ongoing discussions : the Hungarian-Russian negotiations regarding the return of the spent fuel elements to Russia and the debate over planned developments at Paks in the areas of interim storage and possible extension.

In 1989, when the former socialist countries introduced hard currency payments in intra-COMECON trade, several countries decided that it was too expensive to return the spent fuel elements to the USSR and built storage facilities of their own.[30] Hungary, on the other hand, decided that it would continue to return the spent fuel elements to the USSR for reprocessing. In 1992, however, the Russian Parliament passed a law on environmental protection which forbade the import of dangerous wastes. As the clause ensuring the

---

[30] This was the solution chosen by Bulgaria, the Czech Republic and the GDR.

return of the spent fuel[31] was missing from the original Soviet-Hungarian agreement concluded in 1966 upon the purchase of the Paks plant, the Hungarian government found itself in a difficult situation. After several rounds of negotiations, in December 1992 a tripartite agreement was concluded between the governments of Russia, the Ukraine and Hungary for the transport of the spent fuel elements. From time to time new negotiations have been necessary to make sure that Russia accepts the spent fuel.

This difficulty seemed to be solved when in April 1994 Russian Prime Minister Chernomyrdin paid a visit to Hungary. He signed a supplementary protocol, in fact an interpretation of the former Soviet-Hungarian agreement which ensures the continued return of the spent fuel from Paks to Russia as long as the plant is in operation. However, upon Chernomyrdin's return to Russia the ratification of the protocol was strongly challenged by the Russian Minister of Environmental Protection and by the relevant civil organizations. At the time of writing, this problem had not been solved. It has been shown that the protocol is against Russian law, but the Russians have offered new negotiations to resolve the issue.

It is against this background that preparations have been made for the construction of an interim dry repository for the storage of spent fuel elements coming from the Paks plant. The facility is designed to cope with the spent fuel for 50 years. Preparations are at a stage when the storage could be completed by the end of 1995. In 1992 a new interagency National Project was started in Hungary to co-ordinate the scientific, economic, technical, social, legal, financial and international attempts to find a solution to the problem of the safe and socially acceptable treatment and final storage of the low-level and intermediate-level radioactive wastes produced in Paks.[32]

---

[31] This clause is included in every agreement concluded between the other socialist countries and the USSR on the purchase of nuclear power plants.

[32] The co-operation agreement was signed on 26 February 1993, with the participation of the ministers of Industry and Trade, Environment and Regional Policy, Public Welfare, the Chairman of the National Committee for Technological Development and the National Atomic Energy Commission, the Minister without Portfolio acting as the owner of the Hungarian State Holding Co., the Director General of the Hungarian Electrical Network Co. and the Director General of the Paks Power Plant Co.

In March 1994 the Hungarian government discussed the idea of a new basic power plant. Although the decision was put off for two years due to the present state of industrial development and of the national economy, some preparations have already been made. In 1993, with the participation of BELGATOM, regions of Hungary were selected where it would be possible during 1994-95 to look for and study potential sites.

This does not mean, however, that if a decision is made to the effect that a new basic power plant should be built it will necessarily be of the nuclear type. All the more so since public awareness, the "green movements" and also some of the parties object to such plans and argue that the energy should be generated by other, alternative methods.[33]

4.2. Firms and Companies

There are not many Hungarian firms and companies which deal with nuclear materials, goods or technologies other than those related to the Paks plant and all of them are subject to continuous control.[34] These companies were and are accustomed to having their trade activities checked, which is a strong incentive. This may change with increasing privatization, although most of the smaller, privately owned companies are well aware of the consequences. This awareness has been increased by a series of measures.

The Export Control Office regularly organizes seminars for interested companies and, as mentioned before, the National Customs and Excise also informs them on the latest developments in regulation. Those companies which already have international contacts are also aware of the fact that the international export control system is getting stricter, and are therefore unlikely to take any risks. In prob-

---

[33] Such methods include the utilization of wind and solar energy. Another claim is that future energy demands and utilizations are always overestimated, and that it may not be necessary to build another basic power plant at all.

[34] This control is exercised under the terms of Government Decree No.112/1992 and the activity licences issued by the Ministry of Industry and Trade.

lematic cases, they usually consult the Export Control Office or the National Atomic Energy Commission. There is a free flow of information between the authorities and the interested companies. It is a big help to the operation of the system that getting an export licence takes only a short time, so that trade activity is not hindered.

Another incentive is in fact the lack of incentive. In the past, many of the items exported were not licence-bound in Hungary, as only their import was centrally controlled, and when these (e.g. computers) were sold to countries to the east of Hungary, the trade was a lucrative one. Now the countries to the east can import these goods and technologies themselves from the West, so this market has shrunk considerably. Simultaneously, the Hungarian domestic market has improved greatly and can absorb most of the imported goods and technologies.

The staff of a big foreign trade company in engineering, *Transelektro*, was interviewed on the company's non-proliferation behaviour and export control policy. The company has a separate department for trade in nuclear/fissile materials, goods and technologies called the Atomic Department. The head of this department said that they had just one rule, which is to abide by the laws and regulations even if this is sometimes difficult and has a negative effect on business. This view is generally shared by the companies involved in nuclear issues and is one of the reasons why there have been no real cases of violation of the export control regulations, so far at least.

4.3. The (Non-)Cases

There have, however, been a small number of non-cases - none of them nuclear - where the regulations were violated. In the first case a careful investigation found that although chemical materials had been imported into Hungary without a licence, none of them was used for forbidden purposes. In the second instance no verdict could be reached. This latter case involved some computer spare parts which used to be on the COCOM list imported into Hungary without an import licence... By the time the legal process was finished, these goods had been taken off the list and were not licence-bound any more. These cases will lose even this slight relevance when plans to abolish Hungarian import controls altogether are realized.

The non-case that attracted most international attention was the Hafnium case. Hafnium is an element which occurs together with zirconium. It was discovered only in 1922, as it is very difficult to separate the two with the traditional methods. In spite of their great chemical similarity, these two elements behave very differently when facing neutrons. Hafnium absorbs the neutrons very well, and can therefore be used effectively in the control of chain reactions.

In August 1991, 2,000 kg Hafnium of 99.9 % purity in 6 metal bars from the *Pridnyeprovsky Himzavod* in Dnyeprodzerzhinsk in the Ukraine was transported by the all-Union *Techsnabexport* company for a Hungarian firm called *Netto Ltd.* The Hafnium was the property of *Richmond Commercial Services Ltd*, an offshore company registered on the Isle of Man. Between *Richmond* and *Netto* there existed a valid commercial contract, and although no financial guarantees were provided, the Hafnium arrived in Hungary.

At about the same time, another shipment of Hafnium of the same quality, but in this case 9,164.2 kg[35] arrived in Hungary destined for *Duchess Ltd* (Pécs), a subsidiary of *Richmond Commercial Services*.

Since it was of such great commercial value, but meant for re-export, the Hafnium was put into storage in two separate customs-free areas : the 2,000 kg at Tuzsér and the 9,164.2 kg first at Pécs, then in Csepel, Budapest.

Since the whole amount was meant for re-export, at some point the idea occurred of uniting the two consignments. However, while the firms were looking for a buyer, the Hungarian regulations were changed and Government Decree No. 62/1992 was introduced. This

---

[35] The value of this shipment was 4,358,951.73 USD, i.e. 475.65 USD/kg.

meant that from that time on an export licence had to be obtained for the Hafnium. The prospective purchaser cancelled the deal and no other buyers could be found. To make the matter more complicated, it was discovered (with the cooperation of the National Security Office) that the address given by *Richmond Commercial Services Ltd* as their office was only a postal address. In spite of the fact that several small firms were involved, the Hafnium is still under the control of the Customs and Excise. In the meantime, storage costs have been piling up.[36] Some of the firms involved have contacted the Export Control Office for advice on export control regulations and the Customs and Excise on the conditions under which the Hafnium could be re-exported. The same answer was given to all : there is no objection if the firm applies for and obtains an export licence and if the storage fee is paid.

5. Conclusion

Hungary is a non-nuclear weapon state and joined the NPT, as an original signatory, in 1968 in this capacity. It has been Hungary's aim ever since to abide by the commitments it took with the signature of this treaty and to encourage nuclear non-proliferation by every means at its disposal.

Hungary's non-proliferation policy has been continuous since the days of the former socialist regime, and even became more active under the first democratically elected government. Although there is considerable ignorance on the part of Parliament and the parliamentary parties in respect of the non-proliferation aspect of the nuclear issue, they are well aware of the environmental and energy aspects.

Since the change of regime in 1989 and the elections in 1990, a new network of export control regulations has been built with the involvement of all the relevant ministries and administrative bod-

---

[36] To a total of approximately 4-5 million HUF - interview with an officer of the Customs and Excise.

ies. Hungary is not a great nuclear supplier - most of its nuclear exports are related to the Paks nuclear power station - but it may have a role as a potential re-exporter. Hungarian firms and companies involved in the trade in nuclear or nuclear-related materials, goods and technologies are regularly informed by the authorities on changes in the regulations and are fully aware of how the system functions. The Hungarian Penal Code has also been modified in accordance with the newly introduced system.

«Nuclear energy in Hungary can only be used for peaceful purposes»,[37] and it is increasingly and widely used in Hungary in industry, agriculture, medicine and health care, scientific research and power generation. Approximately 50 % of Hungary's energy consumption is provided by the Paks plant, which - notwithstanding the views of the "green" movements and the social tensions in the neighbourhood - cannot be substituted by any other energy source at the moment. To compensate for this, the Hungarian authorities are doing their best to improve the safety of the plant and to make sure that the environment is not damaged. In addition to the regular safeguards inspections performed by the IAEA, the relevant foreign firms and experts are also involved in different projects aiming at the improvement of safety in the plant.

To sum up : Hungary's nuclear policy is built around three main pillars - non-proliferation, the peaceful use of nuclear energy and the need for modern technology, and the export control network developed in the past four years. Taking into account Hungary's first and foremost political priority, integration into the Western world, it is to be expected and it can be assumed that the nuclear issue, including its non-proliferation aspect, will acquire the same place among Hungary's priorities as it has in the West.

---

[37] Law on Atomic Energy of 1980.

POLAND

Genowefa Smagala

1. Introduction

Since the Iraq case, international non-proliferation efforts have been strengthened to reduce the risk related to nuclear materials and sensitive technology. Poland has participated actively in these efforts and has undertaken important international commitments which also have to be incorporated into domestic legislation. Moreover, Poland's attempts to build a modern market economy have forced government to speed up the establishment of a comprehensive trade control system. Poland has nuclear research capabilities and is able to deal with the smuggling problem. Poland also has a well-developed industrial capacity and is able to produce dual-use items (e.g. oscilloscopes, numerically controlled machine tools) for nuclear programmes. This capacity, even if not fully realized, should not be forgotten.

2. Historical Development

The development of nuclear export controls in Poland started after the entry into force of the Non-Proliferation Treaty (NPT), to which Poland acceded in 1969. In 1972 Poland concluded a safeguards agreement with the International Atomic Energy Agency

(IAEA) (based on the IAEA statute and on document INFCIRC/ 153) providing for full-scope safeguards, which means that Poland is obliged to accept international safeguards on all sources and special fissionable materials in all peaceful nuclear activities carried out within its territory. Poland went even further, also placing radioactive sources under its domestic control. In conformity with the commitments undertaken and according to the IAEA recommendations, a State System of Accountancy and Control (SSAC) of nuclear material was established.

At that time implementing export control was relatively easy for the government. The state was the owner of all facilities and trading companies, and distribution of nuclear materials was centralized. The only company authorized to produce radioisotopes and to distribute and transport nuclear materials was located in the Nuclear Research Centre at Swierk. Radioisotopes and nuclear materials could be used after a permit was received from the body responsible for granting such licences, the Central Laboratory for Radiological Protection (CLRP).

Bodies applying for permits had to fulfil some radiological protection requirements. Nuclear material and radioactive sources were subject to recording and controlling procedures. All licences were registered and the material was regularly controlled by the licensing body.

At the same time Poland adopted international rules on the transport of dangerous goods covered by the IAEA Safety Series No.6. As a consequence, a permit for transport of nuclear material has also become obligatory.

Being monopolist the state was able to perform nuclear export control to international standards. It was also quite active in supporting international efforts to strengthen the nuclear non-proliferation regime. Almost from the very beginning Poland participated in the two international groups that have worked to develop common standards on nuclear export control ; Poland joined the Zangger Committee in 1974 and the Nuclear Suppliers Group (NSG, also known as the London Club) in 1976. As a result, in 1978 Poland notified the Director General of the IAEA that it would act as agreed in NSG Guidelines, issued later as the IAEA's document INFCIRC/254. This means that Poland will deliver nuclear material, equipment and technology, as defined in the trigger list, to those non-nuclear weapon states who apply full-scope safeguards to their nuclear activities.

In 1983 Poland acceded to the International Convention on the Physical Protection of Nuclear Material which is intended to ensure the physical security of nuclear materials - especially when they are being transported on international routes.

In the 1980s the Polish government took a decision to build the country's first nuclear power plant. Although the construction was abandoned in 1990, the decision created an urgent need for national legislation covering activities planned and under way as well as international commitments that had been undertaken.

The first piece on domestic legislation on Atomic Law, which deals with activities associated with the peaceful utilization of nuclear energy, was issued in 1986 as an Act of Parliament. This law states that the import, export or transit of nuclear materials, radioactive sources and installations containing such sources will need a permit issued by the governmental body responsible for nuclear safety and radiological protection. The basic provision of this law is that nuclear activities should be performed in such a manner that the requirements on safety and radiological protection are met and the obligations undertaken in Poland's international agreements on the peaceful use of nuclear energy are fulfilled.

The Polish governmental body responsible for dealing with problems arising from the use of nuclear energy is the National Atomic Energy Agency (NAEA), whose President is responsible for establishing detailed principles and requirements for the export, import and transit of nuclear material as well as issuing regulations on these subjects.

Regulations issued by the President of the NAEA under the Atomic Law and state obligations arising from international agreements include the following :

- The Principles of Accountancy and Control of Nuclear Materials (1987)

- The Principles for Keeping Records and Controlling Ionizing Radiation Sources (1987)

- The Terms and Conditions for the Export, Import and Transfer through the Territory of Poland of Nuclear Materials, Radioactive Sources and Equipment containing such Sources (1988)

- The Principles to be followed in the Physical Protection of Nuclear Materials (1988)

The President of the NAEA has entrusted the implementation of these regulations to subordinate bodies.

With the beginning of the Polish transition to democracy the need to introduce some amendments in domestic legislation became obvious, but it was difficult to reconcile meet economic and security objectives often perceived as contradictory. Promotion of the market economy began with the liberalization of foreign trade, with the exception of nuclear materials which were covered by the Atomic Law. However, access to modern technology was still restricted and this situation could only be changed via the introduction of a stringent and more comprehensive export control system designed to meet all newly undertaken international obligations.

This transformation of the export control system was realized in two steps, following discussion and agreement with the COCOM countries. In the first step, new requirements for the import and re-export of goods and technologies from COCOM countries were introduced (September 1990). These requirements were issued by the Ministry of Foreign Economic Relations (MFER), the government body responsible for control of foreign trade. So-called import certificates for commodities covered by the COCOM export restrictions were introduced to give the exporter a guarantee that sensitive goods and technologies would be used solely for civil purposes, and would remain in Poland rather than be re-exported to other destinations. Polish importers applying for an import certificate were obliged to accept pre-licence and post-shipment controls to be performed by Polish customs services and representatives of the government of the exporting country. Moreover, the end-user had to apply for the delivery verification certificate at the local Customs Office and send its copy to the MFER within 7 days if the licence or contract imposed such requirements. The licence was valid for 6 months.

The second step had the goal of removing Poland from the COCOM list of proscribed destinations. A new Act of Parliament was passed on 2 December 1993 - the Law on Special Control of Foreign Trade in Goods and Technologies Subject to International Agreements and Obligations.

Work on this Law started at the beginning of 1991 when the government, at the request of the Ministry of Foreign Economic Relations, established the Inter-ministerial Commission for Foreign Trade Control, which is composed of representatives from :

- the Ministry of Foreign Economic Relations,
- the Ministry of Industry and Trade,
- the Ministry of Foreign Affairs,
- the Ministry of Defence,
- the Office for State Security,
- the Central Board of Customs,
- the National Atomic Energy Agency.

The main task of the Commission was to draw up legislation on foreign trade control in accordance with international obligations undertaken by Poland. The Commission was involved in the implementation of the first step of export control reform, and it has been engaged in the implementation of the new law, which entered into force on 25 March 1994.

This law covers :

- goods and technologies which are important for the nuclear fuel cycle or for nuclear explosive devices ;
- chemicals, micro-organisms, viruses, bacteria and toxins as well as equipment and technology which may be used for chemical and biological weapons production ;
- missile technology ;
- other goods and technologies connected with national security and international commitments.

Lists of goods and technologies subject to special control were published by the Minister of Foreign Economic Relations on the day the Law entered into force.

There is no reference to the intangible transfer of sensitive technology, which is mainly a matter of human capabilities like technical knowledge or consulting services which might pose a proliferation risk. Nor is there any mention of the brokerage, which may initiate the transfer of sensitive technology like human knowledge between different countries.

These lists contain all items as internationally agreed and proposed by :

- the Nuclear Suppliers Group :
     Trigger List (INFCIRC/254/Rev.1/Part 1)
     Dual-use items (INFCIRC/254/Rev.1/Part 2)
- the Missile Technology Control Regime (MTCR)
- the Australia Group (AG) (this list contains 54 items)
- the COCOM countries

Foreign trade in these goods must be carried out on the basis of import certificates or import, export and transit permits.

Import certificates or import and export permits are issued by the Minister of Foreign Economic Relations, but transit permits are dealt with directors of customs offices in order to make it easier for goods which are only in transit to cross borders. Transit permits should be granted exclusively to applicants who present proper documents stating that the consignment registration of all issued import, export and transit permits is obligatory for a recipient outside the territory of Poland. An import certificate is issued only when the regulations of the supplier country impose such a requirement. Granted permits or import certificates may specify some conditions to be fulfilled by exporter, importer or end-user.

According to the enacted law, the licence obligation is linked to the lists of controlled items. This means that it is triggered by technical criteria, and slight deviations from these criteria may make contributions to a nuclear weapons programme possible.

The Minister of Foreign Economic Relations has the licensing and decision-making authority, but his decision must be based on the opinion of experts from many fields. On questions related to nuclear material, equipment, technologies and dual-use items which are important for the nuclear fuel cycle, the National Atomic Energy Agency is involved in the decision-making process. Where country destinations are concerned, the opinion of the Ministry of Foreign Affairs is taken into account and the ministry recently (June 1994) issued a list of banned countries, including countries on which United Nations Security Council export restrictions have been imposed.

3. Penalties

Polish law prescribes penalties in cases of violation of established provisions or requirements. The Atomic Law provides for a term of imprisonment, restriction of liberty or a fine to be imposed on those who engage in controlled activities without a licence or who disregard stipulated conditions. The Trade Control Law provides for penalties of up to 5 years imprisonment. These penalties are applied to bodies who transfer sensitive goods or technology without the required licence. Such punishment is also applied to the manager of a company who breaks the law. Illegal transfers of goods may also result in additional punishment, in the form of forfeiture of goods to the benefit of the state treasury. A fine of PLZ 100 mln, which is about USD 4000, if the conditions specified in the licence have not been fulfilled, the user has one month to put matters right, but if noncompliance continues the Minister of Foreign Economic Relations has the right to confiscate the goods on behalf of the state treasury. Violators can also be punished by being refused future licences.

The Law does not include any provision of penalties for persons or entities, which participate in offences by an instigation or any support of illegal transfers.

4. Implementation

The implementation of the law on export control system has begun. As of this writing, no more regulations have been issued by the Minister of Foreign Economic Relations.

According to the law, regulations should cover :

- application forms for granting certificates or permits ;
- documents to be appended to the applications, ;
- forms of certificates and permits to be granted ;
- forms of the delivery verification certificate.

These regulations are currently under preparation, and the rules and requirements announced during the implementation of the first step of export control reform are being applied.

In April 1993 a special Office for Trade in Goods and Technologies Subject to International Control was established within the MFER. This office is responsible for the implementation of the law and the maintenance of an effective trade control system. The 5-person office is to increase its staff to 25 people and perform such tasks as :

- establishing a database on licences granted and denied and providing access to such information to those who are involved in the licensing and controlling system, ;

- providing advice and training courses for the business and administration communities ;

- supervising and promoting the development of co-operation between bodies and agencies involved in the trade control field.

Goods and technologies under special control are checked by customs officers at border checkpoints, but the end-use control within Poland will be performed by special teams to be appointed by the Minister of Foreign Economic Relations, composed of representatives of governmental agencies or their subordinated units. As establishing an effective end-use control system takes time and additional regulations and provisions to be issued by the Minister of Foreign Economic Relations, current control activities are limited to those performed at the borders by the customs services, in accordance with the Customs Law. Polish customs law regulates control activities carried out by customs services concerning the import, export and transit of goods, as they relate to customs duties or to prohibitions, restrictions, and the observance of international agreements. Checking consignment and clearance documents takes so much time that verification is restricted to random control or occasions when there is a suspicion of illegal transfer.

Parallel and quite independently, control at the borders by the Border Guards (subordinated to the Ministry of Internal Affairs) has been strengthened. Radiation control devices have been systematically installed at the border checkpoints. Thanks to these measures some smuggled nuclear material has been seized. If necessary, the emergency team from the CLRP is asked to provide its expertise. Among the roles of this emergency team is to function as point of contact under the Convention on the Physical Protection of Nuclear Material, so it is responsible for co-ordinating recovery in the event of any unauthorized use of nuclear material. The team performs its duties for 24 hours a day, and is therefore very helpful as a source of advice for customs services and border guards staff.

Implementation of this law in the nuclear field has also begun. International commitments undertaken in respect of the Universal

Reporting of Certain Equipment and Non-Nuclear Material require additional regulations to be issued by the President of the NAEA, as well as some steps to explain the new requirements to actual end-users, who have to submit reports on inventories of equipment and non-nuclear material covered by the Trigger List. Such action is planned for the near future.

5. The Debate on Export Control Policy

Political and economic changes have made it necessary to adjust domestic legislation to new realities or to draft it for the first time. Successive governments have been forced to spend more time than before on drafting this legislation, but export control legislation has not been a priority - at least at the beginning of the transformation process. The legislation process related to export controls was rather long and had to be respected because of the dissolution of parliament in 1993. Since the last elections (September 1993) the situation has changed somewhat because the new ruling parties have a majority in parliament. The growing pressure from western countries, mainly the US and Germany, as well as the revelations about smuggling of nuclear material helped to persuade parliament that trade control legislation should have a high priority. Two parliamentary commissions were involved in drafting this legislation : the Commission on Foreign Economic Relations and the Commission on Education, Science and Development. The law was enacted on 2nd December 1993. Although there was considerable interest in this law and it was supported by all the parliamentary caucuses, there were difficulties over the question of budget allocations for its implementation. However, the Commission on Foreign Economic Relations is still keenly interested in the implementation of the law and has asked for a periodic review of its implementation.

The business community has not been involved in non-proliferation policy-making, and no government - business co-operation has yet been established in this field.

6. Conclusion

Summarizing the development of nuclear export controls in Poland, we can say that a comprehensive export control system in Poland has now been enacted. All international political commitments have been accepted and incorporated into domestic legislation. Western countries provided assistance and exerted pressure (the US, Germany) to encourage the establishment of a comprehensive national law on export controls. These legal foundations of Polish export control made it possible for Poland to be removed from the COCOM list of proscribed destinations. Currently, the law needs effective implementation. However, implementation should be preceded by the creation of regulations, procedures and mechanisms to ensure effective export control and this has not yet been completed. People involved in the export control system have to be trained, especially customs offices staff and border guards staff. Moreover, co-operation between the governmental, business and industrial communities needs to be established.

In general, the legal foundations of Poland's export controls are perceived by international bodies involved in the strengthening of the global nuclear non-proliferation regime as conforming to international standards.

Poland is actively involved in promoting the nuclear non-proliferation regime. One example is Poland's participation in a computer network developed by the Los Alamos Laboratory for testing electronic information exchange. This system may be used as a way of exchanging information on export licence refusals.

ESTONIA

Indrek Tarand

1. Introduction : Estonia and the NPT

Estonia, like the other Baltic states, was unable to take part in international life after the World War II due to its non-existent sovereignty. The number of international obligations deriving from various agreements and conventions has multiplied since September 1991. On September 11, 1994 Estonia became a member of the United Nations. The government declared its intention to join all the major international organizations and conventions. Among the first wave of treaties (52 conventions in all), to which the Estonian Government adhered was the Nuclear Non-Proliferation Treaty, signed on 07.01.1992. At the end of January 1992 Estonia deposited the instruments of accession with the IAEA in Vienna.

However, Estonia's eagerness to sign treaties evidently exceeded the country's domestic capacity to sustain its obligations. The functions of carrying out international obligations in the field of arms control and export control had been performed by the Soviet authorities and Estonians had to start from scratch. In 1992 there was no reliable information about the nuclear and nuclear related items on the territory of the republic of Estonia, and the Russian (ex-Soviet) authorities were not at all eager to reveal their secrets. The functions of the state, such as customs, border security and policing, were not under the control of the Estonian government.

Yet one cannot deny the sincerity of Estonia's intention to carry out its commitments and to take an active stand in preventing the spread of weapons of mass destruction, even though accession to the treaties was also regarded as a tool which could help Estonia in its struggle for independence.

2. Estonian Nuclear Resources

Estonia has no nuclear power plants, and its energy consumption does not exceed the production capacity of thermal power plants which use oil-shale as fuel. Nuclear energy is not regarded as a reliable solution and no political leader has spoken about the nuclear option. This attitude was even strengthened after the Chernobyl catastrophe. Despite this anti-nuclear stance there are two nuclear reactors in Paldiski, remnants of the Soviet military-industrial complex. These reactors were used in training Soviet submarine crews, and their relation to export controls will be examined later.

In 1989 the Estonian public heard allegations about uranium enrichment said to be going on in Sillamäe, formerly a closed Soviet military-industrial city. A year later officials stated that these reports had been exaggerated, and in reality the site was used for producing U_3O_8. This half-product was then shipped back to Russia for enrichment. As this production was discontinued in 1990, public concern about nuclear matters remained low as there were more urgent problems and the sites were still controlled by Russian (ex-Soviet) authorities. Nevertheless, Sillamäe will cause a lot of headache from the point of view of strategic export controls. First of all, the documentation of the former Soviet enterprise has been removed to Russia and the Estonian authorities are unable to obtain reliable data on stocks and equipment. Secondly, the reconstruction of the plant has led to a concentration on the production of earth-metals. According to the latest data, *"Silmet"* (as the factory is now named) is the biggest exporter of niobium in Europe, and zirconium also appears to be an important export item. In June 1994, very rudimentary export control or licensing measures were applied to these products, which are shipped mainly to French and German end-users.[1] Moreover, on September 23, 1994 one of Estonia's leading physicists, Dr. Endel Lippmaa, stated publicly that according to his assessments, 1700 kg of enriched uranium might have been stolen from the Sillamäe factory in 1989.[2] However, the uranium, if indeed stolen, is very likely in Russia and not in Estonia. The theft allegation has not been confirmed.

The possible location of Soviet nuclear weapons on Estonian territory has never been established by the Estonian authorities, although there have been allegations in the newspapers.[3] Most recently, one Estonian journalist suggested that Estonia itself could obtain nuclear weapons, but this has never been considered by the defence planners. Probably the author wanted to stress the feasibility of obtaining materials and technology for nuclear weapons in the aftermath of the plutonium smuggling cases revealed in Germany in summer 1994.[4] On the other hand, this was one of the few newspaper articles to have pointed out the need for efficient border controls, particularly with regard to the collapse of authority in Russian nuclear institutions.

There have been repeated alarms caused by radiation levels in several locations in Estonia, which were usually caused by pieces of irradiated metal, either stolen from various factories where radioactive materials had been used or related to the illegal trade carried out by Russian military personnel. But these incidents also indicated a growing transit trade with metal from Russia to western markets. The radioactive items were taken to the store of radioactive materials in Saku by the National Rescue Board. The Saku depository appears to be the third potential proliferation source on Estonian territory, but the risk is almost non existent, as irradiated items, not radioactive materials themselves, form the major part of the items deposited there.

Estonia's mineral resources include uranium oxide, but even Soviet industry's attempts to process it in Sillamäe appear to have

[1] **Pühapäevaleht**, 13.08.1994.
[2] **Eesti Ekspress** 37(251), 23.09.1994.
[3] **Ohtuleht**, 27.07.1991.
[4] **Rahva Hääl**, 17.08.1994.

been unsuccessful. Consequently there is no reason to consider Estonia as a potential producer of nuclear materials.

3. Nuclear Trade

Although lacking any indigenous production capability, Estonia has recently emerged as one of the leading exporters of rare metals, some of which have nuclear weapons applications. There are numerous reports of Estonia being used as a transshipment point for controlled materials originating in Russia.[5] In the period December 1992 to July 1994, the Estonian Security Police initiated eight investigation processes in connection with the illegal ownership of radioactive materials. The majority of these cases involved cesium-137, and on one occasion cobalt was discovered. In most cases the accused had obtained the materials from the Russian military, who remained on Estonian territory until August 31, 1994. One case had international implications, involving Swedish citizens as well. Two cases came to court and the punishment imposed was relatively soft : Aleksandr Kvinov was sentenced to prison for one month and Juri Aksjonov to an 18 months suspended sentence. Both men were punished according to Article 208 of Estonian Penal Code.[6] According to the estimations of specialists, the likelihood of future smuggling is increasing. On August 26, 1994 there were press reports of the confiscation of 2.95 kg of uranium oxide in Pôlva, a small town close to the Russian border. According to the Estonian Security Police's comment on this occasion, it was the result of a control operation which started at the beginning of August and involved observing Russian citizens linked to the Russian nuclear industry.[7] The results of the analysis of the material seized have not yet been published, but the uranium has been said to be of very low enrichment. All these events underline the need to enforce border controls and customs checks and to impose an appropriate export controls regime. We will examine what has been and what needs to be done in this field.

[5] POTTER W.C., **Nuclear Profiles of the Soviet Successor States**, Program for Nonproliferation Studies, Monterey Institute of International Studies, Monterey, Cal.1993, p.12.

[6] An interview with the Director of the Estonian Security Police.

[7] **Ohtuleht**, 26.08.1994.

4. Legislation and the Administrative Setting

Due to the Soviet legacy, Estonia is facing very complicated problems in the creation of new legislation. The underlying theory has been that even though Estonia was annexed by the Soviet Union in 1940, the continuity of the state remained and independence had only to be re-established. Hence Soviet law, including for instance the traffic regulations, was null and void. However, everyday life demanded some kind of maintenance of existing legislation, and the process of creating new legislation has been rather complicated. The situation was improved by the adoption of the new constitution in June 1992. On that basis elections were held in September 1992 and a new, legitimate parliament began to meet. According to the new Estonian constitution, the legislative initiative can come either from parliament or from the government. The very first chapter of the Constitution states that international agreements have to be incorporated into domestic legislation.[8] Hence the Ministry of Foreign Affairs has to initiate bills about amendments to domestic law or, if needed, new law resulting from international commitments. As the NPT has been generally understood, its Articles III and IV require nuclear export controls.[9] The Estonian procedure foresees that the government proposes a bill to parliament, which has to ratify all international agreements. Hence the MFA suggested six bills to the Government and they were all passed to parliament in February 1994.

On 06.04.1994 parliament decided to enact all six laws at the *second reading*.[10] These regulated Estonia's accession to the following international conventions :

1. Convention on the Physical Protection of Nuclear Material.
2. Joint Protocol Relating to the Application of the Vienna Convention and Paris Convention.

---

[8] Constitution of the Republic of Estonia, chapter 1, p.6.

[9] VAN DASSEN L., Chapter *"Denmark"* in this book, *supra*.

[10] Normally the passing of a law requires three readings, but if there are no amendments it can be adopted at the second reading in parliament.

3. Convention on Assistance in the Case of a Nuclear Accident or Radiological Emergency.
4. Vienna Convention on Civil Liability for Nuclear Damage.
5. Convention on Early Warning of a Nuclear Accident.
6. Law on the Export and Transit of Strategic Goods.

The need for accession to these conventions was determined mainly by the threat posed by the two nuclear reactors in Paldiski. The Russian authorities had been insisting at the bilateral negotiations that they needed more time for the complicated process of dismantling the reactors. Estonia regarded the matter as part of the problem of withdrawal of Russian troops and the Russian military was committed to leaving by the 31 August 1994. Estonia had sought international assistance for dismantling the reactors, but Russia claimed that it was entitled to dismantle its own military installations without external interference. The problem of physical protection of the nuclear materials during the shipment of the fuel rods from Paldiski to Russia established a connection to the export controls system, and this is how the sixth-mentioned bill was included in the package presented to parliament.

There was little active debate in parliament and the bill met practically no opposition. The exporters probably considered the new law normal and the only objection came from a radical nationalist MP, who expressed concern about limitations to Estonian sovereignty.[11]

4.1. The Law on the Export and Transit of Strategic Goods

Until the adoption of this law, exports and transit were regulated by the Customs Law. The new law says in its preamble that it is designed in accordance with international treaties applicable to the Republic of Estonia. It goes on to define strategic goods and makes the government responsible for drawing up the list of strategic goods. Article 3 states that licences will be issued and renounced under the Regulation established by the Government of the Republic. The government has to appoint a special commission for

---

[11] Protocol of the Session of the Parliament on 06.04.1994.

controlling the exports and transit of strategic goods, with the participation of civil servants from the ministries of Economic Affairs, Internal Affairs, Defence, Budget and Finance (as the Customs Board operates under this Ministry), and Foreign Affairs. The commission has to elaborate the rules and set up an institutional framework for issuing International Import Certificates and Delivery Verification Certificates. The government decided to form this commission with a decree issued on 15.06.1994.[12]

The Commission for Control over the Export of Strategic Goods was formed on July 1st, and it consists of officials of the Ministry of Foreign Affairs, Ministry of Defence, Ministry of Economic Affairs, Ministry of Internal Affairs and Ministry of Budget and Finances. Within the ministries the following offices were involved : Foreign Economic Policy Department in MFA ; Department of Strategic Research in MOD ; Department of Licensing in the Ministry of Economics and Security Police Board from the Ministry of Internal Affairs. The Customs Surveillance Department represents the Customs Board, and this the Ministry of Finance. The Commission has put forward proposals for the rules on issuing licences and has drawn up the list of strategic goods.

4.2. The Rules of the Game

The Commission, which will consist of five members representing the ministries mentioned above, will operate under the auspices of the Ministry of Foreign Affairs, even though there was a debate about that arrangement. Formerly the licensing process had been carried out by the Department of Licensing, which operated under the Ministry of Economic Affairs. It would have been fairly logical to continue this way by enlarging the duties of that department, but the decision was taken to set up the Commission within the MFA. This was done mainly because the initiators of the new legislation were employed by the MFA, and their argument was that international cooperation and the necessary assistance with know-how would be more easily obtainable if the Commission remained under the auspices of the MFA. Nevertheless it is not ruled out that

---

[12] **Riigi Teataja** II 1994, 45, 748.

in future the licensing process could be transferred to the Ministry of Economics. For the time being the Commission will be chaired by the deputy undersecretary of the MFA. The proposed Regulation states that the meetings should be held regularly, once every three months, and more often if the Head of the Commission requests it. The decision to grant or refuse a licence should be taken within 60 days. Even though the Commission did not have any staff of its own at the beginning, it now has two people responsible for administering the licensing process.

The exporter has to fill in an application form, indicating his address, and, in case he was not the original importer of the item, the importer's address. Further, a description of the item, its code according to the Codex of Estonian Goods and value in Estonian crowns, and the estimated time of actual delivery are all required. The country of origin of the item, as well as the country of destination, should be indicated. Finally, the applicant has to certify by means of his signature that he is familiar with the terms of the Law on Transit and Exports of Strategic Goods and the government's Decree enacting the List of Strategic Goods. If more details are required, the Commission has the right to ask the exporter for additional information about the particular deal before issuing the licence, in order to establish :

1. that the item was purchased legally and that its documentation is authentic ;
2. that the claimed company of destination has really ordered the item ;
3. that the item's technological parameters correspond to the end-use as shown in the application ;
4. that the company which has ordered the item is trustworthy ;
5. that the export of the item poses no threat to Estonian or international security.

The Commission takes decisions on the basis of consensus, and if this is not reached the Head of the Commission is entitled to decide.

The other major task of the Commission as laid down in the government's decree is the preparation of the List of Strategic Goods and its presentation to government. The list of Strategic Goods was approved and enforced by Estonian Government on 5 October 1994. The codes of goods to the list and forms of international import certificates were enacted by the end of the same month. The amendment and updating of this list is also the responsibility of the Commission. The List is an integral part of the Regulation for the Export and Transit of the Strategic Goods. The List as drawn up by the Commission covers the items specified under all major export control regimes, i.e. Australia Group, Nuclear Suppliers Group, Missile Technology Control Regime, and COCOM. The expertise of Finnish and Norwegian specialists has been extensively drawn upon and the result is basically identical to the Norwegian list of strategic goods. It is not a precise translation of all the major lists, being more general ; the specialists have tried to define common denominators for several items in order to harmonize the list better with the Code of Estonian Goods. This has given rise to the problem that licences are also required for exports which cannot be considered dangerous for international security. However, the specialists involved considered this the only possible way to establish efficient customs control for strategic goods in the Estonian customs area. The Estonian List consists of five parts :

1. Goods related to chemical or biological weapons.
2. Goods related to nuclear technology and equipment.
3. Missiles and related technology and equipment.
4. Weapons, ammunition and other military technology.
5. Strategic goods not included under categories 1 - 4, i.e. dual-use items.

The export control system is thus in existence and has been in operation since November 1994. How it will operate remains to be seen. The initial period will be observed by experts from the USA.

5. Outstanding Problems and Questions

The main current problem for Estonian society is the dismantling of the two nuclear reactors in Paldiski. After two years of protracted negotiation on this question, agreement was finally reached in Moscow on July 26, 1994. According to the agreement, Russia is responsible for shipping the fuel rods to Russia, and Estonia has to take care of the remaining clean-up of the site. The deadline for the Russians' part of the operation is September 30, 1995. By the end of September the fuel rods should be removed from the reactors and packed into containers for transportation. As a consequence of this operation, the Estonian public is becoming more and more aware of the problems of export control. However, the main impetus has been provided by the development of trade relations and the understanding of the fact that without rules Estonia cannot be part of the European game. Despite the fact that the public has been insufficiently informed about the new regulations, the serious exporters comply with them willingly and understand the need for the setting of limits to free trade. The year 1995, when export controls on strategic goods will be applied in practice, is regarded as decisive in forming the consciousness of the population, and consequently of the authorities, about this internationally important matter.

Notes on the Contributors

THANOS DOKOS is a Research Fellow at the Hellenic Foundation for European and Foreign Policy (ELIAMEP), Athens and a lecturer in Strategic Studies at the Hellenic Naval War College.

VICENTE GARRIDO REBOLLEDO is Professor of International Public Law in the Law Faculty at the Centre of University Studies (CEU) and Coordinator of Non-Proliferation Projects at the Peace Research Centre (CIP), Madrid.

DARRYL HOWLETT is a Senior Research Fellow in the Mountbatten Centre for International Studies, University of Southampton and since 1987 he has been the Information Officer for the Programme for Promoting Nuclear Non-Proliferation (PPNN).

ALEXANDER KELLE is Research Associate at Peace Research Institute Frankfurt.

QUENTIN MICHEL is an Assistant in Public administration law and Environmental law at the University of Liège.

HARALD MÜLLER is Director of Research at Peace Research Institute (PRIF) and Director of PRIF's Non-proliferation Programme. He is Associate Professor at the Technical University Darmstadt and Visiting Professor at the Johns Hopkins University Bologna Centre, Italy.

PHILIPPE RICHARD is lecturer at the Institute of Human Rights (Catholic University, Lyon). He is also a Research Associate at the Centre de Documentation et de Recherche sur la Paix et les Conflits (CDRPC, Lyon) and at the Centre d'études sur la Défense et la Sécurité Internationale (CEDSI), University of Grenoble.

ERZSÉBET N. RÓZSA is a Research Fellow at the Hungarian Institute of International Affairs. She used to teach at the Eötvös Loránd University and is a guest lecturer and PhD candidate at the University of Economics at the Department of International Relations, Budapest.

GENOWEFA SMAGALA is a Senior Specialist at the Central Laboratory for Radiological Protection in Warsaw.

INDREK TARAND is a Secretary General of the Ministry of Foreign Affairs of the Republic of Estonia.

LARS VAN DASSEN is External Research Associate at Peace Research Institute Frankfurt and a PhD candidate.

Most used Abbreviations

AA	Auswärtiges Amt ; Foreign Office (Germany)
ABC (weapons)	see NBC
AL	Ausfuhrliste ; Export List (Germany)
AWG	Außenwirtschaftsgesetz ; Foreign Trade and Payments Act (Germany)
AWV	Außenwirtschaftsverordnung ; Foreign Trade and Payments Regulation (Germany)
BAFA	Bundesausfuhramt ; Federal Export Office (Germany)
BAW	Bundesamt für gewerbliche Wirtschaft ; Federal Export Licensing Office (Germany)
BDI	Bundesverband der deutschen Industrie ; German Association of Industries (Germany)
BMWi	Bundesministerium für Wirtschaft ; Ministry of Economics (Germany)
BOE	Boletin Oficial del Estado (Spain)
BWC	Biological Weapons Convention
CAE	Exportability Analysis Committee (Italy)
CANPAN	Nuclear Non-Proliferation Committee (Belgium)
CDI	Confederation of Danish Industries (Denmark)
CEA	Commissariat à l'Energie Atomique (France)
CISD	Interministerial Committee for Defence Exports (Italy)
CLRP	Central Laboratory for Radiological Protection (Poland)
COCOM	Coordinating Committee for Multilateral Export Controls

CPNE	Conseil de politique nucléaire extérieure ; Coucil for Foreign Nuclear Policy (France)
CWC	Chemical Weapons Convention
DTI	Department of Trade and Industry (UK)
ECO	Export Control Organization (UK)
ECS	Energy Conversion Systems
EG(C)O	Export of Goods (Control) Order (UK)
EU	European Union
EUC	End-User Certificate (Italy)
FOA	Försvarets Forskningsanstalt ; National Defence Research Establishment (Sweden)
GAEC	Greek Atomic Energy Committee
GIR	Groupe interministériel restraint ; International Restricted Group (France)
GNP	Gross Net Product
HEU	Highly Enriched Uranium
IAEA	International Atomic Energy Agency
INFCIRC	Information Circular (of the IAEA)
JIMDDU	Interministerial Committee for Trade Regulation of Defence Material, Dual-Use Goods and Technologies (Spain)
KWKG	Kriegswaffenkontrollgesetz ; War Weapons Control Act (Germany)
LBN	Liste des biens nucléaires ; List of nuclear goods (France)
LCN	Liste des biens connexes au nucléaire ; List of dual-use goods (France)
MTCR	Missile Technology Control Regime
NAEA	National Atomic Energy Agency (Poland)
NATO	North Atlantic Treaty Organization
NBC (weapons)	Nuclear, Biological, Chemical
NPT	Non-Proliferation Treaty
NSG	Nuclear Suppliers Group
OCCL	Central Office for Quotas and Licences (Belgium)
OGEL	Open General Export Licence (UK)

SETICE	Service des Titres du Commerce Extérieur ; Export Control Office (France)
SK	Statens Kärnkraft-Inspektion (Swedish Nuclear Power Inspectorate)
UNSCOM	United Nations Special Committee
WMD	Weapons of Mass Destruction
WTO	Warsaw Treaty Organization
ZKA	Zollkriminalamt; Customs Criminal Office (Germany)
ZKI	Zollkriminalinstitut; Customs Criminal Institute (Germany)